Applesoft Language

Dr. George H. Blackwood is a retired Navy pilot and a former college professor with bachelor's, master's, education specialist, and DDS degrees. He now devotes full time to writing.

Brian D. Blackwood has studied computer science and engineering at Michigan State University. For the last four years he has been employed as a supervisor at a large data processing center that services banks and financial institutions.

Applesoft Language

(Detailed Programming Instructions Specifically for the Apple® Computer)

by

Brian D. Blackwood
and
George H. Blackwood

Howard W. Sams & Co., Inc.
4300 WEST 62ND ST. INDIANAPOLIS, INDIANA 46268 USA

FIRST EDITION
SECOND PRINTING—1982

International Standard Book Number: 0-672-21811-9
Library of Congress Card Number: 81-51550

Edited by: *Richard Krajewski*
Illustrated by: *Liane Krajewski*

Printed in the United States of America.

Preface

Programming is detailed, exacting, and thought provoking. Do not expect to become an expert overnight. Some advertisements may lead you to believe that there is nothing to it. This is simply not true. Programming takes effort that many people are not willing or able to expend. Furthermore, because a program written for one brand of computer will probably not run on a different brand of computer you must not only understand the programming language, but the design of the computer as well. You see, many programming language details and functions are applicable only to a specific brand of computer.

In programming, every character, item, formula, punctuation, and format means something specific to the computer. Exact steps must be programmed for each action the computer takes. Any step not correctly programmed, or improperly placed within the program, will cause the program to fail. This failure may be partial or total, but the program will not produce the desired results. Rote memorization will aid in programming, but comprehensive understanding of how the rules interact and relate will produce more efficient programs.

Programming is the truest form of building on a foundation. A solid foundation must be in place to begin the building process. The computer is an inanimate object that is designed according to a set of specifications. The machine does not know anything, nor does it assume anything. The computer does exactly what it is told to do. The programmer must understand machine capabilities and apply proper programming rules to produce correct results.

The lessons in this book are designed to present programming rules in a logical, detailed, progressive method from a beginners level to an advanced level. The lessons attempt to always establish a reference point. If you have trouble with programming errors, you can always return to the last reference point to attempt to understand the correct procedure. When the correct programming procedure is understood, you have to practice it. Practice reinforces the learning experience. With practice comes perfection, and with perfection comes enjoyment.

Do not force the learning experience. Most learning is accomplished by studying in a regular routine. The same surroundings and location aid learning. Some people learn best during the morning, while others learn best at night. Establish your place and time for maximum learning enjoyment.

Unless the computer has a hardware problem, it does not make mistakes. Many times the statement is heard, "It's the computer's fault." Don't you believe it! If an error comes from a computer, it was caused by a person or persons, and a person or persons must correct the error.

Computers are a great part of our daily lives and will be a greater part in the future. The more you understand about computers, their operations, and programming, the better you will understand the future. Much of the future of the world is tied to computer operations.

George H. Blackwood

Contents

Introduction

In November 1978, Brian and I purchased an Apple computer. I looked forward with great anticipation to using the computer to solve all the problems I had never been able to solve. The problems were: how to make a million dollars, how to beat the stock market, and how to solve the energy problem. After working with the computer for a couple of months, I discovered I had an even greater problem. I could not write a program that would solve those problems. As a matter of fact, I could not write a program that would solve a problem of any difficulty. So, I had to learn how to program the computer. I do not have a mathematical background, so the terms *reals* and *integers* didn't mean anything to me. I not only had to learn to program, I had to understand the vocabulary used in relation to the computer. Now, almost two years after the computer was purchased, I can write simple programs. I don't think I could have ever learned to program had it not been for the co-author, Brian. Brian is a computer engineer.

Not everyone is fortunate enough to have a computer engineer answer questions about computers and programming. Neither can everyone study programming on a formal basis. For those who want to learn how to program, don't have access to a computer engineer, and have no opportunity for formal instruction, this book is the answer. It is written for people who have very little comprehension of computer programming and need someone to hold their hand during the struggle. The object is to produce a programming manual for those persons interested in serious programming, but do not have the necessary fundamentals or assistance.

If you can understand and identify with this "most basic" level of computer programming, then this book is for you. If you understand Kunth's *Fundamental Algorithms,* then this book is not for you. Do not waste your time or money.

The book begins on a simple level for the person who has little knowledge of programming, but progresses to the advanced programming techniques that are applied at the highest level of the art. For clarity of presentation, few references are made to the hexadecimal numbering system, assembly language, or machine language. The neophyte programmer has enough to handle mastering BASIC.

We present the book in three sections, Applesoft Language, Programming, and Supplement.

The first section, Applesoft Language, assumes the reader can push the OFF-ON switch to the ON position so the little light on the keyboard glows. Once the light is glowing, Lesson 1 attempts to introduce the user to detailed programming routines. The explanations may be tedious and repetitious, but programming is exact and any detail affects the program. The explanations use lay language and try to avoid ambiguous computer engineering phrases. There is an old computer cliche that covers this situation, "If you can't dazzle them with brilliance, then baffle them with bs."

The second section, Programming, deals with the logic, formulas, and thought that enable interaction among the programmer, the program, and the computer. This section brings the reader from the hand holding stage to the thinking stage. The section stimulates those seldom used brain cells. You can feel the rust breaking loose and the dendrites pull and strain.

The third section, Supplement, presents simulations, games, and graphics.

We have written this book specifically for the Apple II microcomputer, which uses microsoft (Applesoft) language. We are not connected directly or indirectly with Apple Computer Co.® or Bell and Howell.

SECTION I

Applesoft Language

LESSON 1

Load and Save Programs

After completion of Lesson 1 you should be able to:

1. Type a program on the keyboard and store it in memory.
2. Save a program on cassette tape.
3. Load a program from cassette tape into memory.
4. Save a program on disk.
5. Load a program from disk into memory.

VOCABULARY

CRT—This abbreviation stands for cathode ray tube. The picture tube in your television is a CRT. The CRT can be used to display the output from and the typed-in input to your Apple computer.

Cursor—This is a blinking square of white light on a black field in the NORMAL mode. A blinking square of black light on a white field in the INVERSE mode.

Input—This is the process of transferring data, or program instructions, into memory from some peripheral unit. It also can denote the data itself. The word "input" sometimes denotes the signal applied to a circuit or a device, such as a timing signal.

Line Number—This is a positive integer that begins each program statement.

LIST—This command displays the entire program on the screen. LIST 0,100 lists the program statements from 0 to 100 on the screen.

LOAD—This command reads a program from cassette tape and stores it in computer memory. LOAD USA loads a program named USA from disk into computer memory.

NEW—This command deletes the current program and all variables from computer memory.

Program—This is the set of statements or instructions that tell the computer how to solve a given problem or accomplish some other task.

Program Statement—This is a discrete instruction to the computer, stored in memory, that begins with a positive integer.

RUN—This command clears all variables, pointers, and stacks, and begins execution at the line number indicated. RUN generally begins at the lowest number and executes the complete program.

SAVE—This command stores a program on cassette tape. SAVE USA stores a program named USA on disk. (Programmers describe this action as a SAVE *to* tape or a SAVE *to* disk.)

VDM—This abbreviation stands for video display module, which is an electronic screen for displaying data or information.

DISCUSSION

The starting point of this lesson is after Applesoft is in place in the Apple II computer. When Applesoft is loaded into the computer from ROM (read only memory), disk, or cassette tape, the cursor ( ]) and the prompt (■) appear on the left side of the screen.

The older version of the Apple II came with Integer BASIC as standard equipment and Applesoft as an accessory available either on ROM or cassette tape. The present Apple II Plus comes with Applesoft as a standard ROM card and the Integer BASIC language as an accessory to be purchased separately.

Programs typed on the keyboard are stored in memory. Programs of value are SAVEd to cassette tape or disk. From your program library programs are LOADed from tape or disk into memory. Programs are also referred to as software.

After the screen has been cleared, type in the following program.

```
10   PRINT "THIS IS THE USA"
20   PRINT
30   PRINT "THIS IS THE"
40   PRINT "UNITED STATES"
50   PRINT "OF   AMERICA"
60   PRINT
70   PRINT "THIS IS THE",
80   PRINT "USA"
999  END
```

Type in RUN and press RETURN. The output from the program appears on the screen. Study the output in relation to the program statements. Now type LIST and press RETURN. The program is listed on the screen. To save this program on cassette tape follow these steps.

1. Type in SAVE–*DO NOT PRESS RETURN.*
2. Place a cassette into the tape recorder and rewind until the tape stops.
3. Press the stop-pause button.
4. Set the mechanical counter on the recorder to zero.
5. Forward the tape to a specific number on the counter (for example, forward the counter to 005).
6. Set the recorder volume to 6 and the tone to medium.
7. Press record-play buttons (or the combination that will cause your recorder to record).
8. Now press the RETURN key on the computer. The cursor leaves the screen and the computer beeps. This indicates the program is being SAVEd to tape.
9. When the recording is completed, the computer beeps and the cursor returns to the screen.
10. Press the stop-pause button on the recorder.

The program has been SAVEd to tape. To facilitate future location of the program, label the program on the cassette cover in the following manner.

1. Name and description of the program.
2. Starting number (on the counter) of the program.
3. Ending number (on the counter) of the program.
4. Volume and tone of the recording. (generally a volume of 6 and a medium tone from a Panasonic recorder will satisfactorily SAVE and LOAD programs on the Apple II)

Keeping a record of programs on tape aids in finding and LOADing programs. Four programs for each 15 minute tape are sufficient for program protection. Record programs on only one side of the tape. Valuable programs should be duplicated on separate tapes and stored in a safe place.

To check the program just recorded, LOAD the program back into computer memory as follows.

1. Type in NEW. This clears memory.
2. Type in LIST. This checks to see that memory is clear.
3. Type in LOAD–*DO NOT HIT RETURN.*
4. Rewind tape until it stops.
5. Press counter to read zero.
6. Forward tape to 004 (program recording started at 005).
7. Stop tape recorder.
8. Pull out monitor plug from recorder so sound can be heard.

9. Press play button on the recorder.
10. When the shrill sound is heard, press plug into monitor.
11. Now press RETURN.
12. Cursor leaves the screen, the computer beeps, and the program LOADs.
13. When the program is LOADed a beep is heard and the cursor returns to the screen.
14. Type RUN to run or LIST to list the program.

After each operation, the RETURN key must be pressed to complete the operation. From this point when an operation is complete, you must press the RETURN key. Enough said about the RETURN key.

In most cases a volume of 6 and a medium tone will produce a satisfactory LOAD or SAVE. A volume and/or tone that is too low will produce an ERR below the LOAD or SAVE on the screen. A volume that is too high will produce a MEM FULL ERR below the LOAD or SAVE. Persistent difficulty in LOAD or SAVE routines indicates the tape recorder should be checked to determine if the frequency of the recorder synchronizes with the frequency of the computer.

Tapes should be of the highest quality and low background noise. Low quality tapes will give the user great difficulty in LOADing and SAVEing programs.

To SAVE programs to disk, the disk operating system must be booted. To SAVE a program to disk it is necessary to type the program on the keyboard and to store the program in memory. The same program that was SAVEd to tape will be the same program SAVEd to disk. The program will be named "USA".

1. Place initialized disk in the disk drive.
2. Close disk drive door.
3. Type in SAVE USA.
4. Press RETURN.

The program has now been SAVEd to disk.

To clear memory, type NEW, then LIST. This clears memory and prepares the computer to load the program from disk.

1. Type in LOAD USA.
2. Press RETURN.

The program is now LOADed from disk. The main difference between tape and disk is that disk programs must be named.

Here is a suggestion that is slightly off the subject. Many companies advertise vinyl dust covers for your computers, disks, and printers. These valuable machines definitely need dust covers—but dust covers that breathe. Vinyl covers trap moisture under the cover and this condensation falls into the machine. This excess moisture held against the working parts causes an oxide called rust. This excess moisture is also bad for the integrated circuits, capacitors, and other parts of the computer. To keep out the dust, use a canvas material that breathes.

LESSON 2

Print Rules

After completion of Lesson 2 you should be able to:

1. Write a program in Applesoft using PRINT statements.
2. Define and properly use the rules pertaining to PRINT statements.

VOCABULARY

Applesoft II BASIC—This is a more extended, comprehensive, and flexible language than INTEGER BASIC.

Command—Commands are executed immediately and do not require a line number but can be used as program statements in certain cases.

Documentation—This is the total history of a program and its component parts from inception to completion. Documentation enables another programmer to understand the program.

Delimiters—These are the signals that tell the computer how closely the results are to be printed, i.e., the comma and the semicolon.

Format—This is the predetermined arrangement of data, the layout of the printed document.

PRINT—This statement outputs data.

REM—This statement allows comment within the program but produces no action in the program. In other words, "REM" reminds the programmer of what the program does. You can type any comment you like in a REM statement.

Semicolon—This prevents the cursor from moving after output is completed. In other words, it inhibits the automatic repositioning of the cursor.

Statement—Statements are instructions that require line numbers and tell the computer what action to take.

DISCUSSION

The first objective of this lesson is to write a program using a PRINT statement.

A program is a set of instructions developed to solve a specific problem. In this example, the problem is to print out the statement "THIS IS THE USA."

```
5    REM - PROGRAM - PRINT RULES
10   PRINT "THIS IS THE USA"
999  END
```

Now that was simple, wasn't it? This programming sure is easy.

The number "5" in the first line is the line number that identifies a statement of the program for reference use by the programmer. The first line doesn't have to start with the number "1." You can use any number you like up to 63999, the highest line number possible on an Apple II. However, succeeding lines must have higher line numbers than previous lines. The most practical way is to number every line in 5s or 10s. This way you'll be able to insert extra program steps later if you want to expand your program.

The "REM" statement helps the programmer document the program.

The line 10 PRINT "THIS IS THE USA" is a program statement that outputs the information enclosed in quotation marks.

The line 999 END is the end of the program. Apple Company's Applesoft guide states that an END statement is unnecessary and eliminating it is one way to conserve memory space. It is strongly suggested that an END statement always be used in every program. In many cases a program will not run properly without an end statement.

Now type in line 10 without quotation marks.

```
10   PRINT THIS IS THE USA       (no quotation marks)
999  END
RUN
0        (zero)
```

The output is zero (0) because the computer reads THIS IS THE USA as a variable that has a zero (0) value. Variables are used to hold values that change as the program progresses.

Now type in line 10 using a beginning quote and no closing quote.

```
10   PRINT "THIS IS THE USA
999  END
```

```
RUN
THIS IS THE USA
```

THIS IS THE USA prints even though there is no closing quote. Applesoft is flexible enough to let you "get away" without a closing quote.

Now type line 10 with no beginning quote but with a closing quote.

```
10   PRINT   THIS IS THE USA"
999  END
RUN
0
```

The output is zero (0) because the computer recognizes THIS IS THE USA as an uninitialized variable and the ending quote is ignored.

Retype line 10 again, this time spelling PRINT incorrectly, and see what happens.

```
10   PUNT "THIS IS THE USA"
999  END
RUN
SYNTAX ERR #10
```

Now that you have all the errors out of your system—on to the PRINT rules. This program was written and tested line by line so the student can view the results produced by each program statement.

1. Anything in quotation marks is printed exactly as in the PRINT statement when RUN.

```
10   PRINT "THIS IS THE USA"
20   PRINT     (this PRINT causes a line feed — a space between lines)
999  END
RUN
THIS IS THE USA
```

2. PRINT statements with no punctuation following the closing quote cause the output to be printed on one line and causes the computer to line feed (space down). Consecutive PRINT statements with no closing punctuation causes the output to be printed vertically, one output below the other.

```
30   PRINT "THIS IS THE"
40   PRINT "UNITED STATES"
50   PRINT "OF AMERICA"
60   PRINT
RUN
THIS IS THE
```

```
UNITED STATES
OF AMERICA
```

3. A comma placed at the end of a print statement places the output in separate fields on the same line. Applesoft is designed to divide each line into 3 fields. The first field begins at column 1 and ends at column 16. The second field begins at column 17 and ends at column 33. The third field begins at column 34 and ends at column 40.

```
70   PRINT "THIS IS THE",
80   PRINT "USA"
90   PRINT
RUN
THIS IS THE         USA
```

4. A semicolon placed at the end of a PRINT statement causes the output to be packed (no space).

```
100  PRINT "THIS IS THE";
110  PRINT "USA"
120  PRINT
RUN
THIS IS THEUSA
```

5. A comma between the two items in a PRINT statement places the output in the 1st field and the next output in the next available field.

```
130  PRINT "THIS IS THE" , "USA"
140  PRINT
RUN
THIS IS THE       USA
```

6. A semicolon between two items in a PRINT statement causes the output to be packed (no space).

```
150  PRINT "THIS IS THE" ; "USA"
160  PRINT
RUN
THIS IS THEUSA
```

(Note that examples 3 and 5 give the same output, but are produced by a different program statement format. The same is true of examples 4 and 6.

7. Spaces placed between quotation marks and the item will be outputted in the print format. (*X's are placed in the PRINT statement to represent blank spaces*).

```
170  PRINT "XXTHIS IS THEX" ; "USA"
180 PRINT
```

```
RUN
XXTHIS IS THEXUSA      (X's represent blank spaces)
```

8. A PRINT following a PRINT statement closes out the line. (A PRINT following a PRINT statement with no punctuation causes a line feed, i.e., space between the lines. A PRINT following punctuation closes out the line, but does not cause a line feed).

```
190  PRINT "THIS IS THE";
200  PRINT
210  PRINT "USA"
220  PRINT
RUN
THIS IS THE
USA
```

9. To print variables with assigned values NO quotation marks are used and the assigned values are printed.

```
230  A = 5 : B = 10 : C = 15
240  PRINT A
250  PRINT B
260  PRINT C
270  PRINT
RUN
5
10
15

280 PRINT A,B,C
290 PRINT
RUN
5                          10                          15

300  PRINT A; B; C
RUN
51015
```

The same punctuation rules that apply to items enclosed in quotation marks apply to variables.

1. No punctuation prints vertically.
2. Commas after variables print in three vertical columns.
3. Semicolons after variables pack the output leaving no space between numbers.

The complete program and RUN follows.

```
5    REM — PRINT RULES
10   PRINT "THIS IS THE USA"
20   PRINT
30   PRINT "THIS IS THE"
```

```
40  PRINT "UNITED STATES"
50  PRINT "OF AMERICA"
60  PRINT
70  PRINT "THIS IS THE" ,
80  PRINT "USA"
90  PRINT
100 PRINT "THIS IS THE" ;
110 PRINT "USA"
120 PRINT
130 PRINT " THIS IS THE" , "USA"
140 PRINT
150 PRINT "THIS IS THE" ; "USA"
160 PRINT
170 PRINT "XXTHIS IS THEX" ; "USA"
180 PRINT
190 PRINT "THIS IS THE" ;
200 PRINT
210 PRINT "USA"
220 PRINT
230 A = 5 : B = 10 : C = 15
240 PRINT A
250 PRINT B
260 PRINT C
270 PRINT
280 PRINT A, B, C
290 PRINT
300 PRINT A; B; C
999 END
RUN
THIS IS THE USA

THIS IS THE
UNITED STATES
OF AMERICA

THIS IS THE       USA

THIS IS THEUSA

THIS IS THE       USA

THIS IS THEUSA

XXTHIS IS THEXUSA

THIS IS THE
USA

5
10
15

5                             10                            15

51015
```

LESSON 3

HTAB, TAB, and VTAB Statements to Format Output

After completion of Lesson 3 you should be able to:

1. Use HTAB, TAB, and VTAB statements to format output on the CRT, similar to using the tabulators and return on a typewriter.
2. Draw the location of rows and columns on the CRT.
3. Clear the CRT by the use of HOME and CALL statements.

VOCABULARY

CALL—This causes the execution of a machine language subroutine at a memory location whose decimal address is specified in the call expression. CALL -936 clears the screen. CALL -936 causes the same results as HOME.

Colon—The colon separates multiple statements that are on the same line. The colon is also called the program statement separator.

HOME—This clears the screen of all data and moves the cursor to the upper left position within the scrolling window. Produces the same results as CALL -936.

HTAB—This moves the cursor from 1 to 40 spaces over on the current line and prints data at the HTAB numeric expression. HTAB 20 prints data at column 20 on the current line.

Program Statement Separator—This is the colon in Applesoft language that allows multiple statements at the same line number.

TAB—This must be used in a PRINT statement and prints data one column past the numeric expression. PRINT TAB(20) prints data at column 21 of the current line.

VTAB—This moves the cursor to a line that is in the numeric expression. VTAB 12 moves the cursor to row 12 on the screen. The numeric expression in VTAB can range from 1 to 24.

DISCUSSION

HTAB is a function that allows the programmer to place information on a specific vertical column on the VDM. The VDM has columns numbered from 1 to 40.

VTAB is a function that allows the programmer to place information on a specific horizontal row on the VDM. The VDM has 24 rows numbered from 1 to 24.

HTAB and VTAB are generally used together in the same program line and are separated by a colon (:). The colon is used as a separator between two or more program statements with the same line number.

TAB (26) is used only in a PRINT statement and is separated from other statements by semicolons, and it accomplishes the same purpose as the HTAB.

HOME is a command that moves the cursor and the prompt to the upper left hand corner of the screen of all text. Call -936 clears the screen in the same way.

HOME and CALL -936 are discussed because the following program must clear the screen to see the HTAB and VTAB functions executed properly.

```
10   HOME
20   VTAB 1   : PRINT "A"
RUN
```

This clears the screen and prints "A" at VTAB 1 : HTAB 1 (see Fig. 3-1).

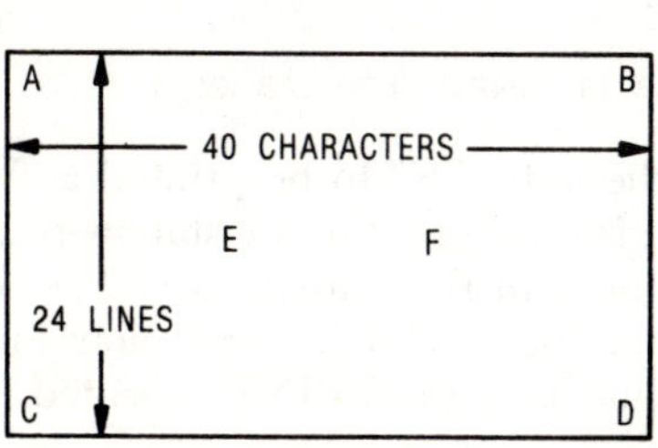

Fig. 3-1. VDM screen.

```
30   VTAB 1  : HTAB 40 : PRINT "B";
RUN
```

This prints "B" at VTAB 1 : HTAB 40. The semicolon is necessary to prevent line feed.

```
40   VTAB 24 : HTAB 1 : PRINT "C"; : VTAB 10
RUN
```

This prints "C" at VTAB 24 : HTAB 1. The semicolon prevents line feed and the colon closes out the line. VTAB 10 shifts the cursor to VTAB 10, because if we didn't, the computer would automatically shift the cursor to the next line when we close out line 40. Since the cursor is already on the last line of the screen, the present screen display must shift up one line to make more room. That will cause us to lose "A" and "B" from the display, and it will shift "C" up one line. To avoid all that, we just tell the computer to move the cursor up instead of down. Of course, if we weren't running this line by itself, the next line could instruct the computer to put the cursor elsewhere. And that's just what we do in the next line, line 50.

```
50   VTAB 24 : HTAB 39 : PRINT "D"; : VTAB 10
RUN
```

This prints "D" at VTAB 24 : HTAB 39. Even though the screen is 40 columns wide it is not possible to print the "D" at VTAB 24 : HTAB 40 without shifting the "A" and "B" characters off the screen, because, immediately after we print there and before we can do anything else, the cursor jumps to the next line.

To clean up the program type LIST 40. Line 40 will be displayed on the screen. Now retype the line.

```
40   VTAB 24 : HTAB 1 : PRINT "C";
```

That leaves out the last colon and the VTAB 10. The program still runs properly because the ":" and VTAB 10 are not necessary with the inclusion of line 50. (The edit function is discussed in further detail in Lesson 15.)

```
60   VTAB 12 : HTAB 13 : PRINT "E" ; TAB (26) ; "F"
```

Line 60 causes the letter "E" to be printed at VTAB 12 : HTAB 13. A TAB function is used in a PRINT statement and the numerical expression is contained in the parentheses. The TAB (26) expression is separated from the PRINT by semicolons on each side. Notice that the "F" does not have the PRINT repeated but is enclosed in quotation marks.

Here is the program written as a unit.

```
10   HOME
20   VTAB 1 : PRINT "A"
30   VTAB 1 : HTAB 40 : PRINT "B" ;
40   VTAB 24 : HTAB 1 : PRINT "C" ;
50   VTAB 24 : HTAB 39 : PRINT "D" ; : VTAB 10
60   VTAB 12 : HTAB 13 : PRINT "E" ; TAB (26); "F"
999  END
```

Type in and RUN the following program to learn more about controlling PRINT statements (see Fig. 3-2).

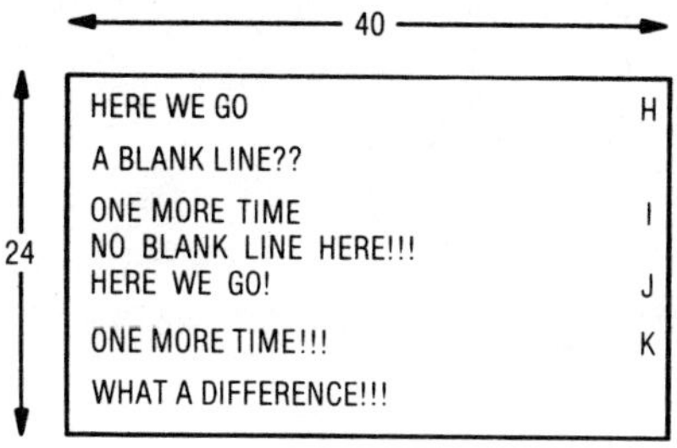

Fig. 3-2. PRINT program results.

```
70   HOME
80   PRINT "HERE WE GO" ; TAB (39); "H"
90   PRINT "A BLANK LINE??"
100  PRINT : PRINT
110  PRINT  "ONE MORE TIME" ; TAB (39) ; "I" ;
120  PRINT "NO BLANK LINE HERE!!!"
130  PRINT "HERE WE GO !" ; : HTAB 40 : PRINT "J"
140  PRINT "ONE MORE TIME !" ;: HTAB 40 : PRINT "K"
150  PRINT "WHAT A DIFFERENCE!!!"
160  END
```

Line 70 clears the screen.

Line 80 prints "H" in column 40 on the top line. PRINT TAB (39) actually prints one column past the value of the TAB statement. After "H" is printed the cursor went to the second line, first column to prepare for the next item. Since the PRINT statement was complete, the second line was closed out.

Line 90 prints on the third line even though the second line is completely blank.

Line 100 leaves 2 blank lines.

Line 110 is almost a duplicate of line 80, except for the semicolon after "I." The semicolon does not close out the line.

Line 120 is printed immediately below "ONE MORE TIME" because the line was not closed out.

Lines 130 through 150 do essentially the same things as lines 80 through 120 except the HTAB function is used instead of the TAB function. The HTAB prints in the place where the HTAB value is assigned. HTAB 40 prints at column 40. TAB (39) prints at one column more than the assigned value. TAB (39) prints at column 40.

You cannot print at VTAB 24 : HTAB 40 without pushing the top line off the screen.

You cannot print at VTAB 24 : PRINT TAB (39) without pushing the top line off the screen.

LESSON 4

Variables

After completion of Lesson 4 you should be able to:

1. Define the variables used in Applesoft.
2. Distinguish between variables and reserved words.
3. Understand the relationship between integers and reals and how truncation affects mathematical calculations.
4. Use INT and DEF functions to round off calculations.

VOCABULARY

DEF FN—This allows the programmer to define functions within the program.

Deferred Execution—This means that a line is to be executed at a later time. Basic statements with a line number are run in the deferred mode.

Immediate Execution—This means that a line is to be executed immediately. Basic commands without a line number are run in the immediate execution mode.

Integer—This is any whole number, its negative, or a zero. Integers never include decimal points, unless they are being expressed as real numbers.

Literal—This is a sequence of characters enclosed in quotation marks. In A$ = "HELLO", A$ is a variable, HELLO is a string, and "HELLO" is a literal. See the definition of *String* below.

Real—This is any number, including integers, that can be written with a decimal.

Scientific Notation—This is the method of expressing numbers as powers of ten. In scientific notation, the number 1234 is 1.234×10^3 and the number 0.001234 is 1.234×10^{-3}. Applesoft uses the symbol "E" to indicate that the number before the E is to be multiplied by ten raised to the power indicated after the E. For instance, 1×10^{11} is expressed by Applesoft as 1 E +11.

String—This is any sequence of characters.

Truncate—This is the act of rounding a number upward or downward to the next whole number. It is also the act of removing a normal or expected element at the end of a number.

DISCUSSION

A variable, according to Webster, is:

1. Something that is variable.
2. A quantity that may assume any one of a set of values.
3. A symbol representing a variable.

In Applesoft, a variable can be an alpha (alphabet) character (A through Z), two alpha characters (AA), or an alpha and a numeric (0 through 9) character unless these characters are part of a word reserved specifically for Applesoft language.

LEGAL APPLESOFT VARIABLES

A	BB	C1	Z2

LEGAL APPLESOFT VARIABLES—but only the first 2 characters are recognized by the language.

DOE	S1M	SU3	PER

ILLEGAL APPLESOFT VARIABLES—that are reserved words.

ABS	AND	CALL	DEL
LET	LOAD	SAVE	VTAB

A complete list of reserved words is found on page 122 of the *Applesoft II BASIC PROGRAMMING REFERENCE MANUAL*, published by Apple Computer, Inc.

What happens when a reserved word is used as a variable?

```
10  FOR = 5
20  PRINT FOR
30  END
RUN
? SYNTAX ERR IN 10
```

The syntax err message is produced and the program does not run. One deficiency of the Applesoft language is that it does not give an error message until the program is run. A better method would be to give an error message when the program statement is input.

TYPES OF APPLESOFT VARIABLES

TYPE	EXAMPLE
INTEGER	A% = 1
REAL	A = 1.23
STRING	A$ = B2.5

An integer is any of the natural, or whole, numbers, the negatives of these numbers, or a zero. The numbers 1, 2, 3, 4, and 5 are integers. Integers must be in the range of −32768 to +32767 or the machine will give an ILLEGAL QUANTITY ERR because you are out of the range of its capabilities. Applesoft uses a percent (%) sign to designate integer variables.

```
10   A% = 10
20   PRINT A%
30   END
RUN
10
```

A real number converted to an integer is truncated. A truncated number is cut short, or lacks an expected or normal element at the end of the number. How does Applesoft handle positive numbers that are truncated?

```
10   B% = 3.1416
20   PRINT B%
30   END
RUN
3
```

Applesoft converts positive reals to positive integers by truncating them *down* toward zero.

3.1416 truncated = 3

How does Applesoft handle negative reals when it converts them to integers?

```
10   C% = -0.843
20   PRINT C%
30   END
RUN
0    (zero)
```

Applesoft converts negative reals to integers by converting them *up* toward zero.

How does truncation affect mathematical computations? The

computation of the area of a circle 3 feet in radius is given as an example.

```
10    PI% = 3.1416 : R = 3
20    A% = PI% * R∧2        The symbol "∧" tells the computer that the following
                            number is an exponent.
30    PRINT A%
40    END
RUN
27
```

The answer 27 is not very accurate compared to the actual answer of 28.27. The integer function is inaccurate when performing mathematical calculations, but it is extremely important in other situations that will be explained later.

Reals are numbers that relate to practical or every day numbers. Dollars and cents, 3.1416, −2.5, and 0 are real numbers. Applesoft prints reals of nine digits or less directly. Numbers requiring more than nine digits, such as 9999999999 or 0.000000009, are converted to scientific notation.

For 9 digits or less, Applesoft prints out a maximum of 9 digits.

```
10    A = 999999999
20    PRINT A
30    END
RUN
999999999
```

Over 9 digits, Applesoft converts to scientific notation with an exponent from 10 to 38.

```
10    A = 9999999999
20    PRINT A
30    END
RUN
1E+10
```

Now that we have all the power of real numbers how do we control it to the number of digits we want?

The number of digits printed when outputting real numbers can be controlled by the INT function. The following program demonstrates how reals can be rounded to a specific number of places.

```
10    P = 1000         (P = a variable to determine the number of
                       places to which the number is rounded)
20    PI = 3.1416 : R = 3
30    A = PI * R∧2
40    PRINT A, INT (A * P + .5)/P, INT (A)
RUN
28.2744          28.274          28
```

In this example, the INT function outputs to one place. For the last time, change line 10

```
10   P = 100
RUN
28.2744            28.27          28
```

In this example, the INT function outputs to two decimal places. Again change line 10.

```
10   P = 10
RUN
28.2744            28.3           28
```

In this example, the INT function outputs to one place. For the last time, change line 10

```
10   P = 0
RUN
? DIVISION BY ZERO ERROR IN 40
```

Remember the old rule? Thou shalt not divide by zero.

An easier way to handle rounding is by using DEF FN. Any function may be defined by using DEF FNA (X), where "X" is a dummy variable that holds the equation and A is the function name.

```
10   DEF FNM (X) = INT (X*1000 + .5)/1000
20   DEF FNN (Y) = INT (Y*100 + .5)/100
30   DEF FNO (Z) = INT (Z*10 + .5)/10
40   PI = 3.1416 : R = 3
50   A = PI* R 2
60   PRINT FNM(A), FNN(A), FNO(A)
99   END
RUN
28.274           28.27          28.3
(line 10)        (line 20)      (line 30)
```

By using the DEF FN the rounding can be controlled and the PRINT statement is much simpler to write. In this example, if you want A to be displayed to three decimal places you must use FNM (A). Similarly, if you want two or one decimal place displays, you must use FNN (A) or FND (A), respectively.

A literal is a set of alphanumeric characters enclosed in quotation marks. The following are examples of literals:

```
"7 - 11 STORE"          "BILL"
"44 - 50"               "SUE"
```

String literals have already been used in the PRINT statement.

A string variable may consist of 255 characters (one row on the screen consists of 40 characters). The following are examples of string variables:

```
A$          Z1$         CC$         COB$
D2468$      HI$         MOLE$       HAIR$
```

A string variable must begin with an alpha character and may be followed by an alpha or numeric character, followed by a dollar sign ($). Remember that only the first two characters are recognized by Applesoft.

```
HA$ is equivalent to HAIR$
Z2$ is equivalent to Z2468$
```

A string is used by placing the string variable on one side of the equals sign and the string literal on the other side.

```
A$ = "HI THERE SUE"
10   A$ = "HI THERE SUE"
20   PRINT A$
999  END
RUN
HI THERE SUE
```

The Apple has a function that tells the number of characters in a string and the length of a literal. To use this function LEN, type in the following:

```
PRINT LEN (A$), LEN ("SUE")      (return)
13              3
```

In this case, *NO* line number is needed. The PRINT is an immediate command that prints out the number of characters in the literal. The length of a literal can be printed by using LEN and placing the literal in parentheses. Did you get a SYNTAX ERR while typing the last PRINT statement? Sure you did! Very few programmers get by with less than a zillion syntax errors.

It should be noted, that A, A%, and A$ are different variables and can be used in the same program.

LESSON 5

Precedence

After completion of Lesson 5 you should be able to:

1. Write the order of precedence of arithmetic operators and show how to modify precedence.
2. Demonstrate three methods to input into a program.
3. Use constants to perform addition, subtraction, multiplication, division, and exponentiation.

VOCABULARY

Arithmetic Operators—These are symbols that instruct the computer to do arithmetic operations, addition, subtraction, multiplication, division, and exponentiation.

ASC—This is the function that converts one string character to a numeric value. PRINT ASC ("A") returns the American Standard Code for Information Interchange (ASCII) value of A which is 65.

*CHR$*—This is the function that converts a numeric value into one string character. PRINT CHR$ (65) returns the character A which is the ASCII value of 65.

Constant—This is an item of data that remains unchanged after each run.

Interactive Mode—This is a method of operation in which the user is in direct communication with the computer and is able to obtain immediate response to his input messages. A display where the user is allowed to input data in response to information displayed is said to be in an interactive mode. Conversational mode (display) is synonymous with interactive mode (display).

LET—This is a replacement statement that allows the value on the right side of the equals sign to be stored in the variable on the left side of the equals sign. LET may be a real, an integer, or a string.

MODEM—This word is a contraction of modulator and demodulator. It means a device that codes or decodes information to send or receive from a remote computer over telephone lines.

Operand—This is the item on which the operation is performed.

Operator—This is the action to be taken on the operand. In A = 5 * 2, times is the operator.

Precedence—This is the order in which things are done.

Replacement Statement—This statement takes the value on the right side of the equals sign and stores it in the variable on the left side of the equals sign (e.g., A = 5 is a replacement statement).

Replacement Operator—In A = 5, the equals (=) sign is the replacement operator.

Unary Operator—This is a processing operation performed on one operand. NOT, plus (+), and minus (−) are unary operators and apply to the sign of a number (−5, +3). It is the same as the monadic operator.

DISCUSSION

The order of precedence is very important in mathematic calculations. Incorrect precedence produces incorrect answers. Correct precedence produces correct answers if all other procedures are correct. The order of precedence of arithmetic operators from highest to lowest is

1. ( ) items enclosed in parentheses are operated on first—highest priority.
2. NOT, +, − NOT, POSITIVE, and NEGATIVE unary or monadic operators.
3. Exponentiation.
4. Multiplication and division.
5. Addition and subtraction.

Operators listed on the same line have the same priority and are executed starting at the left side of the formula and completed on the right side.

Integers and reals are classified as arithmetic variables. Strings are classified as non-arithmetic variables. When integers and reals are used in a formula, the integers are converted to reals before the calculation takes place. The final result can be converted either to an integer or left as a real. String variables (non-arithmetic) cannot be converted directly to integers or reals, but can be converted indirectly by other functions provided for that purpose.

The following program converts a string variable to a numeric variable and converts a numeric variable to a string variable.

```
10   A$ = "A"
20   B = ASC (A$)
30   PRINT B
40   D = 65
50   C$ = CHR$ (D)
60   PRINT C$
70   END
RUN
65
A
```

Line 10 sets A$ = "A". The computer uses coded numbers to represent letters. "A" is converted to the ASCII number. Each letter, number, and symbol on the keyboard has an ASCII number.

Line 20 B = ASC (A$) puts the ASCII number of A (65) into B.

Line 30 PRINT B produces B = 65 which is the conversion of A$ (a string) to a real number.

ASC IS THE FUNCTION THAT CONVERTS ONE STRING CHARACTER TO A NUMBER.

Line 40 D = 65 places the ASCII value of the letter A into D.

Line 50 C$ = CHR$ (D) changes the value of D into a string character in C$.

Line 60 PRINT C$ prints out the letter that was converted from the numeric equivalent of (65) of the letter A.

CHR$ IS THE FUNCTION THAT CONVERTS A NUMBER INTO ONE STRING CHARACTER.

The maximum length of a string is 255 characters.

Now for some examples of precedence.

1. Items enclosed in parentheses can either be variables or numeric values. If the variable is not given a value – a value of zero (0) is returned. The innermost set of parentheses are evaluated first.
   15*(2+(3+2)*3) = 255
   15*(2+ 3+2)*3 = 315
   15* 2+ 3+2 *3 = 39
   Precedence can be modified by using parentheses as demonstrated by the previous example.

2. The monadic or unary operator is the sign (+, –, or NOT) of the number.

+3 +2 = 5 (number is positive when no sign is printed)
+3 −2 = 1
− 3 +2 = −1
−3 −2 = −5

3. Exponentiation.
   3∧2 = 9
   3∧80 = 1.47808831 E + 38
4. Multiplication and division.
   (10 * 5)/(2*5) = 5
   (10 * 5)/ 2*5 = 125
   10 * 5 / 2*5 = 125
5. Addition and subtraction.
   (8 + 2) + (2 + 2) = 14
   8 + 2 + 2 + 2 = 14
   (8 + 2) − (2 + 2) = 6
   8 + 2 − 2 + 2 = 10
   (8 − 2) + (2 − 2) = 6
   8 − 2 + 2 − 2 = 6
   (8 − 2) − (2 − 2) = 6
   8 − 2 − 2 − 2 = 2

There are several ways to get information or data into the computer. The replacement statement and the READ–DATA statement do not require any outside action or external peripherals. The INPUT statement is interactive between the user and the computer. Cassette tape, disk, and modem are external sources to place information or data into the computer.

```
10   LET A = 1 + 2 + 3
20   PRINT A
999  END
RUN
6
```

Line 10 is a replacement statement. The values on the right side of the equals sign are calculated and placed in a memory location that the computer labels "A." The contents of A are 1 + 2 + 3 or 6.

In this case, equals does not mean two equal values on opposite sides of the equals sign, but the value on the right side of the equals sign is transferred to the left side of the equals sign. This is an operation (transfer) for the computer to perform and not an evaluation (decision). The equals is the replacement operator, and the LET is a replacement statement.

Line 20 PRINT A outputs 6, the value stored under the variable label A.

The LET is optional. You get the same results with A = 5 as with

LET A = 5. A = 5 saves memory and is easier to type.

The following program is written to demonstrate the arithmetic operators, print rules, and replacement statements.

```
10   A = 5 : B = 10 : C = 20
20   D = C + B
30   E = C − B
40   F = A * B
50   G = C / A
60   H = A∧2
70   PRINT D : PRINT E : PRINT F : PRINT
80   PRINT F, G, H : PRINT
90   PRINT D; E; F : PRINT
100  D = A : E = B : F = C
110  PRINT D, E, F
999  END
RUN
30        (D, no punctuation, line 70)
10        (E, no punctuation, line 70)
50        (F, no punctuation, line 70)
(line 70, PRINT skips a line)
50     (F comma)          4     (G comma)          25     (H comma)
(line 80, PRINT skips a line)
301050        (D; E; F, semicolons, line 90)
(line 90, PRINT skips a line)
5      (D = A)            10    (E = B)            20     (F = C)
```

Line 100 D = A replaces the existing value of D (30) with the value of A (5). When D is printed, the replaced value 5 is printed. E = B replaces the existing value of E (10) with the value of B (10). These values happened to be the same, so no difference is seen. F = C replaces the existing value of F (50) with the value of C (20).

INPUT is used to place values in the program on an interactive basis. Type in the following lines but leave the rest of the program as it is.

```
6    INPUT "A = ";A
8    INPUT "B = ";B
10   INPUT "C = ";C
RUN
A = 5
B = 10
C = 20
```

The rest of the run is exactly the same as when the replacement statement was used to input the values of A (5), B (10), and C (20).

Now RUN the program using any values that you choose, but do not delete the program because the next step is to use the READ–DATA input method.

When you are through experimenting with different numbers using the INPUT statement type in

```
DEL 6, 10        (return)
```

This deletes the INPUT statements at lines 6, 8, and 10.
Now type in:

```
10  READ A, B, C
120 DATA 5, 10, 20
```

The results of the run are the same as using a replacement statement, INPUT statement, or a READ–DATA statement when the values are A = 5, B = 10, and C = 20.

LESSON 6

Loops

After completion of Lesson 6 you should be able to:

1. Write a program using a GOTO loop.
2. Write a program using a FOR – NEXT loop.
3. Write a program using nested loops.

VOCABULARY

Branch—This is a departure (or the act of departing) from a sequence of program steps to another part of the program. Branching is caused by a branch instruction that can be conditional (i.e., dependent on some previous state or condition in the program) or unconditional (i.e., always occurring). It is also known as a transfer or jump.

Conditional Transfer—See *Branch.*

FOR – NEXT—This is a conditional branch instruction used to make the computer jump to another part of the program.

GOTO—This is an unconditional branch (jump or transfer) to another part of the program. It may be executed in the immediate or deferred mode.

Graphics—This is the art or science of drawing a representation of an object on a two dimensional surface according to mathematical rules of projection.

Increment—This is a fixed quantity that is added to another equivalent quantity.

Initialization—This is a process performed at the beginning of a program or program section or subroutine to ensure that all indicators and constants are set to prescribed conditions and values before that subroutine is run.

Loop—This is a set of instructions that are performed repeatedly until some specified condition is satisfied, whereupon a branch (jump or transfer) instruction is obeyed to exit from the loop.

Nested Loops—These are loops that exist within other loops.

STEP—In a FOR - NEXT loop, STEP is that function that causes the loop to increment by the value designated by the STEP. It may be positive or negative.

Test—This means to examine an element of data or an indicator to ascertain whether some predetermined condition is satisfied.

Unconditional Transfer—See *Branch.*

DISCUSSION

A loop is a series of instructions that are performed repeatedly until a specified condition is satisfied.

Suppose a program was written to count from one to five. One variation of the program could be

```
10   PRINT "1"
20   PRINT "2"
30   PRINT "3"
40   PRINT "4"
50   PRINT "5"
60   END
```

The program would not use the computer very efficiently; writing a program this way to count to a thousand would take all day. A more efficient way to use the computer would be to write a program to count from 1 to 5 by using a GOTO loop.

```
10   X = 1
20   PRINT X
30   X = X + 1
40   IF X>5 THEN 60
50   GOTO 20
60   PRINT : PRINT "I'M THRU COUNTING!"
999  END
RUN
1
2
3
4
5

I'M THRU COUNTING!
```

Line 10 is the initializing top. The loop begins by initializing the variable X to the first value of the count one. If a simple variable is not initialized, the computer initialized the value to zero. The variable could be initialized to any number such as 2, −40, or 308. The programmer must know the correct value to initialize the variable to produce the right answer.

Line 20 prints X each time the loop is executed.

Line 30 is the summing or incrementing statement that keeps track of the number of times the loop has executed. The loop variable was initialized to one. Each time the loop is executed, the summing statement adds one to the initialized value of the variable. In this case, when the summing statement is equal to five, the program (at line 40) jumps out of the loop and executes line 60.

Line 40 is a testing step, a conditional branch or transfer that says, IF the loop has executed five times THEN jump out of the loop to line 60 in the program.

Line 50 is an unconditional branch or transfer that makes the computer go back to line 20.

When the loop has been executed five times and X > 5, line 40 checks that X > 5 and THEN causes a branch to line 60 to print "I'M THRU COUNTING!" and the program ends.

The FOR – NEXT loop program to count from one to five follows.

```
10   FOR X = 1 TO 5        (replacement statement)
20   PRINT X
30   NEXT X
40   PRINT : PRINT "I'M THRU COUNTING!"
999  END
RUN
1
2
3
4
5

I'M THRU COUNTING!
```

This is how the GOTO loop and the FOR – NEXT loop look when they are placed side by side.

GOTO loop

```
10   X = 1
20   PRINT X
30   X = X + 1
40   IF X>5 THEN 60
50   GOTO 20
60   PRINT : PRINT "I'M THRU
     COUNTING!"
END
```

FOR – NEXT loop

```
10   FOR X = 1 TO 5
20   PRINT X
30   NEXT X
40   PRINT : PRINT "I'M THRU
     COUNTING!"
999  END
```

The FOR – NEXT loop program is shorter and more efficient than the GOTO loop program. The GOTO loop is used in cases where the number of times of loop execution is not known beforehand. This will be explained more clearly when the GOTO loop is used with the decision statement in Lesson 7.

The FOR – NEXT loop is used when the number of times of loop execution is known. The FOR – NEXT loop can use loop variables to determine the number of times that the loop is to be executed. In FOR X = 1 TO 5, the number of times the loop will be executed is 5. In FOR X = 1 TO N, the variable "N" determines the number of times the loop will be executed.

In the same FOR – NEXT loop program type in these lines.

```
5    INPUT "COUNT TO # : "; N
10   FOR X = 1 TO N
RUN
COUNT TO # : 3
1
2
3

I'M THRU COUNTING!
```

Line 5 allows the user to input the highest number in the count.

Line 10 causes X to start at the number "1", and go to "N", the highest number to be counted. In this case, X = 1 TO 3.

Now type these lines in the same program.

```
5    READ N
60   DATA 3
RUN
1
2
3

I'M THRU COUNTING!
```

The following program demonstrates how to use loops to print forward, to print forward by steps, and to print backward by steps. It also demonstrates how the HTAB function formats output from loops.

```
10   FOR A = 1 TO 6
20   HTAB (A - 1)*3 + 1 : PRINT A;
30   NEXT A : PRINT
RUN
1  2  3  4  5  6
```

Line 10 designates that the loop executions will go from 1 to 6.

In line 20, the HTAB function sets up the column in which the value of A is to be printed. The "*3" begins a field every three positions ("*4" would begin a field every four positions). The "+1"

Table 6-1. HTAB (A − 1)*3 + 1 : PRINT A;

LOOP EXECUTIONS	A	(A − 1)	(A − 1)*3	(A − 1)*3 + 1	PRINT A;
1	1	0	0	1	1
2	2	1	3	4	2
3	3	2	6	7	3
4	4	3	9	10	4
5	5	4	12	13	5
6	6	5	15	16	6

signifies column one on the left side of the screen. If the "+1" is not used the HTAB tries to print in column zero. Since there is no column zero, the program bombs (a "+2" would signify column two on the left-hand side of the screen). The "*3" controls the positions between the numbers, while the "+1" signifies the number of columns from the left-hand side of the screen. The value of A is printed horizontally because of the semicolon following the A. See Table 6-1 for details.

Line 30 completes the loop and the PRINT closes out the line.

```
40   FOR B = 2 TO 6 STEP 2
50   HTAB (B − 1)*3 + 1 : PRINT B;
60   NEXT B : PRINT
RUN
     2  4  6
```

Line 40 starts with a value of 2, to change the learning experience. STEP 2 causes the loop to be incremented by 2 numbers on each execution. The STEP can be any necessary value, positive or negative, to achieve the solution to the problem.

Lines 50 and 60 are similar to lines 20 and 30.

The next sections of the program use the loop to print the numbers backward.

```
70   FOR C = 6 TO 1 STEP −1
80   HTAB (6 − C)*3 + 1 : PRINT C;
90   NEXT C
100  PRINT
110  FOR D = 6 TO 2 STEP − 2
120  HTAB (6 − D)*3 + 1 : PRINT D;
130  NEXT D : PRINT : PRINT
```

The first PRINT in line 130 closes out the line and the second PRINT causes the program to skip a line between the previous section and the next section of the program printout.

```
140  PRINT "A = ";A; " : B = ";B; ": C = ";C; " : D = ";D
RUN
A = 7 : B = 8 : C = 0 : D = 0
```

The output from line 140 shows the next value of the variable after the loop has completed its executions. In loop A, the values go from 1 to 6, but the loop makes 7 the final value of A. In loop B, the values go from 2 to 6, but the loop makes 8 the final value of B. In loop C, the values go from 6 to 1, but the loop makes 0 the final value of C. In loop D, the values go from 6 to 2, but the loop makes 0 the final value of D. *This is a very important fact.* It is important to keep track of these final values because they can produce incorrect results if the variables are used again and are not initialized. This fact will be detailed in the CASH FLOW program.

The complete program and RUN follows.

```
10   FOR A = 1 TO 6
20   HTAB (A - 1)*3 + 1 : PRINT A;
30   NEXT A : PRINT
40   FOR B = 2 TO 6 STEP 2
50   HTAB (B - 1)*3 + 1 : PRINT B;
60   NEXT B : PRINT
70   FOR C = 6 TO 1 STEP -1
80   HTAB (6 - C)*3 + 1 : PRINT C;
90   NEXT C
100  PRINT
110  FOR D = 6 TO 2 STEP -2
120  HTAB (6 - D)*3 + 1 : PRINT D;
130  NEXT D : PRINT : PRINT
RUN
6  5  4  3  2  1
```

Line 70 sets the loop to go from 6 to 1 and is stepped in increments of −1.

In line 80, since the loop values are to be printed backwards in increments of −1, the value of 6 must be printed on the left side of the screen in column 1. To accomplish this, the value of C must be subtracted from the maximum value of the loop which is 6. (See Table 6-2.)

Line 90 completes the loop.
Line 100 closes the output line.

Table 6-2. HTAB (6 – C)*3 + 1 : PRINT C;

LOOP EXECUTIONS	C	(6 – C)	(6 – C)*3	(6 – C)*3 + 1	PRINT C;
1	6	0	0	1	6
2	5	1	3	4	5
3	4	2	6	7	4
4	3	3	9	10	3
5	2	4	12	13	2
6	1	5	15	15	1

The next section of the program causes the loop to print backwards in steps of −2.

```
110  FOR D = 6 TO 2 STEP −2
120  HTAB (6 − D)*3 + 1 : PRINT D;
130  NEXT D : PRINT : PRINT
RUN
6    4    2
140  PRINT "A = ";A; " :B = ";B; " :C = ";C; " :D = ";D
150  END
RUN
1    2    3    4    5    6
     2         4         6
6    5    4    3    2    1
6         4         2

A = 7 :B = 8 :C = 0 :D = 0
```

Nested loops are a loop within a loop or loops within a loop. In Applesoft, loops can be nested 10 deep.

```
10   FOR S = 1 TO 3 ──────────────────────────────────┐
20   FOR T = 1 TO 5 ────────┐                          │
30   PRINT T; " ";       INNER LOOP               OUTER LOOP
40   NEXT T : PRINT ────────┘                          │
50   NEXT S ──────────────────────────────────────────┘
60   END
RUN
1    2    3    4    5
1    2    3    4    5
1    2    3    4    5
```

Line 20 sets the inner loop to execute 5 times. Line 30 causes the inner loop to print out the value of T on each execution and the quotation marks cause one space to be placed between each of the values in the printout. If two spaces were left between the quotation marks, there would have been two spaces created between the values as they were printed. This gives a second method of spacing in a loop. The first method demonstrated was with the HTAB.

Line 10 and line 50 cause the outer loop to execute three times.

Loops must never be crossed or the program will not execute. Reverse lines 40 and 50 and observe what happens to the program.

```
10   FOR S = 1 TO 3 ──────────────┐
20   FOR T = 1 TO 5 ──────────────┼───────────────────┐
30   PRINT T; " ";          CROSSED LOOP         CROSSED LOOP
40   NEXT S : PRINT ──────────────┘                    │
50   NEXT T ──────────────────────────────────────────┘
60   END
RUN
```

```
1    1    1

?NEXT WITHOUT FOR ERROR IN 50
```

Nested loops give the computer more power in computations and simpler more efficient programming for the programmer. They are very useful in graphics.

The following program uses nested loops and a graphic print to produce the triangle shown in Fig. 6-1.

```
10   FOR S = 1 TO 10
20   HTAB (19 - S)
30   FOR T = 1 TO S
40   PRINT "*";
50   NEXT T : PRINT
60   NEXT S
70   END
RUN
```

```
         *
        **
       ***
      ****
     *****
    ******
   *******
  ********
 *********
**********
```

Fig. 6-1. Triangle.

LESSON 7

Rational and Logical Operators

After completion of Lesson 7 you should be able to:

1. Define and use relational and logical operators in writing a program.
2. Use decision statements in programming.

VOCABULARY

Bug—This is a mistake or malfunction in a computer program.
Debug—This means to remove a mistake, or mistakes, from a computer program or system.
Decision—This is an operation performed by a computer that enables it to choose between alternative courses of action. A decision is usually made by comparing the relative magnitude of two specified operands. A branch instruction is used to select the required path according to the results.
Default—The rule of default states that a computer program runs sequentially according to increasing line numbers unless a branch is executed.
Logical Operator—This is a word or symbol to be applied to two or more operands (AND, OR, and NOT are logical operators).
Relational Operator—This is a method of comparing quantities to make decisions.

DISCUSSION

Program statements have line numbers so the program can run sequentially from the lowest line number to the highest. The program runs sequentially until a program statement containing a relational or logical operator is reached. The program then must weigh the decision. If the decision is true (1 or YES), then the program branches to a line number out of sequence. If the decision is false (0 or NO), then the program continues in its sequential run. The program "falls through" or defaults to the next line number. The rule of default states that unless a branch is executed, the statement with the next highest number is executed. With the computer there are only two decision choices, true or false. There can be no other answer to the decision.

The following relational operators compare two quantities. Based on the result of the comparison, the computer can make a decision.

1. NOT. This is the logical negation of an expression.

1. = Left expression "equals" right expression (in this case, equals is not a replacement statement).
2. < > Left expression "does not equal" right expression.
3. > Left expression "is greater than" right expression.
4. < Left expression "is less than" right expression.
5. >= Left expression "is greater than or equal to" right expression.
6. <= Left expression "is less than or equal to" right expression.
   NOT is a replacement symbol in an IF – THEN statement.

Relational operators are related to logical operators.

1. NOT. This is the logical negation of an expression.
2. AND – IF A>B and C>D THEN 999.
   Expression A>B AND expression C>D must be true for the statement to be true.
3. OR – IF A>B OR C>D THEN 999.
   If either expression A>B OR C>D is true, then the expression is true.

The following program combines PRINT statements, GOTO loops, decision statements, and program sections in one unit to further the learning experience. In Lesson 6 GOTO loops were discussed. This lesson details why a GOTO loop is used in cases where the total number of inputs is not known beforehand. The program deals with applicants who come into a drivers license bureau to apply for an operators permit. The office never knows how many applicants will present themselves on a given day. The GOTO loop accommodates the unknown number of applicants by using decision statements.

An applicant enters the drivers license office and the attendant asks the applicants name and age. The program asks for the age of the applicant. An operators license is issued or not issued on the basis of the age of the applicant. The total number of applicants by age groups and the total number of applicants for the day are printed out and the program terminates.

The program was intentionally written with REM statements in the program to demonstrate how programs can be written in sections to determine if each section runs properly. This is one method of debugging a program. These variables are used in the program:

AGE = age of the applicant

IS 18 = the applicant is 18 years of age

NA = number of applicants

UNDER 18 = the applicant is under 18

OVER 18 = the applicant is over 18

```
10   REM * PROGRAM TO DETERMINE
20   REM * LICENSE ELIGIBILITY AND
30   REM * COUNT THE NUMBER OF APPLICANTS
40   REM * INITIALIZE VARIABLES
50   INPUT "AGE = "; AGE
60   IF AGE <= 0 THEN 190
70   REM * COUNTING VARIABLE
80   IF AGE <18 THEN 130
90   IF AGE = 18 THEN 160
100  REM * COUNTING VARIABLE
110  PRINT "OPERATORS LICENSE"
120  GOTO 50
130  REM * COUNTING VARIABLE
140  PRINT "NO OPERATORS LICENSE"
150  GOTO 50
160  REM * COUNTING VARIABLE
170  PRINT "JUNIOR OPERATORS LICENSE"
180  GOTO 50
190  REM * PRINT HEADINGS
200  PRINT
210  REM * PRINT TOTALS
220  END
RUN
AGE = 36
OPERATORS LICENSE
AGE = 18
JUNIOR OPERATORS LICENSE
AGE = 15
NO OPERATORS LICENSE
AGE = 0
] ■
```

The program RUNs as planned. When age is input, the output shows the eligibility of the applicant. The first program revision counts the number of applicants. Change the program by typing in the following line numbers and program statements.

```
40    NA = 0         (initialize summing variable to zero)
70    NA = NA + 1         (counting statement)
190   PRINT "TOTAL APPLICANTS"
210   PRINT NA
RUN
AGE = 25
OPERATORS LICENSE
AGE = 0
TOTAL APPLICANTS

1
```

It worked just as planned. Now let's try the second revision.

Line 40 initializes the variable NA (number of applicants) to zero.

Line 70 is a replacement statement that is also a counting statement that counts the number of applicants. This will be discussed in detail in Lesson 10. The value of NA (originally zero) is incremented by the value of 1 for each applicant. This incremented value (NA + 1) is placed on the left side of the equals into NA. When processing the first applicant, the counter looks like this: NA = 0 + 1. With the second applicant the process is repeated, so the counter is NA = 1 + 1 and the results are placed on the left side of the equals sign into the variable NA. As each applicant's age is input, the counter is incremented by 1. The incrementing continues until a zero is input, which causes the program to branch to line 190 to print out the totals (see line 60).

The second revision separates the applicants by age, counts and prints out the total number of applicants, and prints out the number of applicants that are UNDER 18, NOW 18, and OVER 18.

Type in the following line numbers and program statements.

```
40  NA = 0 : UNDER 18 = 0 : NOW 18 = 0 : OVER 18 = 0
100  OVER 18 = OVER 18 + 1
130  UNDER 18 = UNDER 18 + 1
160  NOW 18 = NOW 18 + 1
190  PRINT "TOTAL NUMBER  UNDER 18  NOW 18  OVER 18"
210  HTAB 5 : PRINT NA; TAB (16); UNDER 18; TAB (25);
     NOW 18; TAB (33); OVER 18
RUN
AGE = 15
NO OPERATORS LICENSE
AGE = 18
JUNIOR OPERATORS LICENSE
AGE = 25
```

```
OPERATORS LICENSE
AGE = 0
TOTAL NUMBER  UNDER 18  NOW 18  OVER 18
     3            1        1       1
```

The second revision initializes three more counting variables to zero.

```
40   NA = 0 : UNDER 18 = 0 : NOW 18 = 0 : OVER 18 = 0
100  OVER 18 = OVER 18 + 1
130  UNDER 18 = UNDER 18 + 1
160  NOW 18 = NOW 18 + 1
```

Lines 100, 130, and 160 add counting statements to count the number of applicants in each age bracket. The counting statements are placed in the program sections that deal with the specific age of the applicant. The GOTO statements of lines 120, 150, and 180 are the ends of GOTO loops. The statements are unconditional jumps to line 50, the line that accepts the age of the next applicant.

The two program revisions complete the program and solve the problem of totaling the number of applicants and total the applicants by age.

The program section pertaining to applicants UNDER 18 is

```
80   IF AGE<18 THEN 130
130  UNDER 18 = UNDER 18 + 1
140  PRINT "NO OPERATORS LICENSE"
150 GOTO 50
```

The program section pertaining to those applicants who are 18 is

```
90   IF AGE = 18 THEN 160
160  IS 18 = IS 18 + 1
170  PRINT "JUNIOR OPERATORS LICENSE"
180  GOTO 50
```

The program section dealing with those applicants OVER 18 is

```
90   IF AGE = 18 THEN 160      (if the AGE is OVER 18 the statement is FALSE
                                and the program defaults to line 100)
100  OVER 18 = OVER 18 + 1
110  PRINT "OPERATORS LICENSE"
120  GOTO 50
```

Finally, the program section that deals with line 60:

```
60   IF AGE <= 0 THEN 190
190  PRINT "TOTAL NUMBER UNDER 18  NOW 18  OVER 18"
200  PRINT
210  HTAB 5 : PRINT NA; TAB (16); UNDER 18; TAB (25);
     NOW 18; TAB (33); OVER 18
220  END
```

In the operators eligibility program, there are 3 age classifications, UNDER 18, NOW 18, and OVER 18. There are, however, only two decision statements to select the 3 age categories. Line 60 does not select an age category.

```
80   IF AGE <18 THEN 130
90   IF AGE = 18 THEN 160
```

As shown above, line 80 selects applicants UNDER 18. If line 80 is *TRUE* it branches to line 160. If line 80 is *FALSE* the program defaults to line 100.

```
10   REM * PROGRAM TO DETERMINE
20   REM * LICENSE ELIGIBILITY AND
30   REM * COUNT THE NUMBER OF APPLICANTS
40   NA = 0 : UNDER 18 = 0 : IS 18 = 0 : OVER 18 = 0
50   INPUT "AGE = "; AGE
60   IF AGE <= 0 THEN 190
70   NA = NA + 1
80   IF AGE <18 THEN 130
90   IF AGE = 18 THEN 160
100  OVER 18 = OVER 18 + 1
110  PRINT "OPERATORS LICENSE"
120  GOTO 50
130  UNDER 18 = UNDER 18 + 1
140  PRINT "NO OPERATORS LICENSE"
150  GOTO 50
160  IS 18 = IS 18 + 1
170  PRINT "JUNIOR OPERATORS LICENSE"
180  GOTO 50
190  PRINT "TOTAL NUMBER  UNDER 18  IS 18  OVER 18"
200  PRINT
210  HTAB 5 : PRINT NA; TAB (16); UNDER 18; TAB (25);
     IS 18; TAB (33); OVER 18
220  END
```

In Applesoft, an IF – THEN statement that is TRUE executes all statements after the THEN.

```
10   A = 5
20   IF A>4 THEN A = 6 : B = A/12: PRINT : GOTO 90
```

In this case, since A> 4 is TRUE all statements at line 20 are executed before the computer branches to line 90.

```
10   A = 5
20   IF A>4 THEN 90 : A = 6 : B = A/12 : PRINT
```

In this case, since A>4 is TRUE it branches to line 90 *without* executing the other statements at line 20.

With the Age Eligibility Program completed, the following concepts have been reinforced.

1. PRINT statement rules.
2. HTAB and TAB rules.
3. GOTO loops.
4. Operators and decision statements.
5. Initializing variables and counting statements have been introduced and will be discussed in greater detail in Lesson 10.

LESSON 8

Problem Solving and Flowcharts

After completing Lesson 8 you should be able to:

1. Begin using a logical method in problem solving.
2. Flowcart simple problems with flowchart symbols.

VOCABULARY

Hardware—This is the name for all of the physical units of a computer system. Hardware is made up of the apparatus rather than the programs.

Logic Flowchart—This is a chart representing a system of logical elements and their relationship within the overall design of the system or hardware unit. It is the representation of the various logical steps in any program or routine by means of a standard set of symbols. A flowchart is produced before detailed coding for the solution of a particular problem.

Software—In its most general form, software refers to all programs that can be used on a particular computer system.

DISCUSSION

When you write a computer program, you solve a problem. The most basic approach to solving a problem is to first understand the problem. In the program to compute the area of a circle, the formula was discussed and thought out in high school math. The knowledge simplifies the programming of the output. A program to compute and compare three types of depreciation somewhat changes the problem. The first problem in programming is to understand the problem and its ramifications.

Once the problem is understood, the solution must be placed in the proper order. The exact output format must be known. The precise formulas to output the correct answers must be used. The exact language that the computer understands must be programmed in the proper order, and the idiosyncracies and normal operations of the machine must be understood. The computer can only output according to specific input. The excuse is often heard, "It's the computer's fault." Computers seldom (if ever) make errors, it's the human input that is in error. Computers are stupid but exacting. Many programmers pray for a program statement DWIT (do what I think). The DWIT statement is not yet available in Applesoft, so we'll do the best we can with what we have. Remember, the computer does exactly what you tell it to do, nothing more, nothing less.

Once the problem, the language, and the computer are understood, all other problems are relatively simple. The program can now be written to solve the problem.

The output must be tested for correct results with as many different inputs as possible. Simple inputs may produce correct outputs, but are there cases where the outputs are incorrect? The program should be tested and debugged to produce the correct output under all circumstances. What if the program to put a man on the moon had had bugs in it?

Has the program been documented with REM statements and other written records so another person could RUN the program and understand the output? Have the variables been recorded so the computational formulas can be easily understood? Has the program been properly indexed so it can be easily located in the library? The answers to all these questions should be yes. It is easy to forget what problem a program solves, what the variables represent, and where the program can be located.

Flowcharting, or logic flowcharting, is a technique for representing a succession of events in symbolic form. Flowcharting is the first step in logical program development. It aids in thinking the program through from the problem to the computer stage.

In data processing, flowcharts may be divided into two types, system flowcharts and program flowcharts.

System flowcharts, using symbols, show the logical relationship between successive events using hardware. Such symbols include data input (on, for example, magnetic tape, disks, and punched cards) and data output (through, for instance, printers, magnetic tape, or disk).

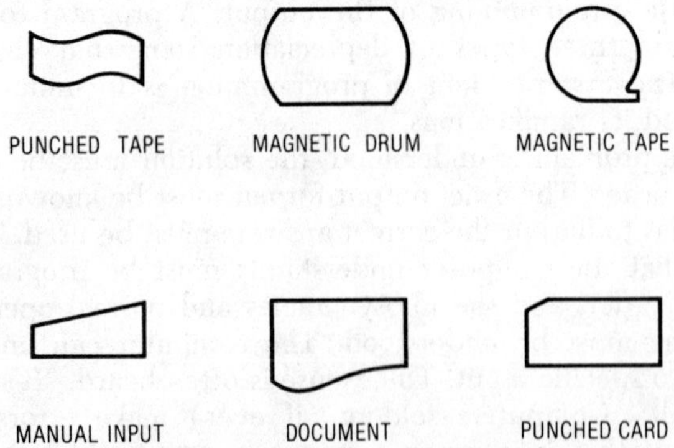

SYSTEM SYMBOLS

Program flowcharts show diagrammatically the logical relationship between successive steps in the program. For most complicated programs, an outline flowchart precedes a detailed flowchart before the program is written.

The purposes of an outline or initial flowchart are to show:

1. All input and output functions.
2. How input and output are to be processed.
3. How the program will be divided into routines and subroutines.

The purposes of a detail or final flowchart are:

1. To interpret the detailed program specifications.
2. To determine the programming techniques to be used.
3. To provide direction for code and comment.
4. To fix the program style for ease of interpretation.

Flowcharting symbols usually conform to some standard set in which each symbol has a specific meaning. Flowchart symbols and definitions are as follows.

PROGRAM FLOWCHART SYMBOLS

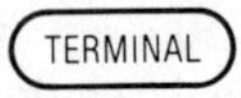

Used for the beginning and ending of a program. A symbol representing a terminal point in a flowchart.

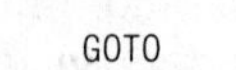

Flowlines show the transfer of control from one operation to another by default, conditional, or unconditional branching.

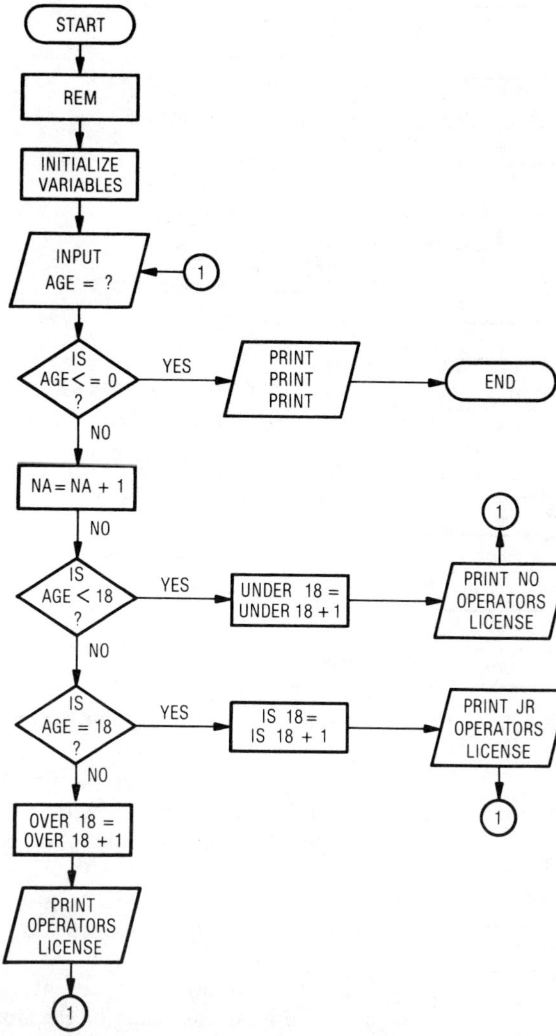

Fig. 8-1. Flowchart for license eligibility program.

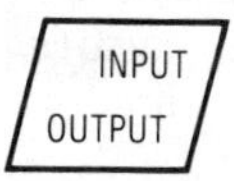

Indicate data entered into the computer and results returned from the computer. INPUT PRINT

Indicates a decision or switching type of operation that determines which of a number of alternate paths to follow. IF – THEN

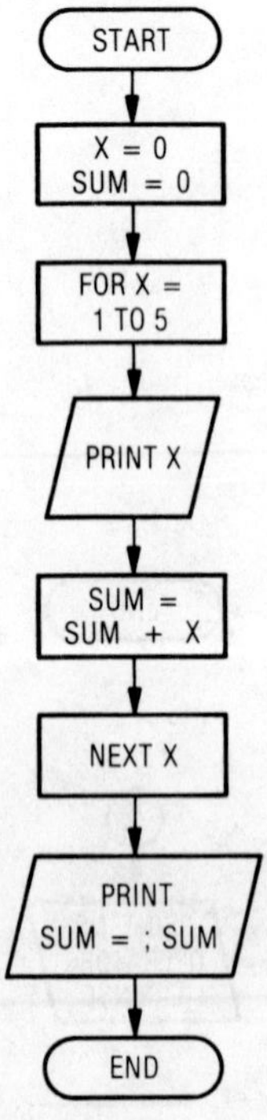


```
10  X = 0
20  SUM = 0
30  FOR X = 0
40  PRINT X
50  SUM = SUM + X
60  NEXT X
70  PRINT "SUM = "; SUM
80  END
```

Fig. 8-2. Sum of the integers 1 through 5 using a FOR–NEXT loop.

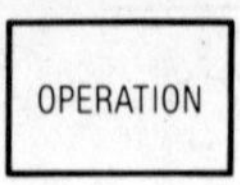

Operation or process symbol that represents any kind of processing function such as initializing, counting, summing, or computing.

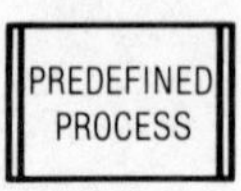

Indicates a sequence of the program statement items in a list. GOSUB

A symbol (pair) to represent the exit or entry from another part of the flowchart. It is used to indicate a transfer of control from one point to another that cannot be conveniently shown on a flowchart because of the confusion of connector lines, or because the flowchart is continued on another page.

Figs. 8-1, 8-2, and 8-3 demonstrate how flowcharts graphically describe a program. Fig. 8-1 represents the driver's license program of Lesson 7. Figs. 8-2 and 8-3 represent new Sum of the Integers programs. The last two figures also show how a FOR – NEXT loop

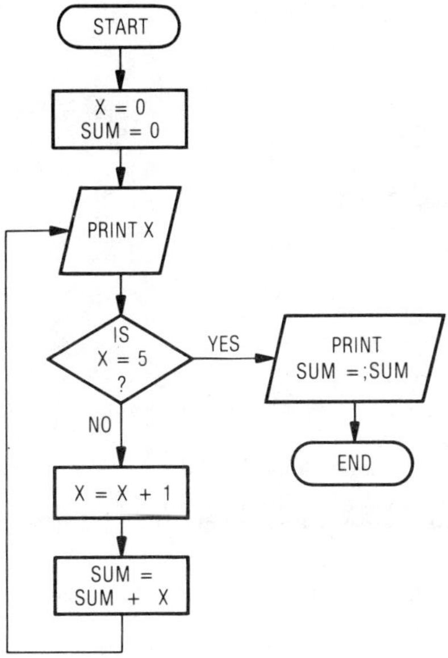


```
10 X = 0
20 SUM = 0
30 PRINT X
40 IF X = 5  THEN 80
50 X = X + 1
60 SUM = SUM + X
70 GOTO 30
80 PRINT "SUM = "; SUM
99 END
```

Fig. 8-3. Sum of integers 1 through 5 using a GOTO loop.

is more efficient than a GOTO loop because it is shorter (program loop efficiency was discussed in Lesson 6).

LESSON 9

Rules for Efficient Programming

After completion of Lesson 9 you should be able to:

1. Write three pairs of opposites to be used with decision statements.
2. Use three rules for efficient programming.
3. Understand how to save memory space and increase the speed at which a program runs.

DISCUSSION

This lesson deals with how to program more efficiently and how to make the program run faster. Efficiency and speed may be well and good, but for the average computer hobbyist speed is not that important. The important thing is to enjoy the hobby and write programs that are readable and can be deciphered six months from now. Place REM statements within the program that will help you understand and remember what that variable represented. Did that single "R" variable stand for RUTH or RAIN? These points are very important if the program is to be reused at a later date. A couple of microseconds lost here and there isn't going to change the world. Write understandable programs. Write programs that jog your memory when you pick them out of your library four months from now. The variable SUM, (even though Applesoft recognizes only the 1st two letters) means something. The variable "S", now what did that stand for? Now back to speed and efficiency.

There are three pairs of opposites that are used to reverse the logic of the IF – THEN statement.

1. > is opposite <=
2. < is opposite >=
3. = is opposite <>

These pairs of opposites select a range. If the range is below age 18, the statement is AGE < 18. If the range includes age 18 and those ages below age 18, the statement is AGE <= 18. If the over 18 group is to include the 18 year olds, the statement is written AGE >= 18.

AGE less than 18 = AGE < 18
AGE less than 18 but
includes the 18 year
old group = AGE <= 18
AGE greater than 18 = AGE > 18
AGE greater than 18 but
includes the 18 year
old group = AGE >= 18
AGE is 18 = AGE = 18
AGE is not 18 = AGE <> 18

Decision statements (IF – THEN) operate on a TRUE (1 or YES) or FALSE (0 or NO) basis and are flowcharted as shown in Fig. 9-1.

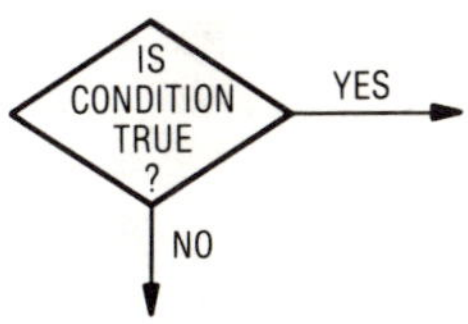

Fig. 9-1. Decision statement flowchart.

Decision statements should select the range from least to greatest by sequential line number for maximum programming efficiency. In other words, the ranges involving the smallest numbers should be programmed first, and the ranges involving the largest numbers should be programmed last.

```
60   IF AGE<= 0 THEN 190
80   IF AGE<18 THEN 130
90   IF AGE = 18 THEN 160
                              (AGE 18 defaults to line 100)
100  OVER 18= OVER 18 + 1
```

Selecting the range from least (line 60) to greatest (line 90) makes programming an orderly endeavor and, thus, easier to perform and interpret.

Memory space can be saved and program speed increased by:

1. Using multiple statements for each line number.

   ```
   100  UNDER 18 = UNDER 18 + 1 : PRINT "OPERATORS LI-
        CENSE" : GOTO 50
   ```

   This saves memory space, but also it sometimes helps to keep track of program sections. In a long program, if short program sections are written with a single line number it eases readability.
2. Using variables within the program instead of constants. PI = 3.1416. If PI is used in the program (instead of 3.1416), it runs faster. It takes more time to convert a constant to a real number than it does to fetch a variable. This is true in computations and in FOR – NEXT loops. Use FOR X = 1 TO PI instead of FOR X = 1 TO 3.1416.
3. Placing items that are used frequently at the beginning of the program. When the program reaches an item that must be converted or fetched, the computer must search through the program sequentially until the item is found. If the item is on line 10, the search is much shorter than if the item is on line 10,000.

There are other methods to save space and increase program speed but they do not increase efficiency greatly. Learn to program efficiently so the programs are usable, accurate, and understandable.

LESSON 10

Summing, Counting, and Flags

After completion of Lesson 10 you should be able to:

1. Write a program using summing and counting variables.
2. Initialize variables in the proper program location.
3. Use a flag to control all or part of a program.

VOCABULARY

Counting Variable—This is a variable used to count within a loop, e.g., C = C + 1. The variable is incremented by 1 on each loop execution.

Flag—This is an additional piece of information added to a data item which gives information about the data itself. An error flag indicates that the data item has given rise to an error condition.

Illegal Value—In Applesoft, this means using a reserved word for a variable, e.g., using TO as a variable when it is a reserved word.

Legal Value—In Applesoft, this means using a variable that meets the requirements of the language, e.g., X = 5.

Summing Variable—This is a variable used within a loop to sum the values of the loop variable, e.g., FOR X = 1 TO 5. The summing statement SUM = SUM + X sums the value of X.

DISCUSSION

Counting variables are used to count some function within the program and are generally initialized to zero. The increment is one if each execution of the loop is to be counted. C = C + 1 is the statement used to increment the count by one and store the count in variable location "C".

Summing, also known as totaling, variables are used to sum or total within a loop. If "T" is the totaling variable, then T is usually initialized to zero, the value at the beginning of the operation. A program that totals daily and adds the daily total to the previous day's total would not be initialized to zero, but to the previous day's total. If the variable is "X", then the totaling statement would be T = T + X. The value of X is added to the total (T + X) and that value is placed in the variable T. The statement T = T + X is placed inside the loop and the total value is outputted outside the loop, after the loop has made its final execution.

Variables are initialized at the beginning of the program. The statements that initialize the variables have no further function in the program. If a GOTO statement returns the program to the line that initializes all variables to zero, each loop execution will initialize all variables to zero. The GOTO statement should go to a line number below the line where the variables are initialized.

The following program demonstrates counting and totaling variables.

```
10   C = 0 : T = 0 : REM * INITIALIZE VARIABLES
20   FOR X = 1 TO 5
30   PRINT X; " ";
40   C = C + 1 : REM * COUNTING STATEMENT
50   T = T + X : REM * TOTALING STATEMENT
60   NEXT X : PRINT : PRINT
70   PRINT "COUNT = "; C : PRINT
80   PRINT "TOTAL = "; T
999  END
RUN
1 2 3 4 5
COUNT = 5
TOTAL = 15
```

Note that the counting and totaling statements are within the body of the loop and the count and total change with every execution of the loop. When the loop has completed its last execution the computer prints out the total count (line 70), prints out the total value of the variable T (line 80), and the program ends.

A flag is a value stored in a variable. Flags are signals to the computer used to start some programmed function. In the following program the flag has a legal value of zero (0), one (1), or minus one (−1). Flag = 0 causes the program to print "# of adds", "# of subtracts", final total, and the program ends. Flag = 1 causes a jump to the section of the program to input a number to add. Flag = −1 causes the program to jump to a section of the program to input a number to be subtracted. After each addition and subtraction there is a GOTO 20 statement that is an unconditional jump to input another flag value.

If an illegal value (any item other than 0, 1, or −1) is typed in the INPUT (20 for instance) the program defaults to line 70. When Flag = 20, the decision in line 40 is false, and the program defaults to line 50. In line 50, the decision is also false and the program defaults to line 60. The same thing happens in line 60 and the program defaults to line 70. Line 70, GOTO 20, is an unconditional jump to line 20 to input another flag value.

The variables used in the program are:

CA = count to be added.
CS = count to be subtracted.
N = number
F = flag
T = total

```
10   CA = 0 : CS = 0 : T = 0
20   PRINT "ENTER FLAG VALUE ( 0 TO QUIT : 1 TO ADD NUMBER :
     -1 TO SUBTRACT NUMBER)"
30   INPUT "?" ;F
40   IF F = 0 THEN 140
50   IF F = 1 THEN 80
60   IF F = -1 THEN 110
70   GOTO 20
80   INPUT "NUMBER TO BE ADDED "; N
90   CA = CA + 1 : T = T + N
100  GOTO 20
110  INPUT "NUMBER TO BE SUBTRACTED "; N
120  CS = CS + 1 : T = T - N
130  GOTO 20
140  PRINT : PRINT "# OF ADDS = "; CA
150  PRINT : PRINT "# OF SUBTRACTS = "; CS
160  PRINT : PRINT "FINAL TOTAL = ", T
170  END
RUN
ENTER FLAG VALUE ( 0 TO QUIT : 1 TO ADD NUMBER : -1 TO SUB-
TRACT NUMBER)
? 1
NUMBER TO BE ADDED 34
ENTER FLAG VALUE (ALL OF LINE 20)
? -1
NUMBER TO BE SUBTRACTED 18
? 0
# OF ADDS = 1
# OF SUBTRACTS = 1
FINAL TOTAL = 16
```

Line 10 initializes the variables to zero. Line 20 prints out the flag values that control a specific part of the program. F = 0 outputs and ends the program. F = 1 adds a number that has been input and keeps a total. F = −1 subtracts a number that has been input and

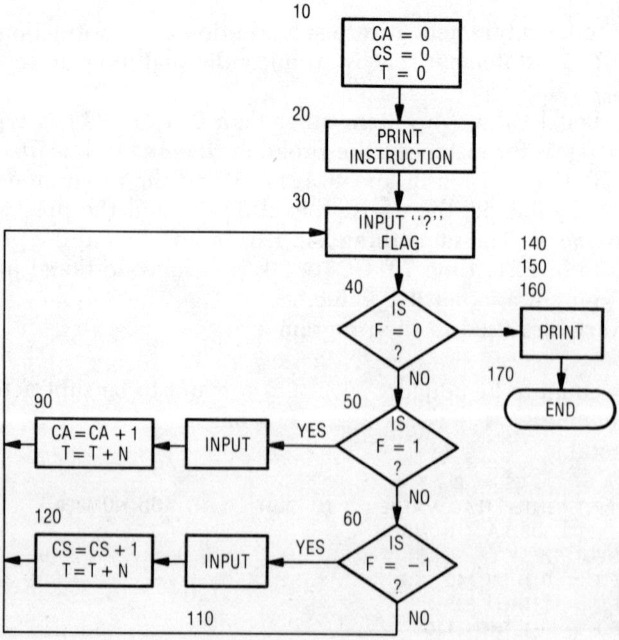

Fig. 10-1. Flowchart for flag program.

keeps a total. Line 30 allows the user to input the flag value. The flowchart for the FLAG PROGRAM is shown in Fig. 10-1.

GOTO lines in Fig. 10-1 are represented by lines from one symbol to another but are not named on the flowchart. Unless F = 0, all GOTO lines return to input another flag value.

Lines 140, 150, and 160 print out the results and the program ends at line 170.

LESSON 11

Single Subscripted Variables

After completion of Lesson 11 you should be able to:

1. Set DIMension limits using constants and variables.
2. Write programs using subscripted variables for numeric lists
   a. To output the list as it was input.
   b. To output the list in reverse order.
   c. To operate on the numbers in the list.
   d. To total the numbers in the list.

VOCABULARY

Array (subscripted variable)—This is an arrangement of items of data, each identified by a key or subscript. It is constructed in such a manner that a program can examine the array in order to extract data relevant to a particular key or subscript. The dimension of an array is the number of subscripts necessary to identify an item. Reservations based on the day of the month would need a (DIM R (31)) subscripted variable R (D), while reservations based on the day and the month would need a (DIM R (31, 12)) doubly subscripted variable R (D, M).

DIM—The DIM statement reserves memory locations for numeric or string arrays, such as A$ (14), B (5), and C% (12). DIM A (15) reserves 16 strings of 255 characters in length, starting from zero. DIM A (N) sets aside N + 1 number of arrays of up to 255 characters in length. The DIM A (N) must be placed in the program after N has been input. The DIM A (N) must not be placed in a loop, except under very special conditions.

List—This is any printing operation in which a series of records on a file, or in memory, are printed one after another.

Operate—This is a defined action by which a result is obtained from an operand.

DISCUSSION

Lesson 11 introduces a new type of variable, the subscripted variable for numeric lists, or array.

SUBSCRIPTED VARIABLE

C(A) C(1)

SIMPLE VARIABLES	CA	X9	CX4	G3H
SUBSCRIPTED VARIABLES	C(A)	X(9)	CX(4)	G3(H)

The variables A, A(O), AB, and A(B) can all be used in the same program successfully. A subscripted variable, like a simple variable, reserves a memory location with a label and contents.

Table 11-1 shows five subscripted variables with the memory locations labeled C(A) with no values in the locations.

Table 11-1. Subscripted Variables

LABEL	CONTENTS
C(1)	
C(2)	
C(3)	
C(4)	
C(5)	

C(A) represents C(1), C(2), C(3), C(4), and C(5).

Suppose the contents of the memory locations whose label is C(A) is filled with random numbers. LET C(1) = 8. LET C(2) = 5. LET C(3) = 19. LET C(4) = 1. LET C(5) = −8.

Table 11-2 shows the five memory locations whose labels are C(A) and whose contents are as stated above.

The subscripted variable, or array, is now filled with a list of numbers.

When you remember that the subscript of a variable can be a

Table 11-2. Subscripted Variables

LABEL	CONTENTS
C(1)	8
C(2)	5
C(3)	19
C(4)	1
C(5)	−8

variable (C(A)), or a constant (C(1)), you begin to realize what a powerful tool the single subscripted variable turns out to be.

IF A = 1 THEN C(A) = C(1)
IF A = 2 THEN C(A) = C(2)
IF A = 3 THEN C(A) = C(3)

Subscripted variables give great processing power to the computer, and make the job of the programmer much easier.

To practice conversion of using constants and variables in the subscripted portion of subscripted variables, complete the following exercises.

L(1)	2	N(1)	6	P	1
L(2)	5	N(2)	3	Q	2
M(3)	7	O(3)	1	R	3
M(4)	−2	O(4)	4	S	4

L(1) =	P =	L(P) =
L(2) =	Q =	O(R) =
M(R) =	N(Q) =	N(Q) =
M(S) =	M(S) =	N(P) =

2	1	2
5	2	1
7	3	3
−2	−2	6

A DIM statement is necessary to reserve memory locations for a numeric array. The array range goes from zero to the number dimensioned. DIM A(15) reserves 16 elements for array A (0 to 15). Each element may be up to 255 characters in length. An array can be up to 11 (0 to 10) elements large without a DIM statement.

Integer arrays A%(N) will not be presented separately because they are handled in a manner similar to real arrays A(N).

In the following program there are only three numbers in the numeric list so a DIM statement is not necessary. However, a DIM statement is used anyway as a teaching example. A DIM statement should always be used in programs with subscripted variables to reserve specific memory locations.

The program allows the user to input N numbers into a list. The list of numbers is printed as input, printed backwards, operated on, and totaled.

```
90   HOME : VTAB 3
100  REM : ARRAYS - SINGLE SUBSCRIPTED
110  REM : VARIABLES - USED FOR LISTS
120  REM : 4 WAYS TO USE THEM
130  REM : INPUT 4 NUMBERS
140  INPUT "HOW MANY NUMBERS = ";N
150  DIM L(N)
160  FOR X = 1 TO N : L(X) = 0 : NEXT X
170  FOR K = 1 TO N
180  PRINT "NUMBER";K; "=";
190  INPUT L(K)
200  NEXT K
210  PRINT "PRINT LIST AS INPUT" : PRINT
220  FOR A = 1 TO N
230  PRINT L(A); " ";
240  NEXT A : PRINT : PRINT
250  PRINT "PRINT LIST BACKWARD" : PRINT
260  FOR B = N TO 1 STEP - 1
270  PRINT L(B); " ";
280  NEXT B : PRINT : PRINT
290  PRINT "TO OPERATE ON THE LIST" : PRINT
300  PRINT "C"; TAB (7); "L(C)"; TAB (14); "L(C)+5"; TAB (23);
     "C*L(C)"; TAB (33); "L(C)∧2"
310  FOR C = 1 TO N
320  PRINT C; TAB (9); L(C); TAB (16); L(C) + 5;
     TAB (24); C*L(C); TAB (34); L(C)∧2
330  NEXT C : PRINT
340  PRINT "THE LIST IS TOTALED" : PRINT
350  T = 0
360  FOR D = 1 TO N
370  T = T + L(D)
380  NEXT D
390  PRINT "TOTAL OF THE LIST = "; T
400  END
RUN
HOW MANY NUMBERS 3
NUMBER 1 = ? 4
NUMBER 2 = ? −5
NUMBER 3 = ? 2.5
PRINT LIST AS INPUT
4 −5 2.5
PRINT LIST BACKWARD
2.5 −5 4
TO OPERATE ON THE LIST
```

```
C       L(C)     L(C)+5     C*L(C)     L(C)∧2
1       4        9          4          16
2       -5       0          -10        25
3       2.5      7.5        7.5        6.25
THE LIST IS TOTALED
TOTAL OF THE LIST = 1.5
```

In this program, the variable L automatically references the list. To reference this list, the variable L must be used, followed by a subscript value, (L(A), L(2), L(N*2–3)) or no subscript value L(0). L(0) is the same as L. The subscript can either be a constant, variable, or an arithmetic expression. This flexibility is what gives arrays their real power. Anything can be placed in parentheses to reference a single part of the list as long as it is $\geqslant 0$ and $\leqslant$ the DIM value.

Line 90 clears the screen and places HOW MANY NUMBERS on line 3 of the screen. The screen holds the complete input and output of the program (if no more than three numbers are placed in the list). When viewed together, the input and output help the user determine if the output is correct in relation to the input.

Lines 100 to 130 are REM statements that partially document the intent of the program.

Line 140 sets up the user request and prepares for the input of the number of numbers to be contained in the list. The user then types in the number.

Line 150 reserves memory locations for N + 1 numbers in List L.

Line 160 initializes the memory locations of N numbers in the list to zero. L(X) could have been initialized to zero by using L(1) = 0: L(2) = 0 : L(3) = 0, etc. The loop is much more efficient. This step is unnecessary in this program but is given to show loop/array flexibility.

Lines 170 to 200 set up the input format of the numbers themselves. Again the loop is used for efficiency.

```
170 FOR K = 1 TO N
180 PRINT "NUMBER"; K; "=";
190 INPUT L(K)
200 NEXT K
```

In line 180, the K variable is placed between the "NUMBER" and the "=" to inform the user which of the numbers in the list to be input. The K in the PRINT statement begins as number 1 and increments by 1 with each execution of the loop.

Lines 210 to 240 set up the list to be printed out as it is input. The loop is used and the loop variable is A, so the subscripted variable is L(A).

```
210  PRINT "PRINT THE LIST AS INPUT" : PRINT
220  FOR A = 1 TO N
230  PRINT L(A); "  ";
240  NEXT A : PRINT : PRINT
```

Line 230 prints the numbers in the list by placing them in the subscripted variable (L(1) = 4) and printing one number on each loop execution. The “ ” represents 2 spaces enclosed in quotation marks. The “ ” causes two spaces to be left between each printed number each time the loop executes.

Line 240 closes out the loop, and the first PRINT closes out the line after all the numbers in the list have been printed. The second PRINT statement leaves a blank line between program sections in the printout.

Lines 250 to 280 print out the list backward.

```
250  PRINT "PRINT LIST BACKWARD" : PRINT
260  FOR B = N TO 1 STEP -1
270  PRINT L(B); "  ";
280  NEXT B : PRINT : PRINT
```

Line 250 is the PRINT statement.

Line 260 sets up to print the list out backwards in increments of 1 on each print.

In line 270, the list is referenced by the letter L. The loop variable B becomes the subscript, so the subscripted variable is L(B). The value of the number contained in L(B) is printed out on each execution of the loop. Again, the “ ” leaves two spaces between each number as they are printed.

Line 280 completes the loop. The first PRINT statement closes out the line after all numbers in the list are printed. The second PRINT leaves a blank line between the output sections.

Lines 300 to 330 operate on the numbers.

Line 300 PRINTS the headings.

Line 310 is the beginning loop statement.

Line 320 prints the operation results and tabs those results so they are printed out below the proper headings. The list variable L is combined with the loop variable to produce the subscripted variable L(C).

Line 330 closes out the loop and leaves a blank line between output sections.

Lines 340 to 390 total the list and print out the results.

Line 350 initializes the totaling variable T to zero.

Line 370 is the totaling statement that places the list values in the subscripted variable L(D) and adds one list number on each loop execution.

Line 380 is the ending statement of loop D.

When loop D has completed its last execution, the program defaults to line 390 to print out the total of the list of numbers and line 400 ends the program.

To change the program from an INPUT mode to a READ–DATA mode, delete lines 100 to 200.

The command DEL 100,200 leaves line 90 in place.

Type in these lines:

```
160  RESTORE
170  READ N        (in line 400 — N = 3 — the first data value in the line)
180  PRINT "NUMBER OF NUMBERS = "; N : PRINT
190  FOR K = 1 TO N
200  READ L(K) : NEXT K
--------------------
400  DATA 3, 4, −5, 2.5
410  END
```

Line 160 is not applicable in this program but it should be introduced at this point. If the arrays were to be read two or more times the RESTORE statement would reset the data and make it available for further program executions.

Line 180 prints out the number of numbers in the list after it had been READ from DATA.

Lines 190 and 200 are a loop that READS the list of numbers through the subscripted variable L(K).

```
190  FOR K = 1 TO N
200  READ L(K) : NEXT K
```

When the last number in the list is READ, the program defaults to line 210 to print out the list as it was READ.

Line 400 DATA 3(N), 4(K), −5(K), 2.5(K) sets up the data to be READ in the proper order.

READ statements may contain integer, real, and string variables. To be read properly the READ variables must be aligned with the items in the DATA statement.

```
10   READ A%,  A,   A$
20   DATA 4,   1.7,  HELLO ( or "HELLO")
```

A$ will print out HELLO or "HELLO" in either form as HELLO.

```
10   READ A%, A, A$, B$
20   PRINT A%, A, A$, B$
30   DATA 4.5, 2.5, HELLO, "BYE"
RUN
4  (input as a real but truncated to an integer)
4                 2.5                HELLO
BYE
```

A string variable in a READ statement will READ a literal or a string in a DATA statement but outputs only in the literal form.

LESSON 12

Double Subscripted Variables

After completion of Lesson 12 you should be able to:

1. Discuss double subscripted arrays.
2. Write programs using double subscripted arrays.

DISCUSSION

Double subscripted arrays are arrays that have two subscripts. Double subscripted arrays are used for outputting data or information in table form. The following are examples of double subscripted arrays:

CF(1,4)   X(0,0)   JANE(R,C)   FOB(L,S)

Tables and arrays have rows and columns. Columns are positioned vertically on the screen. Rows are positioned horizontally on the screen. Fig. 12-1 shows how an array of three columns and three rows is arranged.

CF = array name
R = row subscript
C = column subscript

CF(R,C)	COLUMN 0	COLUMN 1	COLUMN 2
ROW 0	CF(0,0)	CF(0,1)	CF(0,2)
ROW 1	CF(0)	CF(1,1)	CF( )
ROW 2	CF( )	CF( )	CF( )

Fig. 12-1. CF (R, C) array.

The double subscripted array references a memory location that holds a value, the same as an ordinary variable. Values for CF(R,C) could be assigned as follows:

CF(1,1) = 20	CF(1,2) = 30	CF(1,3) = 40
CF(2,1) = 25	CF(2,2) = 35	CF(2,3) = 45
CF(3,1) = 30	CF(3,2) = 40	CF(3,3) = 50

An array can use variables as subscripts instead of constants. For instance, if R = 1 and C = 3, then CF(R,C) = CF(1,3). Subscripts can also be combined with arithmetic operators (e.g., CF(R+1, C−1) or CF(R*2, C/3)).

Values input into the program as constants can be stored in subscripted arrays.

```
10   INPUT "GROSS INCOME = ";GI
20   INPUT "EXPENSES = "; EX          (EXP is a reserved word)

30   CF(C,1) = GI
40   CF(C,2) = EX
```

Whole columns or rows in an array can be added or subtracted the same as ordinary variables. As a matter of fact, any arithmetic operator that can be used on ordinary variables can be used on arrays. In the following example, column 2 is being subtracted from column 1 to produce column 3 in array CF.

```
CF(C,3) = CF(C,1) - CF(C,2)
```

Variables, single subscripted arrays, and double subscripted arrays can be handled in a similar fashion.

The program written for this lesson is a very elementary business program. The user inputs the amount of his gross income, expenses, and years (months or days) to operate. From these three inputs is output the period of operation, in this case years, the gross income, expenses, net income, and the totals for each column.

A FOR–NEXT loop is used to compute and print the figures on a yearly basis. After the yearly figures are outputted, double nested loops are used to output the totals of each column.

Some large computers have the capacity to handle arrays with up to 16 subscripts. In the automobile industry, each style of automobile could have 15 items of optional equipment. The subscripted variable might look like this.

CAR (MODEL,STYLE,AIR CONDITIONER, RADIO,
HEATER, ENGINE, TIRES,SPORTS PACKAGE,
COLOR OF PAINT,HUBCAPS)

From the subscripted variable, the manufacturer could keep track of what is produced. The reports could then break down sales percentages into the most popular models and options. This information could be fed back to the computer to aid the production department to produce the cars the public was buying.

Now back to our elementary program.

```
100  REM:PROGRAM TO DEMONSTRATE
110  REM:DOUBLE SUBSCRIPTED VARIABLES
120  HOME: VTAB 2:HTAB 6:PRINT "DOUBLE SUBSCRIPTED VARIABLES"
130  H1$ = "GROSS INCOME   EXPENSES YEARS TO OPERATE"
140  VTAB 4 : PRINT H1$
150  VTAB 5 : HTAB 3 : INPUT " ";GI : VTAB 5 :
     HTAB 17 : INPUT " "; EX
160  VTAB 5 : HTAB 30 : INPUT " "; YRS : PRINT : PRINT
170  DIM CF(YRS,3)
180  FOR R = 1 TO YRS
190  FOR C = 1 TO 3
200  CF(R,C) = 0
210  NEXT C, R
220  H2$ = "YEAR  GROSS INCOME  EXPENSES  NET INCOME"
230  PRINT H2$
240  FOR C = 1 TO YRS
250  CF(C,1) = GI : CF(C,2) = EX
260  CF(C,3) = CF(C,1) - CF(C,2)
270  HTAB 2 : PRINT C; TAB (8); CF(C,1); TAB (21);
     CF(C,2); TAB (30); CF(C,3)
280  TYRS = TYRS + C : NEXT C
290  FOR R = 1 TO YRS
300  FOR C = 1 TO 3
310  CF(0,C) = CF(0,C) + CF(R,C)
320  NEXT C,R
330  PRINT "_____   __________   __________   __________"
340  HTAB 1 : PRINT TYRS; TAB (8); CF(0,1);
     TAB (21); CF(0,2) TAB (29) CF(0,3)       (There are no semicolons between the last
                                              three items)
350  END
RUN
            DOUBLE SUBSCRIPTED ARRAYS
GROSS INCOME  EXPENSES  YEARS TO OPERATE
   1500.21        875.35           4

YEAR   GROSS INC.  EXPENSES  NET INCOME
  1       1500.21     875.35     624.86
  2       1500.21     875.35     624.86
  3       1500.21     875.35     624.86
  4       1500.21     875.35     624.86
_____  __________  ________  __________
 10       6000.84    3501.40    2499.44
```

The variables used in the program are:

CF = cash flow   R = row
C = column   GI = gross income

EX = expenses	YRS = years to operate
H1$ = print heading	H2$ = print heading

The program was designed so the input and output would be visible on the screen at the same time.

Lines 100 and 110 are used to partially document the teaching objective of the program, namely double subscripted variables.

Line 120 HOME clears the screen and prints on line 2 of the screen VTAB 2, DOUBLE SUBSCRIPTED VARIABLES.

Line 130 places the string into H1$ for ease of output. This is especially valuable if the same heading is to be printed many times during the program.

Line 140 tabs to line 4 on the screen and prints out the heading.

Lines 150 and 160 ask for input below the subject in the heading, thereby cluing the user as to what input is requested. In Applesoft, the statement INPUT GI could be used, but it leaves a question mark on the screen in front of the data. INPUT " "; GI is used because it leaves no question mark on the screen in front of the data.

The DIMension statement of line 170 would not be necessary if fewer than 12 array elements were needed, since Applesoft automatically sets aside up to 11 array element memory locations. But because the array CF requires 15 elements (five rows, including the totals row, and three columns), a DIM statement must be used. The DIM statement that we use allows a variable number of rows (CF(YRS,3)) to be allocated. If we knew that the number of rows needed would never be more than five, we could have written line 170: DIM CF (4,3). This version allocates 4 + 1 rows and 3 + 1 columns, or 20 real number elements to the array (don't forget that the computer uses zero as a counting number, so that when you tell it four, the computer counts five places including zero).

Lines 180 to 210 initialize the locations in the table to zero.

```
180  FOR R = 1 TO YRS
190  FOR C = 1 TO 3
200  CF(R,C) = 0
210  NEXT C, R
```

The double nested loop is the most efficient method to initialize the locations in the table to zero. The table locations could have been initialized by listing every element in the array and setting them equal to zero.

```
CF(1,1) = 0
CF(1,2) = 0
CF(1,3) = 0
CF(2,1) = 0
CF(2,2) = 0
CF(2,3) = 0
```

```
CF(3,1) = 0
CF(3,2) = 0
CF(3,3) = 0 , etc.
```

Or a FOR–NEXT loop could have been used.

```
FOR C = 1 TO 3
CF(1,C) = 0
CF(2,C) = 0
CF(3,C) = 0
CF(4,C) = 0
NEXT C
```

Line 220 is the header to be printed before the output of data. The header must be printed before the loop executes. If the header is within the loop, it will be printed each time the loop is executed.

Line 230 prints out the header. There is no VTAB statement because the table is printed below the input information. Two blank lines separate the input information from the output data. The two PRINT statements in line 160 cause the two blank lines below the input.

In line 240, the number of years on which to compute the table was input.

In line 250, CF(C,1) = GI is a replacement statement that stores the input variable on the left side of the equals sign into CF(C,1), the column that is to hold the yearly gross income. CF(C,2) = EX is a replacement statement to place the expenses into the cash flow CF(C,2) column.

Line 260 is a replacement statement that sets up the third column of the table. The column (C,3) is to hold the net income, which is the gross income (C,1) less the expenses (C,2).

Line 270 places the results of each execution of the loop in the proper location under the header. The CF(C,1) is used directly in the PRINT statement to print out the results of that column.

Line 280 totals the number of years in the period. NEXT C is the ending statement of the loop.

Lines 290 through 320 compute the totals for each column by using double nested loops.

```
290  FOR R = 1 TO YRS
300  FOR C = 1 TO 3
310  CF(0,C) = CF(0,C) + CF(R,C)
```

The elements (0,1), (0,2), and (0,3) have not been used in this table yet, but are available in the dimension arrangement. The locations (0,1), (0,2), and (0,3) are used to place the totals of (C,1), (C,2), and (C,3), respectively. Line 310 inside the double nested loops is the totaling statement that totals each of the columns.

Line 320 is the ending statement of the double nested loops.

Line 330 draws a line under the columns and the totals are placed below the lines.

Line 340 prints the totals in the proper positions below the lines. Notice that some of the semicolons between the TAB statements and the PRINT statements are missing. Applesoft is flexible enough to accept the instructions without semicolons and still operate properly.

Line 350 ends the program.

LESSON 13

String Arrays

After completion of Lesson 13 you should be able to:

1. Use LEFT$, MID$, and RIGHT$.
2. Use string arrays (or string subscripted variables) in loops.
3. Output alphanumeric lists by using string arrays.
4. Write programs using string arrays to print lists of names and addresses.

VOCABULARY

Concatenate—This means to link together in a set, series, or chain.

GOSUB—This is a statement that causes a branch to a subroutine at a specific line number.

Null String—This is a string which contains no characters. Strings are initialized with zero characters. A$ = " " is a null string and a PRINT A$ will not print any characters on the screen, nor will the cursor advance on the screen.

ON ERR GOTO 430, 440, etc.—This is a statement that causes an unconditional GOTO branch when a particular error is encountered. Error #1 jumps to line 430, error #2 jumps to line 440, etc. The equivalent statement for a GOSUB branch is ON ERR GOSUB 430, 440, etc.

String Array—This is a complex variable used to manipulate all or part of a string.

Subroutine—This is a discrete part of a program that performs a logical section of the overall function of the program and that is available whenever the particular set of instructions is required.

The instructions forming the subroutine do not need to be repeated every time they are needed, but can be entered by means of a branch from the main program. Subroutines may be written for a specific program or they may be written in general form to perform operations common to several programs. In Applesoft, the statements GOSUB or ON (ERR) GOSUB direct the program to the subroutines. The last line of a subroutine is a RETURN statement, that jumps to the line in the main program directly below the GOSUB (or ON (ERR) GOSUB). Subroutines can be called from the main body of the program or from other subroutines. GOSUBs can be nested 25 levels deep in Applesoft.

DISCUSSION

String variables were introduced in Lesson 4 with the other simple variables, integers and reals. The complex variables, integer arrays and real arrays were discussed in Lessons 11 and 12.

The complex variable (also known as the string array, or string subscripted variable) is a variable with a subscript. The string array is used to output alphanumeric information, such as lists of names and addresses.

A$ = a string variable.
HI SUE = a literal.
"HI SUE" = a literal enclosed in quotation marks (a string).
LEFT$ (A$.J) = string function having 2 arguments.
RIGHT$(A$,J) = string function having 2 arguments.
MID$(A$,J,1) = string function having 3 arguments.

In a string array, a dollar sign ($) follows the name of the array. The Applesoft language uses three functions to retrieve all or part of a string, or to print all or part of a string. A function is that part of a computer instruction that specifies the operation to be performed. An argument is a variable factor, the value of which determines the value of the function. The three functions used to manipulate strings are LEFT$, MID$, and RIGHT$.

When string arrays are manipulated as single entities they are handled in this manner.

LEFT$(A$,2)

function — A string — 2 characters are printed beginning at the first character.

MID$(A$,1,2)

function — A string — 1 = first character in the string. 2 = two characters are printed beginning at character #1.

LEFT$(A$,2) = MID$(A$,1,2)

RIGHT$(A$,3)

function — A string — prints last three characters in the string.

The following program demonstrates the use of LEFT$, MID$, and RIGHT$. The printout caused by each line is printed next to the line for your convenience.

```
100  A$ = "HI SUE"
110  PRINT LEFT$(A$,2)         HI
120  PRINT RIGHT$(A$,3)        SUE
130  PRINT MID$(A$,1)          HI SUE
140  PRINT MID$(A$,2)          I SUE
150  PRINT MID$(A$,3)            SUE
160  PRINT MID$(A$,4)          SUE
170  PRINT MID$(A$,5)          UE
180  PRINT MID$(A$,6)          E
190  PRINT MID$(A$,1,1)        H
200  PRINT MID$(A$,2,1)        I
210  PRINT MID$(A$,3,1)        space
220  PRINT MID$(A$,4,1)        S
230  PRINT MID$(A$,5,1)        U
240  PRINT MID$(A$,6,1)        E
250  PRINT MID$(A$,4,1)        S
260  PRINT MID$(A$,4,3)        SUE
999  END
```

This program also demonstrates that the function MID$ can output the same characters as LEFT$ and RIGHT$. With proper manipulation the programmer does not need LEFT$ or RIGHT$. MID$ alone will do the job.

LEFT$, MID$, and RIGHT$ functions can be used in loops to output all or parts of a string. A loop variable J is used in this example. The L variable holds the value of the length of the string.

```
FOR J = 1 TO L (L = LEN(A$))
```

LEFT$(A$,J)

function — A string — loop variable. Prints forward from left to right.

MID$(A$,J)

function — A string — loop variable. Prints complete A$ on 1st loop pass and decrements by 1 for each character in the string beginning from the left side of the string.

RIGHT$(A$,J)

function — A string — prints string from right to left, i.e., backwards.

```
100  A$ = "HI SUE"
110  PRINT LEN(A$), LEN("HI SUE")
120  FOR J = 1 TO LEN(A$)
130  PRINT LEFT$(A$,J)
140  NEXT J : PRINT : L = LEN(A$)
150  FOR J = 1 TO L
160  PRINT RIGHT$(A$,J)
170  NEXT J : PRINT
180  FOR J = 1 TO L
190  PRINT MID$(A$,J)
200  NEXT J : PRINT
210  FOR J = 1 TO L : PRINT MID$(A$,4) : NEXT J : PRINT
220  FOR J = 1 TO L : PRINT MID$(A$,J,2) : NEXT J : PRINT
230  FOR J = 1 TO L : PRINT MID$(A$,J,1); : NEXT J
999  END
RUN
(PRINT LEN(A$), LEN("HI SUE")) NOT PRINTED FROM PROGRAM
6            6
H
HI
HI S                                      PRINT LEFT$(A$,J)
HI SU
HI SUE

E
UE
SUE                                       PRINT RIGHT$(A$,J)
 SUE
I SUE
HI SUE

HI SUE
I SUE
 SUE                                      PRINT MID$(A$,J)
SUE
UE
E
SUE
SUE
```

```
SUE                                       PRINT MID$(A$,4)
SUE
SUE
SUE

HI
I
  S                                       PRINT MID$(A$,J,2)
SU
UE
E

HI SUE                                    PRINT MID$(A$,J,1);
```

To concatenate is to link together in a set, series, or chain. Applesoft has the ability to concatenate. Strings can be altered to produce desired output.

```
10   A$ = "HI SUE"
20   B$ = A$ + " " + "AND JIM"
30   PRINT A$
40   PRINT B$
50   C$ = LEFT$(A$,3) + RIGHT$(A$,3) + "!!!"
60   PRINT C$
999  END
RUN
HI SUE
HI SUE AND JIM
HI JIM!!!
```

(3 includes the space after HI—if 2 was used the output would be HIJIM!!!)

The balance of this lesson is on program development. The objective is to produce a program that accepts a person's name and address for the purpose of compiling and printing a mailing list. The program has error checking to notify the input operator if the input is incorrect. Once the input is correct the name and address is output in the proper format.

A correct program is not usually written on the first attempt. In this example, an unusable program is written as a first attempt. The program is then revised. The lesson presents an outline for program development and shows some of the steps you should follow when writing usable programs.

The original program is inflexible. A$ holds the name and address of the individual. If an individual with another name and address was placed in A$, the output is not formatted correctly. As an extra, the program demonstrates the use of MID$ to replace LEFT$, and RIGHT$.

```
15   REM: NEXT PROGRAM CHANGE - INPUT A$ AT LINE 20
20   A$ = "JOHN DOE 2200 MAIN ST. ANYTOWN  USA  00000"
30   PRINT A$
40   PRINT LEFT$(A$,8)
```

```
50   PRINT MID$(A$,10,13)
60   PRINT RIGHT$(A$,18) : PRINT
70   PRINT MID$(A$,1,8)
80   PRINT MID$(A$,10,13)
90   PRINT MID$(A$,24,19)
999  END
RUN
JOHN DOE 2200 MAIN ST. ANYTOWN,  USA  00000
JOHN DOE
2200 MAIN ST.
ANYTOWN  USA  00000

JOHN DOE
2200 MAIN ST.
ANYTOWN  USA  00000
```

When the program is typed and RUN, it can be readily understood that the program is useful only if the name and address input is JOHN DOE 2200 MAIN ST. ANYTOWN USA 00000.

When line 20 is changed to

```
20   INPUT A$
```

the input must be the same number of letters and characters in the original JOHN DOE name and address to be output in the correct format.

For a program to be valuable, it must be flexible. The name line of the program must accept any name, no matter if it has three characters or 255 characters. The address field must be able to accept different numbers of characters for different street numbers and street names. The city, state, and zip line must also be able to accept different numbers of characters. To achieve this flexibility, a delimiter (;) is used after each line of the name and address.

```
JOHN DOE;2200 MAIN ST.;ANYTOWN  USA  00000(L)
```

As a step toward developing a flexible program, an inflexible formula is first demonstrated.

```
20   INPUT A$
30   N = 9 : A1 = 23 : L = LEN(A$)
40   PRINT A$
50   PRINT LEFT$(A$,N-1)
60   PRINT MID$(A$,N+1,A1-(N+1))
70   PRINT RIGHT$(A$,L-A1)
999  END
RUN
JOHN DOE;2200MAIN ST.;ANYTOWN  USA  00000
JOHN DOE
2200 MAIN ST.
ANYTOWN  USA  00000
```

The semicolon (;) is used as a delimiter separating the fields in A$. The variables locate the delimiters at the end of each field. No spaces are left between the contents of the field and the delimiter.

The following is an explanation of the expressions used in this program.

N = 9	N = variable of the delimiter at the end of the first field. Nine (9) is the column the delimiter occupies.
A1 = 23	A1 = variable of the delimiter at the end of the second field. Twenty-three(23) is the column the delimiter occupies.
L = LEN(A$)	L points to the end of the third field. The column that L occupies is determined by the length of the city, state, and zip code.

Table 13-1. Where Lines Start and End

Line	Start	Symbol	End	Symbol
1	Position #1	LEFT$(A$,	Before 1st del	N−1
2	After 1st del	N+1	Before 2nd del	A1−1
3	After 2nd del	A1+1	Length of string	L

```
Line 1    LEFT$(A$,N-1)
Line 2    MID$(A$,N+1,A1-(N+1))
Line 3    RIGHT$(A$,L-A1)        (the closing delimiter should be A1+1, but Apple-
                                 soft picks up the delimiter position as A1)
```

In this sequence of learning events, the first string function used, LEFT$(A$,8), had constants within the parentheses that printed out the first through the eighth characters in the string. The second type of string function, LEFT$(A$, N−1), had a constant and a variable with a fixed value in relation to the delimiter and a fixed A$ input. The program to be studied next has a variable length input and a delimiter that is determined by the variable input LEFT$(A$, D1C−1). The variable length input and input error checks produce a useful program.

Developing a complicated program is a detailed, exacting, and thought provoking experience. Not all the programmer's thoughts can be written on paper. The following program is presented in the detailed manner in which it was developed. The final program varies from the outline flowchart and this is a feature of progressive changing thought. For the benefit of the learning programmer, the initial flowcharts were not changed to conform to the finished program. The differences from one step to the next emphasize how development occurs.

I. GENERAL OUTLINE FOR PROGRAM DEVELOPMENT

A. What is the problem?
B. Detailed input format
C. Detailed output format
D. Outline flowchart
E. Assignment of variables
F. Start and end of lines
G. Basic flowchart
H. Error checking
    1. Number of delimiters
    2. Length of lines
        a. Length of line 1
        b. Length of line 2
        c. Length of line 3
I. Write error checking section of outline flowchart
J. Write final flowchart
K. Write program
L. Debug and modify the program
M. Code the final program

The explanations and details of the logic use the same code and headings as the outline.

I. A. What is the problem? The problem is to input three lines of variable length separated by a delimiter (;) to allow any length of name, any length of street number and address, and any length of city, state, and zip code up to 255 characters each.

I. B. Detailed input format. Line of input = A$

JOHN DOE;2200 MAIN ST.;ANYTOWN USA 00000

I. C. Detailed output format.

JOHN DOE
2200 MAIN ST.
ANYTOWN USA 00000

I. D. Outline flowchart. (Shown in Fig. 13-1.)

I. E. Assignment of variables. The variables use the logic that a delimiter (D) is used after line 1 to close the line, hence, D1C means the delimiter that closes line 1. A delimiter (D) is used after line 2 to close the line, hence, D2C. L = LEN(A$) is the delimiter used at the end of line 3. The entire list of variables is as shown below:

ASSIGNMENT OF EXPRESSIONS

1 (st column)	Beginning of line 1–LEFT$(A$,
D1C	Points to the delimiter at the end of line 1.

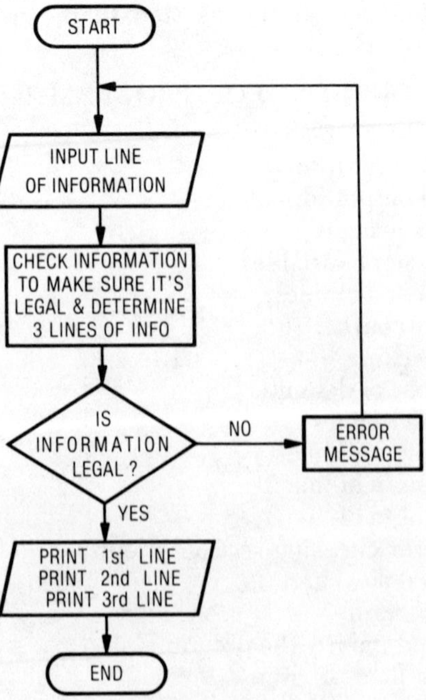

Fig. 13-1. Outline flowchart.

D1C−1	End of line 1.
D1C+1	Beginning of line 2.
D2C	Points to the delimiter at the end of line 2.
D2C−1	End of line 2.
D2C+1	Beginning of line 3.
L	End of line 3.
ERR	Variable that is assigned a value when an input error has occurred, and the value is used to print the type of error.
J − (J,J)	Loop variable or subscript variable.

I. F. Start and end of lines. Once the delimiter variables are assigned, they are placed at the start and at the end of the lines.

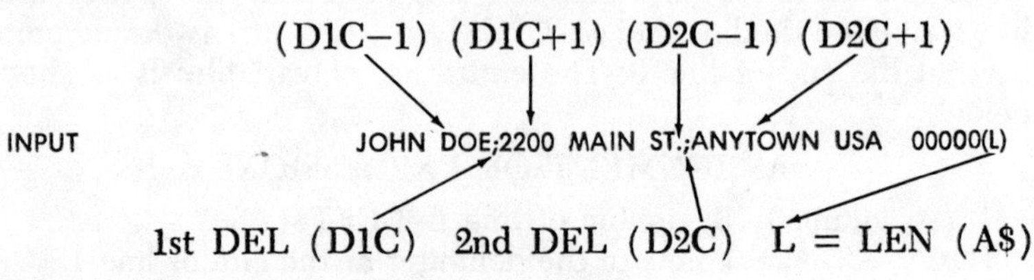

Table 13-2. Showing Where Lines Start and End

Line	Start	Symbol	End	Symbol
1	Beginning col. 1	LEFT$(A$,	Before 1st del.	D1C − 1
2	After 1st del.	D1C+1	Before 1st del.	D2C−1
3	After 2nd del.	D2C+1	At end of string	L

Line 1 LEFT$(A$,D1C−1)
Line 2 MID$(A$,D1C+1,D2C−(D1C+1))
Line 3 RIGHT$(A$,L−D2C)

I. G. Basic flowchart. This is shown in Fig. 13-2. The basic flowchart shows the beginning pattern to develop the program. A$ is in-

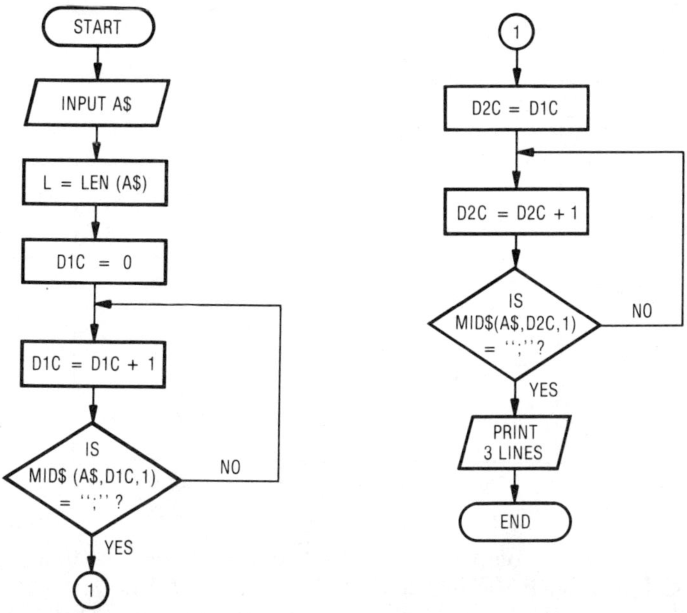

Fig. 13-2. Basic flowchart.

put by the user. The length of A$ is stored in the variable L. The first delimiter D1C is initialized to zero. A$ starts at the first character and ends at L (L = LEN A$). The statements D1C = D1C + 1 and IF MID$(A$,D1C,1) = ";" THEN–branch to D1C = D1C + 1, counts the number of characters in the first line of A$. This looping continues until the first delimiter (;) is found. The numeric value stored in D1C is then transferred to D2C. If after the end of line 1, D1C has a value of 10, then 10 is transferred to D2C. D2C = D1C. D2C is then initialized to a value of 10. The second line starts after the first delimiter (11). The same logic is applied to count the number of characters in line 2. D2C = D2C + 1 and IF MID$(A$, D2C,1) = ";" THEN–branch to D2C = D2C + 1 and count the number of characters in line 2 until the second delimiter is reached. These two delimiters set the end of the first and second lines. The third line is composed of all the characters between D2C and L.

I. H. Error checking. For a program to be effective and efficient, those sections that interrupt the flow must be eliminated. The algorithm from section I. G. specifies that the input section (A$) must have two delimiters separating three lines. The first error check is to determine if D1C is greater than the length of the line. IF D1C>L THEN. If D1C>L, the loop has searched through A$ completely, and has not found a delimiter. Fig. 13-3 shows input with

DOE MAIN USA

D1C	MID$(A$,D1C,1)
1	D
2	O
3	E
4	
5	M
6	A
7	I
8	N
9	
10	U
11	S
12	A
13	ILLEGAL QUANTITY ERR (when D1C = 256)

Fig. 13-3. Input with no error check.

no error check. Compare Figs. 13-4 and 13-5 to see how this process looks logically. If the first loop finds a delimiter, the flowchart goes to the second loop to search for the second delimiter. If D2C>L, the second delimiter was not found. This is another error. If two delimiters are found there is no error, but logic dictates a search for a third delimiter. Another error would occur if there are three semicolon delimiters. Another error would occur if the 1st delimiter was the first character in line 1. Line 1 would be zero length. If the second delimiter is the next character after the 1st delimiter, line 2 would be zero length. If line 3 had no characters between D2C and L, another error would occur. This gives a total possibility of six errors, three delimiter errors, and three line length errors.

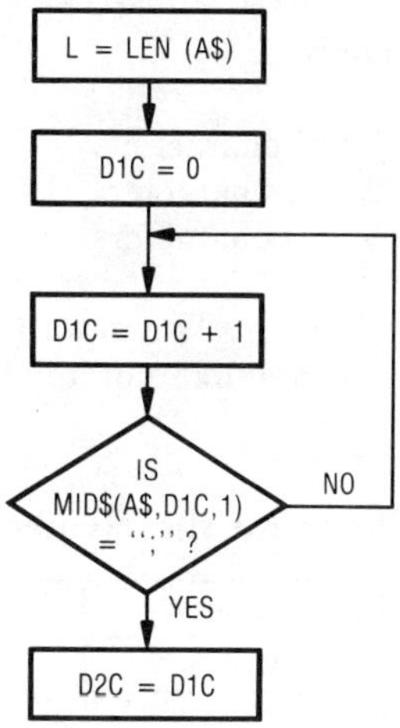

Fig. 13-4. Case No. 1—flowchart with no error checking.

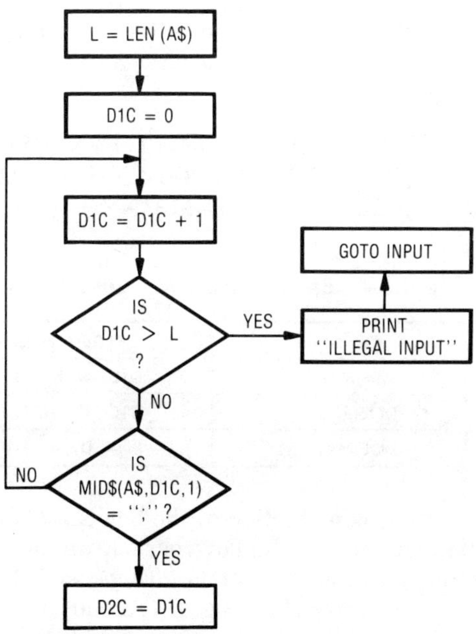

Fig. 13-5. Case No. 2—flowchart with error checking statement.

ILLEGAL CONDITIONS

1. Delimiters—not exactly 2.
2. Length of lines
   a. Length of line 1 = 0 characters.
   b. Length of line 2 = 0 characters.
   c. Length of line 3 = 0 characters.

I. H. 1. Number of delimiters. The input format has two, and only two delimiters. If there are any more or any less than two delimiters, the input is illegal.

Table 13-3. Check for the Number of Delimiters

# of Delimiters	Test	Decision Statement
0	ILLEGAL	D1C>L
1	ILLEGAL	D2C>L
2	LEGAL	
3	ILLEGAL	FOR J = D2C+1 TO L IF MID$(A$,J,1) = ";" NEXT J

I. H. 2. Length of lines. There are 3 lines of input separated by delimiters. If any, or all, of these lines are zero length, the input is incorrect.

Line 1 = 0 ;2200 MAIN ST.;ANYTOWN USA 00000(L)
Line 2 = 0 JOHN DOE;;ANYTOWN USA 00000(L)
Line 3 = 0 JOHN DOE;2200 MAIN ST.;(L)

Table 13-4. Error Check for Line Length

Line	Condition	Decision Statement	
1	;MAIN;USA	D1C = 1	ILLEGAL
2	DOE;;USA	D1C+1=D2C	ILLEGAL
3	DOE;MAIN;(L)	L = D2C	ILLEGAL

I. I. Write error checking section of the flowchart. Fig. 13-6 shows the error checking aspects in the flowchart. Examine Fig. 13-6 carefully to determine where each error case is checked. Fig. 13-3 shows what happens with no error checking. If there are no delimiters separating the name and address fields in "DOE MAIN USA" (A$), the D1C = D1C + 1 loop executes until D1C is greater than L. When D1C>L, the computer prints ILLEGAL QUANTITY ERR because it is telling the machine to compare a nonexistent character with “;”.

Table 13-5. Errors

Error #	Condition
1	IS D1C > L ?
2	IS D1C = 1 ?
3	IS D2C > L ?
4	IS D1C + 1 = D2C ?
5	IS D2C = L ?
6	IS A 3rd DELIMITER FOUND IN THE LAST PART OF THE INPUT ?

I. J. Final flowchart. The final flowchart is an incorporation of all the details, charts, ideas, and logic to this point. The final flowchart should be written so very few changes are needed to code the program. The final flowchart is shown in Fig. 13-6.

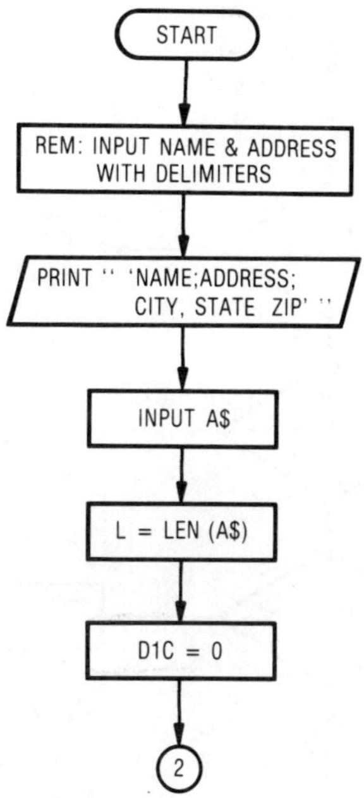

Fig. 13-6. Final flowchart.

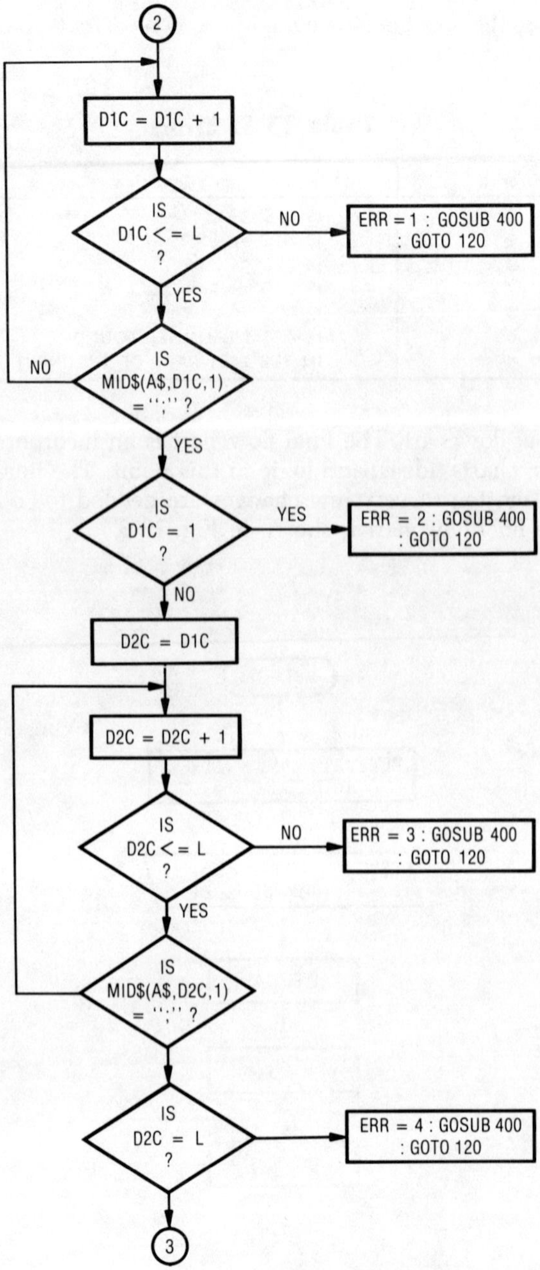

Fig. 13-6. (Cont) Final flowchart.

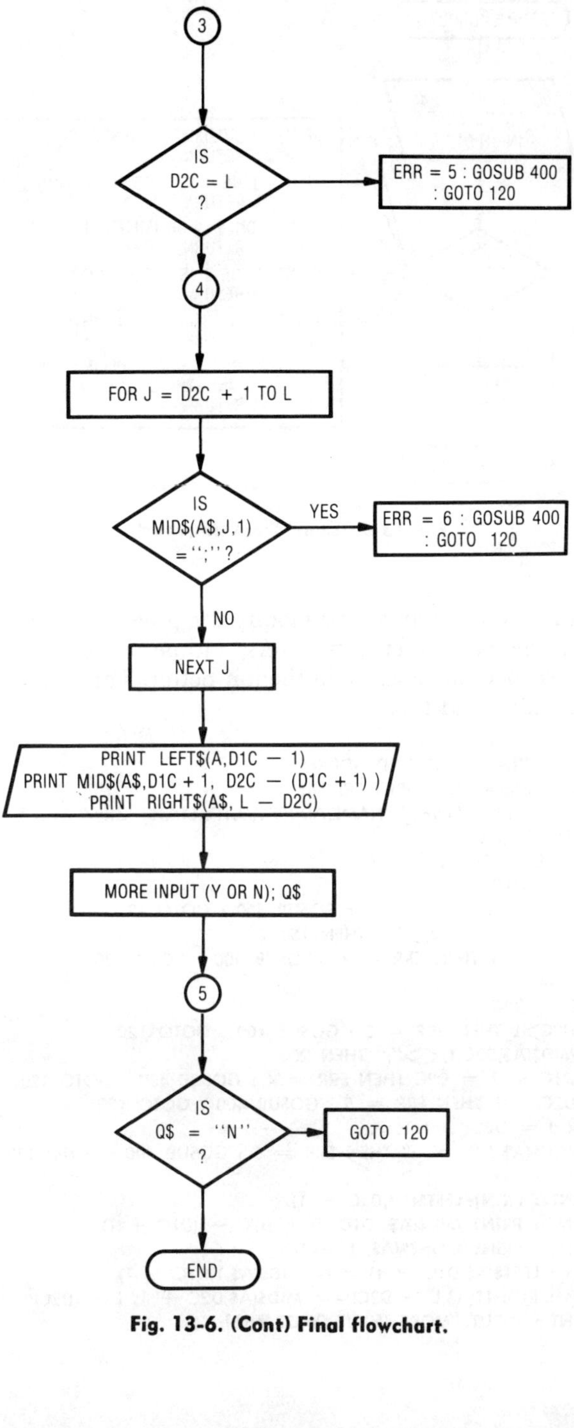

Fig. 13-6. (Cont) Final flowchart.

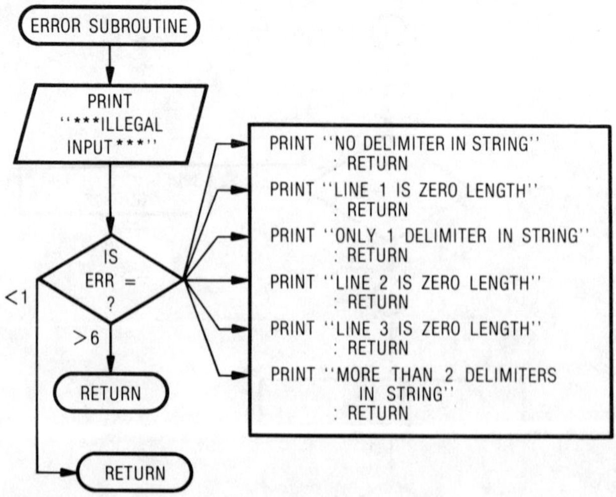

Fig. 13-6. (Cont) Final flowchart.

I. K. L. M. Write, debug, and modify the program. Most programmers are perpetual students, tinkerers, and perfectionists. They will usually seek modifications to do the job better. This is the real idea of programming and life.

```
100  REM : PRINT NAME AND ADDRESS
110  REM : CHECK FOR INPUT ERRORS
120  PRINT : PRINT "INPUT 'NAME;ADDRESS;CITY,STATE  ZIP' "
130  INPUT "?";A$
140  L = LEN (A$) : D1C = 0
150  D1C = D1C + 1
160  IF D1C>L THEN ERR = 1 : GOSUB 400 : GOTO 120
170  IF MID$(A$,D1C,1)<>";" THEN 150
180  IF D1C = 1 THEN ERR = 2 : GOSUB 400 : GOTO 120
190  D2C = D1C
200  D2C = D2C + 1
210  IF D2C>L THEN ERR = 3 : GOSUB 400 : GOTO 120
220  IF MID$(A$,D2C,1)<>";" THEN 200
230  IF D1C + 1 = D2C THEN ERR = 4 : GOSUB 400 : GOTO 120
240  IF D2C = L THEN ERR = 5 : GOSUB 400 : GOTO 120
250  FOR J = D2C + 1 TO L
260  IF MID$(A$,J,1) = ";" THEN ERR = 6 : GOSUB 400 : GOTO 120
270  NEXT J
280  PRINT : PRINT LEFT$(A$,D1C - 1)
290  PRINT : PRINT MID$(A$, D1C + 1, D2C - (D1C + 1)
300  PRINT : PRINT RIGHT$(A$, L - D2C)
301  REM : LEFT$(A$,D1C - 1) = = MID$(A$,1,D1C - 1)
302  REM : RIGHT$(A$,L - D2C)== MID$(A$,D2C + 1, L - D2C)
310  PRINT : INPUT "MORE INPUT (Y OR N)" ; Q$
```

```
320  IF Q$<>"N" THEN 120
330  END
400  PRINT "***ILLEGAL INPUT***"
410  ON (ERR) GOTO 430, 440, 450, 460, 470, 480
420  RETURN
430  PRINT "NO DELIMITER IN STRING" : RETURN
440  PRINT "LINE 1 IS ZERO LENGTH" : RETURN
450  PRINT "ONLY ONE DELIMITER IN STRING" : RETURN
460  PRINT "LINE 2 IS ZERO LENGTH" : RETURN
470  PRINT "LINE 3 IS ZERO LENGTH" : RETURN
480  PRINT "MORE THAN 2 DELIMITERS IN STRING" : RETURN
RUN
INPUT 'NAME;ADDRESS;CITY STATE  ZIP'
?JOHN DOE 2200 MAIN ST. ANYTOWN USA  00000
***ILLEGAL INPUT***
NO DELIMITER IN STRING

INPUT 'NAME;ADDRESS;CITY STATE  ZIP'
$;2200 MAIN ST.;ANYTOWN USA 00000
***ILLEGAL INPUT***
LINE 1 IS ZERO LENGTH

INPUT 'NAME;ADDRESS;CITY STATE  ZIP'
?JOHN DOE;2200 MAIN ST. ANYTOWN USA  00000
***ILLEGAL INPUT***
ONLY ONE DELIMITER IN STRING

INPUT 'NAME;ADDRESS;CITY STATE  ZIP'
?JOHN DOE;;ANYTOWN USA  00000
***ILLEGAL INPUT***
LINE 2 IS ZERO LENGTH

INPUT 'NAME;ADDRESS;CITY STATE  ZIP'
?JOHN DOE;2200 MAIN ST.;
***ILLEGAL INPUT***
LINE 3 IS ZERO LENGTH

INPUT 'NAME;ADDRESS;CITY STATE  ZIP'
?JOHN DOE;2200 MAIN ST.;ANYTOWN ;USA  00000
***ILLEGAL INPUT***
MORE THAN 2 DELIMITERS IN STRING

INPUT 'NAME;ADDRESS;CITY STATE  ZIP'
?JOHN DOE;2200 MAIN ST.;ANYTOWN USA  00000
JOHN DOE
2200 MAIN ST.
ANYTOWN USA  00000
```

This is how the logic developed from conception to completion. The following explanation of statements may be repetitious but it may also be helpful.

FLOWCHART NORMAL LOGIC	PROGRAM EXPEDIENT LOGIC
D1C <= L	D1C > L
MID$(A$,D1C,1) = ";"	MID$(A$,D1C,1)<>";"
MID$(A$,D2C,1) = ";"	MID$(A$,D2C,1)<>";"
D2C <= L	D2C > L
Q$ = "N"	Q$ <> "N"

The flowchart was written with normal logic. The program was coded with expedient logic. Once the flowchart is developed, the sections are broken down to determine the most efficient and fastest way for the program to run. A flowchart is simply a tool to help clarify the logic involved in solving a problem. When converting a flowchart to a program it is sometimes useful to reverse the "IF" check to save memory. The common practice is to use MID$(A$, D1C,1) = ";". The program must search for ";" until it is found. When = ";" is not true the program must unconditionally branch (GOTO) backwards to increment D1C. Expedient logic MID$(A$, D1C,1)<>";" causes the program to search for <>";". If it is not found, the program conditionally branches to increment D1C, thus saving a GOTO statement with each decision. This not only saves program statements, but makes the program more efficient, run faster and uses less memory. Expedient logic makes the program simpler and more efficient. It gets the job done better and faster.

Lines 100 and 110 are REM statements that document the program to print the name and address of an individual and to check for input errors.

Line 120 prints out the exact input format for the user. The user is soon aware that the name and address must be input exactly the same way as the input header. If the input is different, the user is given an error message why the input is incorrect. The program will not accept the name and address unless it is correctly input.

Line 140 is a programming convenience. It is much easier to type L than it is to type LEN (A$). D1C = 0 initializes the first delimiter to zero. The D2C and L delimiters are not initialized to zero, because in line 190 D2C = D1C takes the value of D1C at the end of line 1 and stores it in D2C. This value maintains the continuity of the program in checking for the relationship with L (LEN (A$)).

Line 150 is a counting statement that is incremented on each character of line 1 of A$ until it detects the delimiter (;).

In line 160, if the counting statement increments until the value of D1C is greater than L, the THEN is executed to send the program to ERR = 1. In Applesoft when the statement (IF D1C > L) is true, all statements at that line number are executed (unless there is an unconditional branch THEN 400). GOSUB 400 branches to the subroutine beginning at line 400. ***ILLEGAL INPUT*** is printed. The ERR = 1 sends the program to line 430. The error-line number relationship is shown in Fig. 13-7.

ERROR #	ON (ERR) GOTO
1	430
2	440
3	450
4	460
5	470
6	480

Fig. 13-7. Error-line number relationship.

At the end of line 430 is a RETURN statement. A RETURN statement must be placed at the end of a subroutine. The RETURN causes the program to branch to the program statement immediately after the GOSUB.

The sequence of events that occur after ERR = 1 is

1. GOSUB 400 — Branch to line 400.
2. ERR = 1 — ON (1) GOTO 430 to print the input error. RETURN follows the error printout.
3. RETURN — GOTO 120–line immediately following GOSUB 400.

The ON–GOTO (ON–GOSUB) is a relationship programmed into Applesoft. A specific ERROR number relates to a specific line number in the program.

In line 170, the decision statement checks to see if the delimiter (;) at the end of the first line has been reached. If the character is not the delimiter, the program branches to line 150 to increment the value of D1C.

In line 180, if there is only one delimiter in A$, the ERROR = 2. The statement GOSUB 400 sends the program to line 400 to print out ***ILLEGAL INPUT*** and then to line 440 to print out the input error, LINE 1 IS ZERO LENGTH.

In line 190, the value held in the delimiter D1C is stored in D2C. This statement maintains the value relationship from one delimiter to the next. This value relationship is continued as the program moves to L, the delimiter at the end of line 3.

In line 210, if the present value stored in D2C is greater than L, THEN input error #3 is printed on the screen. The program executes GOSUB 400, ON 2 GOTO 450, to print, ONLY ONE DELIMITER IN STRING. The RETURN statement branches to the line immediately after GOSUB 400. The statement is GOTO 120, and immediately branches to line 120, for more input.

In line 220, if the decision statement does not find the D2C delimiter, it branches to line 200 to increment D2C.

In line 230, if the two semicolon delimiters are together with no characters in between, line 2 is missing. ERR = 4. GOSUB 400 executes to line 400 to print out ***ILLEGAL INPUT***, ON 4 GOTO 460, prints out, LINE 2 IS ZERO LENGTH. RETURN branches to GOTO 120 (line 230) to input the correct information.

In line 240, if D2C = L there are no characters in line 3, and ERR = 5, causes a branch to the subroutine to print ***ILLEGAL INPUT***. ON 5 GOTO 470 prints, LINE 3 IS ZERO LENGTH.

Line 250 to 270 is a loop to check the number of delimiters from D2C to L. The program has checked that there are 2 delimiters to this point. Line 170 checks the delimiter at the end of line #1. Line 220 checks the delimiter at the end of line #2. If the loop FOR J = D2C + 1 TO L executes and finds another semicolon delimiter then ERR = 6. The program branches to line 400, prints out ***ILLEGAL INPUT***, ON 6 GOTO 480, MORE THAN 2 DELIMITERS IN STRING. The RETURN is executed to GOTO 120, and GOTO 120 branches to input information.

Lines 280, 290, and 300 print out the name and address of the individual in the correct format.

Lines 301 and 302 are inserted to inform the user the correct MID$ functions to replace the LEFT$ and RIGHT$ to print out lines #1 and #3.

Line 310 PRINT : INPUT "MORE INPUT (Y OR N)" ;Q$ queries the user, is another name and address to be input, or does the user want to end the program?

Line 320 IF Q$<>"N" THEN 120 is a decision statement to branch to line 120 for more input, or to end the program. This line could be flowcharted in either of two ways with equal efficiency as shown in Fig. 13-8.

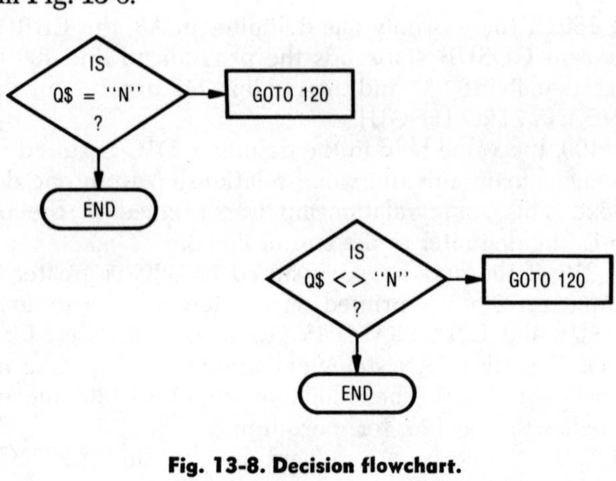

Fig. 13-8. Decision flowchart.

Lines 400 to 480 are the subroutines and the ON (ERR) GOTO statements. Subroutines placed after the main body of the program do not clutter up the main body of the program. Applesoft indicates an END statement is optional and need not be used. Experience shows that complicated programs will not always run properly without an end statement. The subroutines perform better when the program branches past the end statement of the program. The subroutine runs and the RETURN branches to the statement immediately after the GOSUB in the main body of the program. Use an END statement with all programs.

LESSON 14

Functions

After completion of Lesson 14 you should be able to:

1. Use arithmetic functions in programming.
2. Convert radians to degrees by using the DEF FN.
3. List and define language, string, and numeric functions.

VOCABULARY

Argument—This is a variable factor, the value of which determines the value of the function.

Function—This is that part of the computer instruction that specifies the operation to be performed.

Radian—This is a unit of plane angular measurement that is equal to the angle at the center of a circle subtended by an arc equal in length to the radius.

DISCUSSION

In this lesson, the arithmetic functions will be placed alphabetically in a program to demonstrate their use, and they will be clarified by explanation.

A function, as explained in the vocabulary, is that part of the computer instruction that specifies the operation to be performed. Functions act upon the input to a function. The function then performs some operation on the argument, and outputs the result. The operation itself may involve many program steps. Calling a function automatically makes use of these preprogrammed steps.

The following program shows how functions work. The output of each function is placed beside the function, rather than at the end of the program, for clarity.

```
100  M = -4 : N = 2.5 : P = 3 : Q = 0
110  PRINT  ABS (M)          (4)
120  PRINT EXP (P)           (20.0855369)
130  PRINT LOG (P)           (1.09861229)
140  PRINT RND (P)           (.889939655)
150  PRINT SGN (M)           (-1)
160  PRINT SGN (Q)           (0)
170  PRINT SGN (N)           (1)
180  PRINT SQR (P)           (1.73205081)
190  REM: GEOMETRIC ARGUMENTS GIVEN IN RADIANS
200  REM: USE DEF FN TO CONVERT DEGREES TO RADIANS
210  PRINT SIN (P)           (.1411200008)
220  DEF FN SD(X) = SIN (X/57.2958)
230  PRINT FN SD (P)         (.0523359375)
240  PRINT COS (P)           (-.989992497)
250  DEF FN CD (X) = COS (X/57.2958)
260  PRINT FN CD (P)         (.998629665)
270  PRINT TAN (P)           (-.142546543)
280  DEF FN TD (X) = TAN (X/57.2958)
290  PRINT FN TD (P)         (.0524077605)
300  PRINT ATN (P)           (1.24904577)
310  DEF FN AD (X) = ATN (X/57.2958)
320  PRINT FN AD (P)         (.0523120883)
999  END
```

ABS—returns the absolute or positive value.

EXP—raises the value to 6 places to the indicated power of 2.718289. This is used in hyperbolic and exponential functions in biology, chemistry, physics, and engineering. EXP (P) = 20.0855369.

LOG—This function in Applesoft is the natural log. In mathematics, LOG = log to base 10. LN = the natural log. The conversion factor from the natural log to the log base 10 is 2.302585093.

LOG BASE 10—10 LOG = 1.

NATURAL LOG—10 LNX = 2.30258093.

RND—returns a real number greater than zero and less than one. RND (P) = .889939655. M = −4. RND (M) = 2.99214662E−08.

SGN—if the expression is less than zero, a value of −1 is returned. If the expression is zero, a zero is returned. If the expression is greater than 1, a value of 1 is returned.

SQR—returns the square root of the number.

SIN, COS, TAN, ATN—are trigonometric functions. Their arguments are in radians. A radian is an angular measurement that is equal to the angle at the center of a circle subtended by an arc equal in length to the radius. Many people work in degrees, so the DEF FN function is used to convert radians to degrees.

Language, string, and numeric functions are listed and defined below.

ASC ("A")—returns the ASCII code for the character in the argument. Strings cannot be converted directly to numerics. ASC ("A") is used to convert the character of the string to an ASCII numeric value, which is 65.

CHR$ (65)—numerics cannot be converted directly to strings. CHR$ (65) converts the ASCII value 65 to the string character A.

FRE (0)—returns to the user, the number of bytes of memory available. PRINT FRE (0)—must be used to return the amount of memory. Changing the argument from 0 to 10 has no effect on the amount of memory returned.

INT—returns the largest integer in the number. PRINT INT (3.14) returns the number 3.

LEFT$—function detailed in Lesson 13.

LEN—returns the length of the string. A$ = "HI SUE". PRINT LEN (A$), LEN ("HI SUE") returns the number 6 for each LEN, the number of characters and spaces in the string.

MID$—function detailed in Lesson 13.

POS—returns the position of the cursor. If the cursor is in column 1, PRINT POS (0) returns 0. VTAB 20 : HTAB 30. PRINT POS (0) returns the cursor location as 29.

RIGHT$—function detailed in Lesson 13.

STR$—returns a string that represents the value in the argument. PRINT STR$ (3.14) returns 3.14.

VAL—interprets a string value. PRINT VAL ("3.14") returns 3.14.

LESSON 15

List and Edit

After completion of Lesson 15 you should be able to:

1. List programs or parts of programs, and delete parts of programs or a whole program.
2. Edit using escape cursor moves mode and pure cursor moves mode.
3. Comprehend three types of program statements to edit.
4. Insert text into an existing line.

VOCABULARY

DEL—This is a command to remove a line or lines from a program. DEL 20-70 or DEL 20,70 removes lines 20 through 70 from the program.

Edit—This means to arrange data into a format required for subsequent processing. Editing may involve deletion of data not required, conversion of fields into a machine format (e.g., value fields converted to binary), and preparation of data for subsequent output (e.g., zero suppression).

Escape Cursor Moves Mode—In this mode, the ESCAPE key must be pressed at the same time a cursor move key is pressed. If ESCAPE is not pressed simultaneously with a cursor move key, the computer will not move the cursor. Cursor move keys are A, B, C, and D. Escape cursor moves mode is used by Apple computers supplied with Applesoft on tape or disk.

LIST—This command lists all the line numbers and program statements in a program. LIST 50,100 lists lines 50 to 100 of a program.

Prompt—This is any message given to an operator by an operating system.

Pure Cursor Moves Mode—In this mode, the ESCAPE key does not have to be pressed at the same time as the cursor move keys. Instead, ESCAPE is pressed only once to enable the cursor move keys. To leave this mode, any character key but the cursor move keys must be pressed. Cursor move keys are I, J, K, and M. This mode can only be used by Apple computers with Applesoft supplied by firmware, rather than by tape or disk.

DISCUSSION

In editing, probably the most used keys are the left arrow, the right arrow, and the repeat keys. The left arrow key, when pressed, moves the cursor one space to the left. The right arrow key, when pressed, moves the cursor one space to the right. When the repeat key is pressed, the last character printed is repeated on the screen. To prevent this undesirable reprinting, a shift arrow key should be pressed and released. The repeat and shift arrow key (or desired key) can then be held down simultaneously to move the cursor (or chosen character). When the repeat key and any other key are pressed simultaneously, the character is repeated until the keys are released.

Type in this program.

```
10   PRINT "THIS IS THE USA"
20   END
```

To list the program, type LIST and the total program appears. To list only one line of the program, type LIST and the line number.

```
LIST 10
10   PRINT "THIS IS THE USA"
```

To list a long section of a program, type LIST and the beginning line number, followed by a comma, and the last line number.

```
LIST 10,20   (for a long program LIST 50,100—the screen only holds 24 lines of the
              program statements)
10   PRINT "THIS IS THE USA"
20 END
```

In the list function, a minus sign (−) may be used to replace the comma between the line numbers.

```
LIST 50,100 = LIST 50-100
```

To list those lines above 500 (program runs from 0 to 1000) type

LIST −500. To list those lines below 500 type LIST 500−. This convenient feature saves a great deal of typing.

To delete a single line of the program, type in DEL and the line number, followed by a comma, and the same line number.

DEL 10,10—deletes line 10 of the program.

Another way to delete line 10 is to type 10, and press RETURN.

The minus sign (−) cannot be used to replace the comma (,) in the DEL command.

Type in DEL 10 to delete line 10. The computer gives a ? SYNTAX ERR for this illegal command, because the command did not include a comma and the repeat of the line number.

Sections of a program can be deleted by typing in: DEL *first line number, comma, second line number.*

DEL 100,200 deletes all lines from 100 to 200, including 100 and 200.

To delete the total program from memory, type NEW. To check that the program has been deleted from memory, type LIST. If no program appears on the screen, the program has been deleted from memory.

There are two types of edit functions, (1) escape cursor moves, and (2) pure cursor moves.

The escape cursor moves require the escape key be pressed, and held down before the key to move the cursor is pressed. To move the cursor again, the escape key must be pressed before the key to move the cursor is pressed. The routine is press the escape key and then press the cursor move key. The escape cursor move mode works on Applesoft that is loaded from tape or disk.

The keys that control the cursor in the escape cursor moves mode are:

KEY	DIRECTION
ESCAPE A	RIGHT
ESCAPE B	LEFT
ESCAPE C	DOWN
ESCAPE D	UP

If the escape key is not pressed before the A key, the letter A will be printed on the screen. When the escape key is pressed and the A key is pressed, no letter is printed on the screen; only the cursor is moved one space to the right.

The pure cursor moves mode edit function is available on Applesoft firmware, and does not work on Applesoft loaded from tape or disk.

The pure cursor moves mode requires the escape key be pressed once and the proper character key is pressed to move the cursor.

The cursor can be moved in any direction until some key other than I, J, K, or M is pressed.

The keys that control the cursor in the pure cursor moves mode are:

KEY	DIRECTION
ESCAPE (pressed only	once)
K	RIGHT
J	LEFT
M	DOWN
I	UP

To recover from the pure cursor moves mode, any key (other than I, J, K, or M) may be pressed one time. The second time the key is pressed the operator regains control of the computer.

For example, in editing line 10:

```
LIST 10
10   PRINT "THIS IS THE USA"
```

ESCAPE is pressed and released. Key J is pressed one time to bring the cursor to column 1 of the screen. Key I is pressed twice to place the cursor over the 1 in line 10. The pure cursor moves mode is exited by pressing the right arrow key twice. The right arrow and repeat keys are then pressed to place the cursor over the area to be changed. The changes are made by typing in the proper character. The cursor is moved past the closing quote to complete the edit. Did you print an incorrect character in the statement? Go back and do it correctly.

There are three types of statements that can be edited. They are the statements containing,

1. Characters enclosed in quotation marks that occupy one line on the screen.
2. Characters not enclosed in quotation marks that occupy more than one line on the screen.
3. Characters enclosed in quotation marks that occupy more than one line on the screen.

In editing Applesoft loaded from tape or disk, only the escape cursor moves mode can be used.

Statements with characters enclosed in quotation marks that occupy one line and characters not enclosed in quotation marks that occupy more than one line offer no editing problems. The cursor must be past the last character in the line before RETURN is pressed. If the cursor is before the last character and RETURN is pressed, all characters after the cursor are deleted.

The editing problems come in statements with characters enclosed in quotation marks occupying more than one line.

```
10   PRINT "THIS IS THE UNITED STATES OF
AMERICA"
20   END
RUN
THIS IS THE UNITED STATES OF AMERICA
```

Now type LIST 10

```
10   PRINT "THIS IS THE UNITED STA
     TES OF AMERICA"
```

The LIST causes line 10 to break in the middle of STATES. If not edited correctly, spaces will be left in the printout when the program is run. The method to eliminate spaces is to use the escape cursor moves mode, in the areas where spacing is possible.

Press ESCAPE and B. This moves the cursor to column 1 of the screen. Press ESCAPE and D. This moves the cursor one row up. Pressing ESCAPE and D moves the cursor over the 1 in line 10.

Press repeat and right arrow keys simultaneously. D is printed on the screen over the 1. The repeat key repeats the last character key pressed. To prevent printing D (or the last character pressed), the right arrow key must first be pressed and released. The right arrow key and the repeat key can then be pressed simultaneously without printing a character.

To erase the D, press the left arrow key and retype the number 1. Press the right arrow key and the repeat key simultaneously until the cursor moves past the ending quotation mark on the 2nd line. Now press RETURN and type LIST 10.

```
10   PRINT "THIS IS THE UNITED STA
                    TES OF AMERICA"
```

The spacing between the A and the T in STATES has been changed. Now type RUN.

```
RUN
THIS IS THE UNITED STA        TES OF AMERICA
```

The spacing in the RUN has also been changed. To prevent this error the line must be edited to look like this:

```
10   PRINT "THIS IS THE UNITED STATES OF
AMERICA"
RUN
THIS IS THE UNITED STATES OF AMERICA
LIST 10
```

```
10  PRINT "THIS IS THE UNITED STA
    TES OF AMERICA"
```

To edit line 10 so the proper spacing is maintained, the following procedure is used:

1. Press ESCAPE and B to bring the cursor to column 1.
2. Press ESCAPE D three times to bring the cursor over 1 in line 10.
3. Press right arrow key and release.
4. Press right arrow key and repeat key simultaneously until the cursor rests immediately past the A in STA.
5. Press ESCAPE and A in proper sequence and the correct number of times to bring the cursor over the T in TES (on the second line of the statement). Sounds like a galloping horse, doesn't it?
6. Press right arrow key and release it.
7. Press right arrow key and repeat key simultaneously until the cursor is past the closing quotation mark in the statement.
8. Press RETURN.

Type LIST 10

```
10  PRINT "THIS IS THE UNITED STA
    TES OF AMERICA"
```

The statement lists all right. Now type RUN

```
RUN
THIS IS THE UNITED STATES OF AMERICA
```

The printed line now has the correct spacing. The ESCAPE and A must be used to prevent changed spacing on statements with characters enclosed in quotation marks that occupy more than one line.

For Apple computers with Apple firmware using the pure cursor moves mode, editing is very simple. The same procedure is used for the pure cursor moves mode as is used for the escape cursor moves mode, but ESCAPE is pressed once and then I,J,K, or M is used to place the cursor over the character to be edited. After the statement is edited, the RETURN key must be pressed twice for the operator to regain control of the computer.

To delete a character in an existing line using the escape cursor moves mode, type in the line.

```
10  PRINT "THIS IS THE USA"
```

Place the cursor over the I in IS. Press ESCAPE and A. The I is still visible and the cursor moves over the letter S in IS. Move the cursor past the closing quote. Another way to edit the I is to place the cursor over the I in IS, and press the space bar. Type LIST 10.

```
10    PRINT "THIS S THE USA"         (the letter I has been deleted)
```

To insert the letter I in IS, type LIST 10.

```
10    PRINT "THIS S THE USA"
```

Place the cursor over the letter S. Press ESCAPE and B to prepare to insert the word IS. Type IS THE USA. Press RETURN and type LIST 10.

```
10    PRINT "THIS IS THE USA"
```

To delete a letter using the pure cursor moves mode, type in line 10.

```
10    PRINT "THIS IS THE USA"
```

Bring the cursor over the letter I in IS. Press ESCAPE and K. The cursor moves over the S and the I is still visible. Move the cursor past the closing quotation mark. Press RETURN and type LIST 10. The I can also be deleted by placing the cursor over the I and pressing the space bar.

```
10    PRINT "THIS S THE USA"
```

To type in the letter I in the existing line, place the cursor over the letter S. Back the cursor into the space between the THIS and the S. Press ESCAPE and B for escape cursor moves mode, and then ESCAPE and J for the pure cursor moves mode. Type in I. Press the right arrow once and release. Press the right arrow and repeat keys simultaneously to place the cursor past the closing quote. Press RETURN. Type LIST 10.

```
10    PRINT "THIS IS THE USA"
```

The IS is in proper spacing in the literal again.

To insert text into an existing line, place the cursor over the letter where the inserted item is to be placed. In the case of line 10, GOOD OLE is to be placed before USA.

```
10    PRINT "THIS IS THE USA"
```

1. Place the cursor over the letter U in USA.
2. Use the escape cursor moves mode. Press ESCAPE D to move the cursor one line above the statement.
3. Type in GOOD OLE leaving a space after OLE (space).

4. Press ESCAPE C to move the cursor back to the statement line.
5. Press ESCAPE B to back the cursor over the U in USA.
6. Press right arrow key and release it.
7. Press right arrow and repeat keys simultaneously to place the cursor past the closing quote.
8. Press RETURN.

```
RUN
THIS IS THE GOOD OLE USA

LIST 10
10   PRINT "THIS IS THE GOOD OLE U
     SA"
```

Great! This programming is moving in the right direction.

LESSON 16

Play Computer

After completion of Lesson 16 you should be able to:

1. Play computer and RUN a program manually, or mentally, to determine the output.
2. Play computer to determine why a program doesn't RUN or why a program doesn't run properly (debug).
3. Use TRACE function to aid in debugging programs.
4. Use NOTRACE function to counter the TRACE function.

VOCABULARY

NOTRACE—This command turns off the TRACE mode (see TRACE below).

Pass—This means the single execution of a loop, or the passage of magnetic tape across the read or write heads of a recording device.

TRACE—This is an aid in following the sequence of execution of a program. It is used as an aid in debugging programs. TRACE causes the line number and output data to be printed on the screen in the sequence of line number execution. TRACE is turned off by NOTRACE. TRACE and NOTRACE are immediate commands.

DISCUSSION

The primary purpose of this lesson is to "think" like a computer. When you think like a computer and run the program mentally and manually, you will be able to determine what the actual output of the program will be, rather than what you think it should be. You must think like a computer if you are going to understand and outsmart this exacting machine. When you play computer the program is RUN exactly as it is written. If the rule of default applies, use the rule of default. If the program uses a decision statement, you must make the proper decision to branch or default. Tables should be made to determine how the variables change with each pass. RUN the program mentally several times to get the feel of the program. Complete the chart to see if you think like a computer. The RUN and TRACE are shown in Fig. 16-1.

```
RUN
6          10          -8
7          10          -6
8          10          -4
9          10          -2
10         10           0
10         8            1
10         8           -9
TRACE
RUN
#10  #20  #20  #20  #30  #40  #90  #100  #110  6
10             -8
#120  #30  #40  #90  #100  #110  7
10             -6
#120  #30  #40  #90  #100  #110  8
10             -4
#120  #30  #40  #90  #100  #110  9
10             -2
#120  #30  #40  #90  #100  #110  10
10              0
#120  #30  #40  #50  #60  #70  10
8               1
#80  #30  #130  #140  10          8
-9
#150
```

Fig. 16-1. RUN and TRACE.

```
10  REM : PROGRAM TO PLAY COMPUTER
20  A = 5 : B = 10 : C = -10
30  IF C > 0 THEN 130
40  IF (B > A) THEN 90
        (without parentheses: IF B > A THEN 90, produces a SYNTAX ERR because
        AT is a reserved word—to correct this, use parentheses around B > A)
50  IF C < = 0 THEN C = C + 1
60  B = B - 2
70  PRINT A, B, C
80  GOTO 30
90  A = A + 1
100 C = C + 2
110 PRINT A, B, C
120 GOTO 30
```

```
130  C = C - 10
140  PRINT A, B, C
150  END
```

Chart 16-1. Variable Chart

Assign value of variables	A	B	C
from line 20	5	10	−10
Values—1st pass			
Values—2nd pass			
Values—3rd pass			
Values—4th pass			
Values—5th pass			
Values—6th pass			
Values—7th pass			

After the chart has been completed and you are satisfied you understand how and why the program functions, RUN the program to get the correct results. Did you do as well as the computer?

Type in the immediate command TRACE. When the program is RUN, the line numbers, and variable values, are printed on the screen. If a program does not RUN, TRACE can aid in determining why it doesn't run. The error messages built into the language can also aid in debugging programs. If a program stops at line 120, and no error message is given, many times the TRACE mode can aid in correcting the problem.

TRACE function can be removed by typing NOTRACE on the screen. The next program RUN will be without the line numbers on the screen to give an example of how TRACE and NOTRACE are typed on the screen.

```
RUN
```

```
TRACE
RUN
```

```
NOTRACE
```

LESSON 17

Reserved Words

After completion of Lesson 17 you should be able to:

1. Use reserved words in programs in their proper relationship.
2. Use parentheses to separate characters that the computer interprets as reserved words.

VOCABULARY

Reserved Words—These are words programmed into the language to aid in carrying out the programming functions.

DISCUSSION

Reserved words are used to aid in programming. These words cannot be used as variables. Applesoft tokenizes reserved words to a decimal number similar to the decimal number that represents an ASCII symbol. For example,

```
40   IF B = A THEN 90.
```

When the program is RUN, the program is stopped at line 40 and SYNTAX ERR is printed on the screen. When line 40 is LISTed it appears as:

```
40   IF B = AT HEN90.
```

The variable A attaches to T in THEN to become the reserved AT. To overcome this problem and use the variable A in the same sequence, use parentheses around B = A.

```
40 IF (B = A) THEN 90
```

The list of reserved words is taken directly from *Applesoft II, BASIC PROGRAMMING REFERENCE MANUAL,* page 122, by the Apple Computer Inc., 10260 Bandley Dr., Cupertino, California 95014.

RESERVED WORDS IN APPLESOFT

&

ABS AND ASC AT ATN

CALL CHR$ CLEAR COLOR= CONT COS

DATA DEF DEL DIM DRAW

END EXP

FLASH FN FOR FRE

GET GOSUB GOTO GR

HCOLOR= HGR HGR2 HIMEM: HLIN HOME

HPLOT HTAB

IF IN# INPUT INT INVERSE

LEFT$ LEN LET LIST LOAD LOG LOMEM:

MID$

NEW NEXT NORMAL NOT NOTRACE

ON ONERR OR

PDL PEEK PLOT POKE POP POS PRINT PR#

READ RECALL REM RESTORE RESUME RETURN

RIGHT$ RND ROT= RUN

SAVE SCALE= SCRN(SGN SHLOAD SIN SPC(

SPEED= SQR STEP STOP STORE STR$

TAB(TAN TEXT THEN TO TRACE

USR

VAL VLIN VTAB

WAIT

XPLOT XDRAW

LESSON 18

Menu Selection and Coding Formulas

After completion of Lesson 18 you should be able to:

1. Write programs using a menu selection.
2. Translate formulas to computer code for computational purposes.

VOCABULARY

Code—This is the representation of data or instructions in symbolic form. It is sometimes used as a synonym for instructions. Coding is the act of converting data or instructions into program statements.

Comment—This is a written note that can be included in the coding of computer instructions in order to clarify the procedures, but has no effect on the computer itself.

GET A$—This stops the program in order to view the output until any key is pressed.

Menu Selection—This is a method of using a terminal to display a list of optional facilities that can be chosen by the user in order to carry out different functions in the system.

DISCUSSION

Many people have little knowledge of computers. For these people, the programs must be written to tell them what input is required, and in what format. One way to aid these people with the correct selection is to use a menu. A menu selection is a method of using a terminal to display a list of optional facilities that can be chosen by the user in order to carry out different functions in the system.

The following program computes depreciation by using either the straight line method, double declining balance method (200%), or the sum of the years digits method. The variables are shown in Fig. 18-1.

STRAIGHT LINE DEPRECIATION

BV	Book value
DY	Depreciation per year
GA	Gross amount or gross cost of the asset
GET A$	Stops the program to allow the user to view the output.
LA	Life of the asset
P	Rounded to 2 places (100)
S	Selection
SV	Salvage value
TD	Total depreciation

DOUBLE DECLINING BALANCE

BV	Book value
DY	Depreciation per year
GA	Gross amount or gross cost of the asset
GET A$	Stops the program to allow the user to view the output.
K	Constant
LA	Life of the asset
SV	Salvage value
TD	Total depreciation

SUM OF THE YEARS DIGITS

BV	Book value
DY	Depreciation per year
GA	Gross amount or gross cost of the asset
GET A$	Stops the program to allow the user to view the output.
K	Constant
LA	Life of the asset
SV	Salvage value
TD	Total depreciation
Z	Variable to hold (LA − Y). Z = (LA − Y) + 1. A method to compute and print the years forward, after they computed backwards.

Fig. 18-1. Variables.

The program shows the menu selection. The user selects which method of depreciation is to be used for computation. The menu section of the program is contained in lines 500 to 560.

```
500  HOME : VTAB 3 : HTAB 8 : PRINT "***DEPRECIATION***" :
     PRINT : PRINT
510  HTAB 5 : PRINT "1.  STRAIGHT LINE DEPRECIATION" : PRINT
520  HTAB 5 : PRINT "2.  DOUBLE DECLINING BALANCE" : PRINT
530  HTAB 5 : PRINT "3.  SUM OF THE YEARS DIGITS" : PRINT
540  HTAB 8 : INPUT "SELECTION PLEASE!" : PRINT
```

```
550  IF S < 1 OR S > 3 THEN 500
560  ON S GOTO 1500, 2500, 3500
```

Line 500 clears the screen and sets the position at which ***DEPRECIATION*** is to be printed. The two PRINT statements leave two blank lines below ***DEPRECIATION***.

Lines 510 through 530 print out the three types of depreciation. The user selects one choice.

STRAIGHT LINE DEPRECIATION

$$\text{DEPRECIATION/YEAR} = \frac{\text{COST OF ASSET} - \text{SALVAGE VALUE}}{\text{NUMBER OF YEARS}}$$

YEAR	DEP/YR	TOTAL DEP.
1	200	200
2	200	400
3	200	600

DOUBLE DECLINING BALANCE (the numbers have been rounded)

3 year straight line = 1/3 .333 (K)
200% double declining balance = 2 * 1/3 .667 (K)

YEAR	CONSTANT		COST	DEP/YR	BOOK VL.	TOTAL DEPRECIATION
1	.667	*	625	417	208	417
2	.667	*	208	139	69	554
3	.667	*	69	46	25	600

SUM OF THE YEARS DIGITS (the numbers have been rounded)

$$\text{SYD} = \frac{n\,(n + 1)}{2} \qquad \text{SYD} = \frac{3 * (3 + 1)}{2} = 6$$

YEAR	CONSTANT		GA − SV	DEP/YR	Book VL.	TOTAL DEPRECIATION
1	.500	*	600	300	325	300
2	.333	*	600	198	125	500
3	.167	*	600	100	25	600

PRINT YEARS	Z = (LA − Y) + 1
1	3 − 3 = 0 + 1 = 1
2	3 − 2 = 1 + 1 = 2
3	3 − 1 = 2 + 1 = 3

Line 3560 uses the INT function to round off the results to 2 places. DEF FN was used to round off to 2 places in line 2560. The two different methods expose the student to the fact that either method will accomplish the same rounding results.

Fig. 18-2. Formulas and computations.

Line 540 allows the user to select any number. The number does not necessarily have to be 1, 2, or 3.

Line 550 is a decision statement that causes a branch to line 500 if a number other than 1, 2, or 3 is input. This is a form of error checking that limits the input choices that will be accepted by the program. Since there are three choices, the machine is programmed so only an input of 1, 2, or 3 will allow the program to continue.

In line 560, the input value is placed in the variable S. When S = 1 the program branches to line 1500. When S = 2 the program branches to line 2500. When S = 3 the program branches to line 3500. The ON S GOTO type of statement was discussed in Lesson 13 and was the method used to print the input errors.

When a correct menu selection has been input, the program branches to line 1500, 2500, or 3500. At each of these lines is a GOSUB 100. The GOSUB 100 causes a branch to line 100 of the program. Line 100 is the beginning of the input subroutine. This subroutine is placed at the beginning of the program because it is used by each type of depreciation. The program is more efficient because fewer lines are searched before the input information is found. The headings are printed, and the input information is requested.

```
100  INPUT "GROSS AMOUNT = $" ;GA : PRINT
105  IF GA < 1 THEN 100
110  INPUT "SALVAGE VALUE = $" ;SV : PRINT
115  IF SV < 0 THEN 110
120  IF GA < SV THEN 100
130  INPUT "LIFE OF ASSET = " ;LA : PRINT
135  IF LA < 1 THEN 130
140  RETURN
```

In line 105, the gross amount of the asset cannot have a negative value to be used in the formula.

In line 115, the asset may be valued at zero at the end of the depreciation period, but the formula will not properly compute assets with a negative salvage value.

In line 120, if the gross cost of the item is less than the salvage value, the formula will not compute the depreciation properly.

In line 135, the asset must have a useful life of at least one year or some period greater than zero.

The depreciation formula must compute positive real numbers greater than zero. The error checks attempt to eliminate any input that would not give a meaningful computation to the user.

Line 140 causes a branch to the section of the program that requested the input information.

If 1 is input from the menu selection, the program branches to line 1500. Line 1500 branches to the input subroutine. After input is received, line 140 causes a branch to line 1510 to begin calculation of straight line depreciation. The numbers have been rounded. The numbers used for all examples are: cost of asset (GA) = $625, salvage value (SV) = $25, and life of the asset (LA) = 3 years.

```
1500  GOSUB 100
1510  TD = 0
```

```
1520  PRINT "YEAR          DEP/YR          TOTAL DEP." : PRINT :
      P = 100
1530  FOR X = 1 TO LA
1540  DY = (GA - SV)/ LA
1550  TD = TD + DY
1560  PRINT X; TAB (10); INT (DY*P + .5)/P; TAB (25);
      INT (TD*P + .5)/P
1570  IF X = INT (X/8) * 8 THEN GET A$
1580  NEXT
2400  GOTO 9990
```

STRAIGHT LINE DEPRECIATION

$$\text{DEPRECIATION/YEAR} = \frac{\text{COST OF ASSET} - \text{SALVAGE VALUE}}{\text{NUMBER OF YEARS}}$$

DEPRECIATION INFORMATION	PROGRAM STATEMENT
LIFE OF THE ASSET = 3	FOR X = 1 TO LA
DEP/YR = GA − SV / LA	DY = (GA − SV)/LA
DEP/YR = $200	TD = TD + DY
TOTAL DEPRECIATION = $600	1580 NEXT X

Line 1560 prints the year, the amount of each year's depreciation, and the total depreciation. Line 1560 is included within the loop, so the results will be printed for each year's computation.

Line 1570 performs the same function in lines 1570, 2570, and 3570. It causes the loop to stop after every eight executions (as shown in Table 18-1). This is useful when the life of the asset is a long period (over 10 years) of time and the user needs to study sections of the printout. The integers could be any number such as 10, 12, or 20, as long as the number is less than the number of lines on the screen.

GET A$, from line 1570, is a function to stop the program to allow the user to view the output. GET A$ allows the user to press any key on the keyboard to continue the program. The key pressed does not print a character on the screen. RETURN does not have to be pressed.

Table 18-1. IF X = INT(X/8) * 8 THEN GET A$

X	INT(X/8)	INT(X/8) * 8
1	0	0
2	0	0
7	0	0
8	1	8
9	1	8
10	1	8
15	1	8
16	2	16
17	2	16

The conversion of straight line depreciation to program statements uses no decision statements. The complete program is shown in Fig. 18-6 at the end of the lesson.

The double declining balance method of depreciation applies a constant depreciation rate to a reducing book value. This method charges off high depreciation in the early years and lower amounts in later years. The rate used in this example is 200%, or twice the straight line depreciation, as expressed in the formula K = (1/ LA) * 2. The formula for the 150% rate is K = (1/ LA) * 1.5. The formula for the 125% rate is K = (1 / LA) * 1.25.

Please be aware that this is a programming manual, not an accounting text. The double declining balance formula is taken from an accounting text and has been checked by a qualified accountant. The computed figures in the final year of the depreciation schedule may cause questions. The final book value does not equate with the salvage value, nor does the total depreciation equate with the allowable depreciation. Adjustments must be made to the figures computed in the final year of the life of the asset.

In the double declining balance method, the constant (K) is multiplied by the initial cost of the asset to determine the amount of yearly depreciation. The cost (Book Value) is reduced by the depreciation amount each year, but the book value cannot be reduced below the salvage value. The total depreciation cannot be greater than the cost of the asset less the salvage value.

This example uses the input: cost of the asset (Book Value) = \$625, salvage value = \$25, and the life of the asset = 3 years.

The double declining balance routine begins at line 2500, and ends at line 3400.

```
2500  GOSUB 100
2510  K = ( 1/ LA) * 2 : BV = GA
2512  TD = 0
2515  PRINT "YEAR     CONST.     DEP/YR     BK. VAL.     TOT DEP"
2520  FOR X = 1 TO LA
2530  DY = BV * K
2540  BV = BV - DY
2545  TD = TD + DY
2550  DEF FN A(X) = INT (X*100 + .5)/100
2560  PRINT X; TAB (5); FNA(K); TAB (14); FNA(DY); TAB (22);
      FNA(BV); TAB (31); FNA(TD)
2570  IF X = INT (X/8) * 8 THEN GET A$
2580  NEXT
3400  GOTO 9990
```

Line 2500 branches to the input routine. The input routine RETURNs to line 2510 (K = (1/ LA) * 2 : BV = GA). The constant (K) is computed by the formula (1/ LA) * 2 for 200% straight line depreciation. BV = GA is the gross cost of the asset stored in the variable BV. The constant times the reducing book value will give the yearly depreciation.

Line 2512 initializes the total depreciation to zero, and line 2515 causes the headings to be printed.

Line 2520 is the beginning statement of the loop for the computations.

Line 2530 computes the depreciation for one year and stores that value in the variable DY (depreciation per year).

Line 2540 computes the reducing book value by subtracting off the depreciation each year.

Line 2545 is a summing statement that adds each year's depreciation to the previous year's and stores the total in the total depreciation variable, TD.

RUN

YEAR	DEP/YR	TOTAL DEP.
1	200	200
2	200	400
3	200	600

Fig. 18-3. Straight line depreciation run.

Line 2550 rounds the print calculations to two places.

Line 2560 causes the information to be printed in table form on each loop execution.

Line 2570 is the same as line 1570 and is shown in Table 18-1.

Line 3400 branches to line 9990, which cues the user for more input.

RUN

YR	CONST.	DEP/YR	BK.VAL	TOT DEP
1	.67	416.67	208.33	416.67
2	.67	138.89	69.44	555.56
3	.67	46.3	23.15	601.85

Fig. 18-4. Double declining balance run.

The third type of depreciation is the sum of the years digits. In this method, the years of the asset's life are listed numerically and totaled. The highest year in the life of the asset is then divided by the total to compute the depreciation constant for the first year. The changing yearly constant is multiplied by a fixed gross amount of

RUN

YEAR	CONSTANT	DEP/YR	TOTAL DEP.
1	.5	300	300
2	.33	200	500
3	.17	100	600

Fig. 18-5. Sum of the years digits run.

the asset less the salvage value. The method is shown in the program lines 2500 to 3600 in Fig. 18-6, and the RUN in Fig. 18-5.

DEPRECIATION INFORMATION	PROGRAM STATEMENTS
Total years 3 + 2 + 1 = 6	FOR X = 1 TO LA : T = T + X : NEXT X T = LA * (LA+1)/2
3/6 = 1st year maximum depreciation 2/6 = 2nd year depreciation 1/6 = 3rd year minimum depreciation	FOR Y = LA TO 1 STEP −1 : K = Y/T
DY TD .500 * \$600 = \$300 \$300 .333 * 600 = 200 500 .167 * 600 − 100 600	DY = K * BV TD = TD + DY

```
50    GOTO 500
100   INPUT " GROSS AMOUNT = $" ; GA : PRINT
105   IF GA < 1 THEN 100
110   INPUT "SALVAGE VALUE = $" ;SV : PRINT
115   IF SV < 0 THEN 110
120   IF GA < SV THEN 100
130   INPUT "LIFE OF ASSET = " ;LA
135   IF LA < 1 THEN 130
140   RETURN
500   HOME : VTAB 3 : HTAB 8 : PRINT "***DEPRECIATION***" :
      PRINT : PRINT
510   HTAB 5 : PRINT "1. STRAIGHT LINE DEPRECIATION" : PRINT
520   HTAB 5 : PRINT "2. DOUBLE DECLINING BALANCE" : PRINT
530   HTAB 5 : PRINT "3. SUM OF THE YEARS DIGITS" : PRINT : PRINT
540   HTAB 8 : INPUT "SELECTION PLEASE!" ; S : PRINT
550   IF S < 1 OR S > 3 THEN 500
560   ON S GOTO 1500, 2500, 3500
1500  GOSUB 100
1510  TD = 0
1520  PRINT "YEAR        DEP/YR        TOTAL DEP." : PRINT :
      P = 100
1530  FOR X = 1 TO LA
1540  DY = (GA - SV)/LA
1550  TD = TD + DY
1560  PRINT X; TAB (10); INT (DY*P + .5)/P; TAB (25);
      INT (X*P + .5)/P
1570  IF X = INT (X/8) * THEN GET A$
1580  NEXT
2400  GOTO 9990
2500  GOSUB 100
2510  K = (1/LA) * 2 : BV = GA
```

Fig. 18-6. Menu—depreciation.

```
2512  TD = 0
2515  PRINT " YR       CONST.       DEP/YR       BK.VAL.       TOT DEP"
2520  FOR X = 1 TO LA
2530  DY = BV * K
2540  BV = BV - DY
2545  TD = TD + DY
2550  DEF FN (A(X) = INT (X*100 + .5)/100
2560  PRINT X; TAB (5); FNA (K); TAB (14); FNA (DY);
      TAB (22); FNA (BV); TAB(31); FNA (TD)
2570  IF X = INT (X/8) * 8 THEN GET A$
2580  NEXT
3400  GOTO 9990
3500  GOSUB 100
3510  T = 0 : P = 100 : BV - GA = SV : TD = 0
3520  PRINT "YEAR       CONSTANT       DEP/YR       TOTAL DEP." : PRINT
3530  FOR X = 1 TO LA : T = T + X : NEXT X
3535  REM : T = LA * (LA+1)/2
3540  FOR Y = LA TO 1 STEP -1 : K = Y/T
3550  DY = K * BV
3555  TD = TD + DY
3558  Z = (LA - Y) + 1
3560  PRINT Z; TAB (7); INT (K*P + .5)/P; TAB (18);
      INT (DY*P + .5)/P; TAB (26 + (TD < 100));
      INT (TD*P + .5)/P
3570  IF Z = INT (Z/8) * 8 THEN GET A$
3600  NEXT
9990  PRINT
9991  INPUT "ANOTHER PROBLEM? (Y OR N)" ; A$ :
      IF A$ = "Y" THEN 500
9999  END
```

Fig. 18-6. (Cont) Menu—depreciation.

LESSON 19

Program Outline

After completion of Lesson 19 you should be able to:

1. Comprehend that all computer programs are written according to a general outline, but no program will exactly follow such an outline.

VOCABULARY

Data—This is a general expression used to describe any group of operands that denote any conditions, values, or states (i.e., all values and descriptive data operated on by a computer program but not part of the program itself). The word data is used as a collective noun and is usually accompanied by a singular verb: "data are" may be pedantically correct but is awkward to understand. Data is sometimes contrasted with information, which is said to result from the processing of data, so that information derives from the assembly, analysis, or summarizing of data into a meaningful form.

DATA—This statement contains a list of items that can be used by a READ statement. DATA statements can contain literals, strings, reals, and integers. The item in the DATA statement must contain the same relationship and position as the item in the READ statement.

READ—This is a statement used by the program to read data into memory.

DISCUSSION

The outline for program structure must be considered very general and probably no program will rigidly comply with the outline. There must be a starting point to writing a program. The logical start to writing a program must exist within the framework of an outline.

Computer program general outline.

A. Start the program.
B. Initialize the variables.
   1. C = 0 counting variable
   2. S = 0 summing variable
   3. F = 0 flag variable
   4. DEF FN
   5. DIM—where constants are used—DIM CF (3,20)
   6. DIM CF (R,C)—must be placed in the program after R & C have been given values either by a program statement, INPUT, or READ.
   7. RESTORE—resets the "data list pointer" to the first element of DATA. Causes the next READ statement encountered to re-READ the DATA statements from the first one.
C. Print general program headings.
D. Menu
E. INPUT – READ
   1. DIM CH (R,C)—after variables are input.
F. Beginning statement for FOR – NEXT loop, or GOTO loop.
G. Decision statements
H. Computation statements
I. Incrementing statements
   1. C = C + 1—counting statement
   2. T = T + X—summing statement
J. PRINT—in this position the information is printed each time the loop executes.
K. End of loop—NEXT for FOR—NEXT loop, and GOTO for GOTO loop.
L. PRINT—in this position the information totals are printed after the last execution of the loop.
M. DATA statements are placed anywhere in the program. Generally placed close to the END.
N. END
O. Subroutines

The FOR – NEXT loop will be used to demonstrate the effects of statements within, and outside, the loop structure.

```
10   SUM = 0                   (initialize variable)
20   FOR X = 1 TO 5            (FOR – NEXT loop beginning)
30   PRINT X                   (print variable inside the loop)
40   SUM = SUM + X             (summing statement)
50   NEXT X                    (end of loop statement)
60   PRINT "SUM = ";SUM        (print statement outside the loop)
70   END                       (end of the program)
RUN
1
2
3
4
5
SUM = 15
```

The program generally conforms to the outline.

Lines 30 and 40 should be reversed according to the outline. Does it make a difference if they are reversed?

```
30   SUM = SUM + X
40   PRINT X
RUN
1
2
3
4
5
SUM = 15
```

No, the reversal of lines 30 and 40 within the loop make no difference. Generally, the PRINT X statement comes after the FOR statement.

Now reverse lines 40 and 30 to return to the original program. From the original program, make these changes:

```
DEL 30,30
55   PRINT X
```

The entire program is:

```
10   SUM = 0
20   FOR X = 1 TO 5
40   SUM = SUM + X
50   NEXT X
55   PRINT X
60   PRINT "SUM = ";SUM
70   END
RUN
6
SUM = 15
```

The loop runs from 1 to 5 and prints the next number in the series, namely 6. This is a very important point to realize. Because the general outline was violated, the program did not produce the desired results, namely, printing X at every iteration of the loop.

To the original program, make these changes:

```
DEL 60,60
45    PRINT "SUM = " ; SUM
```

The entire program is:

```
10    SUM = 0
20    FOR X = 1 TO 5
30    PRINT X
40    SUM = SUM + X
45    PRINT "SUM = " ; SUM
50    NEXT X
70    END
RUN
1
SUM = 1
2
SUM = 3
3
SUM = 6
4
SUM = 10
5
SUM = 15
```

Since the SUM was within the loop, SUM = was printed with each execution of the loop. Make the following changes to the original program:

```
DEL 10, 10
25    SUM = 0
```

The entire program is now:

```
20    FOR X = 1 TO 5
25    SUM = 0
30    PRINT X
40    SUM = SUM + X
50    NEXT X
60    PRINT "SUM = " ;SUM
70    END
RUN
1
2
3
4
5
SUM = 5
```

In this case, the summing variable was initialized to zero each time the loop executed, so the final SUM = 5. The initialized variable must be outside the loop or it will be reset to zero each time the loop executes.

LESSON 20

Clean Up

After completion of Lesson 20 you should be able to:

1. Open the closet door and have all the final tidbits of the Applesoft language fall out for your inspection and pleasure.

VOCABULARY

Print Field Definition—This is the technique of printing output to fit a standard pattern or form, thus making the output more readable.

Right Justify—This means to format output so the printed field is aligned on a right hand boundary.

Zero Suppression—This is the elimination before printing of non-significant zeros, e.g., those to the left of significant digits. The suppression is a function of editing. It is also known as zero elimination.

DISCUSSION

This lesson "cleans up" many parts of the language not covered in the first 19 lessons. Here we go with all the bits and pieces.

Applesoft does not align columns of different numbers to the power of ten. All numbers are printed starting from one selected space and printed to the right.

```
|.7
|284.6
|98.3
|2
|3.47
```

The following program makes numbers align in the proper columns, so the units are aligned, the tens are aligned, etc. The program causes the printout to right justify by two methods, (1) by aligning the right hand number, and (2) by aligning the decimal point. Either method of justification can be used in a program as a routine or a subroutine. Lines 60 to 80 right justify any number. Lines 90 to 130 right justify the decimal of numbers that are greater than or equal to .1 but less than 10^9.

```
5    D = LOG (10)
6    DEF FN MA (X) = INT (LOG (M)/ D)
10   HOME
20   INPUT "ENTER?" ;M
30   IF M = 0 THEN END
40   GOSUB 60
50   GOTO 20
60   L = LEN (STR$ (M)) : PRINT "R JUST =";
70   FOR J = L TO 12 : PRINT ":" ; : NEXT J
80   PRINT M;
90   L = FN MA (M)
100  FOR J = L + (L < -1) TO 8 : PRINT "$" ; : NEXT J
120  PRINT M;
130  PRINT : RETURN
]RUN
ENTER?2.34
R JUST =:::::::::::::::::2.34$$$$$$$$$2.34
ENTER?234.69
R JUST =::::::::::::::234.69$$$$$$$234.69
ENTER?.5678
R JUST =::::::::::::::::.5678$$$$$$$$$$.5678
ENTER?3456789
R JUST =::::::::::3456789$$$3456789
ENTER?2123.5678
R JUST =::::::2123.5678$$$$$$2123.5678
ENTER?0
```

Lines 5 and 6 are used together to compute the magnitude of the number to be printed. D holds a constant value which is 2.30258509. That is the value used to compute the power to which base 10 is raised. The power is used to right justify on the decimal point in lines 90 to 130.

DEF FN MA (X) = INT (LOG (M) / D) is the function that computes the magnitude of the number.

$$\begin{aligned} M &= 2.34 \\ D &= 2.30258509 \\ \text{LOG } (M) &= 3.17805383 \\ \text{LOG } (M) \;/\; D &= 3.17805383 \;/\; 2.30258509 \\ \text{INT } (\text{ LOG } (M) \;/\; D \;) &= 1 \end{aligned}$$

Line 10 clears the screen. Line 20 asks the user to input a number. Line 30 is a decision statement that ends the program.

In this example, the number 2.34 will be input and the results will be discussed as it is justified.

In line 60, STR$ converts the number 2.34 into a string. This conversion allows the string "2.34" to be evaluated. The number of characters (4) is then stored in the variable L. PRINT "R JUST ="; prints out the header that is printed in the first eight columns of the screen.

Line 70 computes the number of colons to be printed before the number (M) is printed. FOR J = L TO 12 outputs 13 places (0-12) and subtracts off the length of the string. R JUST = occupies the first eight columns. The string contains four characters, so FOR J = 4 TO 12 will print nine colons before printing the number.

```
COLUMN 8,9, ... 17...21
R JUST =:::::::::2.34
```

Line 80 prints the number after the colons so all numbers are right justified. The semicolon after the M keeps the line open to print the next section that is to justify on the decimal point.

The right justification is based on adding the number of columns occupied by R JUST =, plus the number of colons to be added to R JUST =, less the number of columns occupied by the string. All numbers are right justified to column 21 on the screen.

Lines 90 to 130 justify by placing the decimal in column 32 and aligning the numbers in the proper columns in relation to the decimal point.

In line 90, the power of the number is determined by the formulas in lines 5 and 6. The value of the power is stored in the variable L. The value stored in L, shown in Fig. 20-1, is then used to determine how many places to print.

Line 100 is a loop to print dollar signs ($) from column 21 to nine places (0 – 8) (L +, the number of $ signs, = 9). The power of the

CASE	M	FN MA (M)	
0	0 ILLEGAL VALUE		
1	> 0 to ⩽ .01	−2	This case causes special handling by (L < −1)
2	> .01 to ⩽ 1	−1	
3	> 1.0 to ⩽ 10	0	
4	> 10 to ⩽ 100	1	
5	> 100 to ⩽ 1000	2	
6	> 1000 to ⩽ 10000	3	
	> 1 E +8 to ⩽ 1 E −9		

Fig. 20-1. L = FN MA (M).

number is placed in the variable L and L TO 8 determines the number of dollar signs to be printed before the number is printed. The number input is 2.34.

```
COLUMN 8,9, ... 17,21 ... 32
R JUST =:::::::2.34$$$$$$$$$2.34
```

In this case, 2.34 has a power of zero (see Fig. 20-1). FOR J = 0 TO 8 prints out 9 dollar signs.

Line 120 prints 2.34 immediately after the ninth dollar sign so the decimal falls in column 32.

Line 100 must handle a special case when the decimal input is less than .01 and greater than .099 (see Case #1, Fig. 20-1). This special case is handled by (L < −1). FOR J = L TO 8 works in all cases where L is greater than or equal to .1 . When L is less than .1, a one has to be added back to align the decimal points.

A simpler, but less effective, method of controlling the column printout is to use decision statements. Using N as a variable to hold the value of the number, the decision statements are as shown in Chart 20-1.

Chart 20-1. Decision Statement Chart

	COLUMN	32	33	34	35	36	37
N = .78	IF N < 1.00 THEN HTAB 35				.	7	8
N = 1.78	IF N > .99 THEN HTAB 34			1	.	7	8
N = 11.78	IF N >= 10.00 THEN HTAB 33		1	1	.	7	8
N = 111.78	IF N > = 100 THEN HTAB 32	1	1	1	.	7	8

With these four statements the number to be placed in columns must be less than 1000. Decision statements can cause any number to be printed in specific columns as long as the number is in the range of the computer.

CONT is an immediate command that causes the program to continue RUNning after it has been stopped by a STOP, END, or Control C. CONT causes the program to continue at the next instruction. If the program was stopped on line 40, a GOTO 100 statement, the program will execute line number 100, not the default line after line 40. CONTinue will not be successful in continuing the program if the program line has been modified, or if an error message has occurred since the execution stopped. A ?CAN'T CONTINUE ERROR will be printed when no further instructions exist, after an error has occurred, or after a line has been changed or deleted in the existing program.

FLASH, INVERSE, and NORMAL functions are demonstrated in the FLASH SCREEN program. The program combines FLASH, NORMAL, INVERSE, and RND functions to randomly print the letters of the alphabet and change the video mode surrounding the character.

```
4     REM FLASH SCREEN
5     HOME
10    FOR J = 1 TO 653
20    I = INT (RND (1)*39) + 1
30    K = INT (RND (1.) * 23) + 1
40    L = INT (RND (1.) * 3) + 1
50    ON L GOTO 60, 70, 80
60    INVERSE : GOTO 100
70    NORMAL : GOTO 100
80    FLASH
100   HTAB I : VTAB K : PRINT CHR$ (RND (1.) * 26 + 65);
110   N = RND (1.) : NEXT J : NORMAL
120   END
```

Line 10 is the loop that sets the number of times the program is to be executed. The number 653 was selected at random. Any number could be used.

Line 20 randomly selects the column in which the character is to be printed. The screen has a line 40 characters long. RND returns a number from zero to less than one. RND (1) * 39 always returns a number less than 39, from zero to 38. RND (1) * 39 + 1 always returns a number greater than zero and less than 40. The "+ 1" is used to prevent the illegal value zero from being generated. The screen has 40 columns, from 1 to 40. If the RND function generated a zero, the program would stop and an ILLEGAL QUANTITY error would be printed. It is important to remember the parameters and limits of each function.

Line 30 randomly sets the limit of the rows on the screen. The screen has 24 rows, from 1 to 24. RND (1.) * 23 + 1 sets the limit to 22 + 1 which prevents the screen from scrolling while the program is running. In line 20, RND (1) is used. In line 30, RND (1.) is used. Either 1 or 1. can be used without changing the function.

The program is designed so that no character is printed at column 40, nor is any character printed in row 24. A print at column 40, row 24 causes the screen to scroll.

In line 40, the positive argument of RND returns a different sequence of numbers each time. RND (1.) * 3 returns the numbers 0, 1, 2. The "+ 1" changes this sequence to 1, 2, and 3.

The 1, 2, or 3 generated by the program in line 40 is used by line 50 to send the program to line 60 for L = 1, line 70 for L = 2, and line 80 for L = 3.

Line 100 prints the characters and the video mode randomly according to VTAB I (line 20), and HTAB K (line 30). The PRINT CHR$ (RND (1.) * 25 + 65) changes the 26 characters of the alphabet

(0 − 25) + 65, from the ASCII numeric code to the alphabetic characters.

A = 65
B = 66
C = 67
D = 68
etc.

In line 110, N = RND (1.) seems to serve no useful purpose. It is included because the function that the Apple computer uses to generate the random numbers may get into an endless loop that generates the same series continuously. N = RND (1.) prevents the random number generator from continued repetition of the same series. This knowledge comes from two sources: (1) previous programming experience with the theory of algorithms that generate random numbers, and (2) from viewing the program not printing any new positions, but printing the same position over and over. NEXT J is the last statement in the loop, and NORMAL brings the screen back to its normal mode. The program ENDs at line 120.

There is no RUN on this program because it would be impossible to type this hypnotic eye blinker. You have to RUN it to see and believe.

The next program introduces ONERR GOTO, POKE, PEEK, and RESUME.

```
10    ONERR GOTO 8000
20    PRINT "DISCO KID" : STRIKESAGAIN
30    READ D, A, B
40    DATA 1007, 34.5
50    INPUT "LETTER?" ;A
60    POKE 216, 0
70    NEXT J
8000  Y = PEEK (222) : L = PEEK (218) + PEEK (219) * 256
8010  IF Y = 16 THEN PRINT "SYNTAX ERROR IN LINE" ;L :
      PRINT : GOTO 30
8020  IF Y = 42 THEN PRINT "OUT OF DATA IN LINE" ;L :
      PRINT : GOTO 50
8030  IF Y = 254 THEN PRINT "ANSWER THE CORRECT TYPE IN
      LINE" ;L : PRINT : RESUME
RUN
DISCO KID
SYNTAX ERROR IN LINE 20
OUT OF DATA IN LINE 30
LETTER?A        (letter E—reserved for exponentiation)
ANSWER THE CORRECT TYPE IN LINE 50
LETTER?5
NEXT WITHOUT ERROR IN LINE 70
```

Line 10 is a declaration statement that tells the computer what to do when an error is detected. The computer handles errors in a normal fashion until it executes an ONERR GOTO statement. The ONERR GOTO statement is similar to TRACE in that it affects the entire program during its execution. After an ONERR GOTO statement has been executed, anytime an error is detected, the program branches to the line specified. The computer remembers line 10 for all errors. This program handles three error conditions. Given time, all seventeen possible errors could be placed in the program.

Line 60 places a zero into memory location 216. POKE 216, 0 is the statement that clears the error flag so that normal error messages may occur. When information is to be placed in a specific memory location the POKE command is used.

In line 8000, Y-PEEK (222) returns the contents of memory location 222. The value of Y is stored in a variable to make its use easier. L = PEEK (218) + PEEK (219) * 256 sets the value of the line number in the program where the error occurred.

In linc 8010, the number 16 is the value for the error code SYNTAX ERROR.

In line 8020, the number 42 is the value that prints the OUT OF DATA error.

In line 8030, the number 254 is the Y value that gives a bad response to an INPUT statement.

Pause loops cause a delay in the program to allow the user to view the information.

GET A$ pause loops were discussed in Lesson 18.

A simple pause loop that allows the program to continue without user participation is:

```
FOR P = 1 TO 10000 : NEXT P
```

A nested loop pause that allows the program to continue without user participation is:

```
FOR N = 1 TO 1000
FOR P = 1 TO 100
NEXT P, N
```

A pause loop (similar to GET A$) that stops the program after a certain number of printouts, 50 in this example, and requires the user to press RETURN is:

```
FOR I = 1 TO 1000
IF I = INT (I/50) * 50 THEN INPUT Q$
NEXT I
```

HTAB and VTAB are used for spacing in loops. VTAB and TAB are used for straight spacing not in loops. HTAB, TAB, and VTAB tab from the #1 position of the column or row. SPC (6) leaves six spaces between the items.

HTAB (I*2) + 1 leaves 2 spaces between items printed and the + 1 starts in column #1. Zero is an illegal value.

The use of VTAB and HTAB in loops is illustrated in the following program. Line 40 prints the numbers 1 through 5 beginning in column 1 of the screen, with two spaces between each number. This printout is used as a reference with which to compare the spacing in line 70. Line 70 produces similar output and spacing as line 40. Line 72 causes the first print in column 5 rather than in column 1, with two spaces between each number. Line 74 produces the first print in column #1 with 5 spaces between each number. This program RUN demonstrates that the times (*5) produces the number of spaces between printed items, while the plus (+1) determines in which column the first item is to be printed.

```
10    HOME
20    FOR X = 1 TO 5
30    FOR I = 1 TO 5
40    VTAB 10 : HTAB (1 - 1 ) * 2 + 1
50    PRINT I;
60    NEXT I : VTAB 12
70    HTAB (X - 1 ) * 2 + 1 : REM : 1ST RUN
72    REM :HTAB (X - 1 ) * 2 + 5 : REM : 2ND RUN
74    REM :HTAB (X - 1 ) * 5 + 1 : REM : 3RD RUN
80    PRINT X;
90    NEXT X
100   END
RUN - LINE 70
(I) 1  2  3  4  5
(X) 1  2  3  4  5
RUN - LINE 72
(I) 1  2  3  4  5
(X)        1  2  3  4  5
RUN - LINE 74
(I) 1  2  3  4  5
(X) 1     2     3     4     5
```

The following three programs produce identical spacing results. Those results are produced by three different methods:

1. Decision statements.
2. Loops.
3. HTAB formula.

```
5     REM: DECISION STATEMENT SPACING
10    FOR X = 1 TO 3
20    FOR Y = 1 TO 5
30    PRINT Y; " ";
40    IF X > 1 THEN PRINT " ";
50    IF X > 2 THEN PRINT " ";
60    NEXT Y : PRINT : PRINT
70    NEXT X
80    END
```

```
RUN
1 2 3 4 5
1  2  3  4  5
1   2   3   4   5
5     REM : LOOP SPACING
10    FOR X = 1 TO 3
20    FOR Y = 1 TO 5
30    PRINT Y;
40    FOR M = 1 TO X
50    PRINT " ";
60    NEXT  M
70    NEXT  Y
80    PRINT : PRINT
90    NEXT X
100   END
RUN
1 2 3 4 5
1  2  3  4  5
1   2   3   4   5
5     REM : HTAB FORMULA SPACING
10    FOR X = 1 TO 3
20    FOR Y = 1 TO 5
30    HTAB ( X + 1 ) * Y - X
40    PRINT Y;
50    NEXT Y
60    PRINT : PRINT
70    NEXT X
80    END
RUN
1 2 3 4 5
1  2  3  4  5
1   2   3   4   5
```

Applesoft suppresses leading and trailing zeros. Suppressing trailing zeros leaves a blank space in the column where the trailing zero was supposed to be. It leaves the same feeling as reading a suspense story without learning how it ended, you know, an empty feeling in the pit of your stomach.

The final program in this lesson was initially written to print a zero in the position where the zero had been suppressed. As it turned out, the program not only demonstrated printing the zero in the trailing position, but also reenforced HTABing by decision statements and print rules and introduced the rudiments of print field definition.

```
10    DEF FN A(X) = INT (X*100 + .5)/100
20    PI = 3.1416
30    FOR R = 1 TO 100 STEP 10
40    A = PI * R 2
50    IF A < = 10 THEN HTAB 20 : REM : FIG. 20-2
60    IF A > 10 THEN HTAB 19
70    IF A > 100 THEN HTAB 18
80    IF A > 1000 THEN HTAB 17
```

```
90   IF A > 10000 THEN HTAB 16
100  PRINT FN A(A);
110  IF (INT(A*100 + .5) - INT (A*10 + .5)*10) = 0 THEN PRINT "0";
120  PRINT
130  NEXT R
140  END
RUN       (see Fig. 20-2)
```

The important line in the program for overcoming zero suppression and printing the trailing zero is line 110.

CASE	COLUMN 20
1	3.14
2	380.13
3	1385.45
4	3019.08
5	5281.03
6	8171.30***
7	11689.89
8	15836.81
9	20612.04
10	26015.59
*** ZERO PRINTING	

Fig. 20-2. Zero-printing right justify by decision statements.

```
110  IF (INT (A*100 + .5) - INT (A*10 + .5)*10) = 0 THEN PRINT "0";
```

Case #6 of the RUN (Fig. 20-2)
Without line 110 8171.3
With line 110 8171.30

The key to line 110 is to subtract the integer of A from itself. If the result equals zero, then a zero is printed in the last column, as shown in Fig. 20-3.

Line 10 sets up to round the print to two decimal places.

The rudiments of print field definition involve printing a sup-

CASE	INT (A*100 + .5)	INT (A*10 + .5)*10	COLUMN 20
1	314	310	3.14
2	38013	38010	380.13
3	138545	138540	1385.45
4	301908	301910	3019.08
5	528103	528100	5281.03
6	817130	817130	8171.30***
7	1168989	1168990	11689.89
*** ZERO PRINTING			

Fig. 20-3. If (INT (A*100+.5) − INT(A*10+.5)*10) = 10, then PRINT "0".

pressed trailing zero so the printout looks normal. The technique of printing the trailing zero reenforces the print rules of Lesson 2. To print the zero and not disrupt the printout format the print rules must be diligently applied. The value held in A must be printed and the line left open for the possibility of printing a zero. If the zero is printed the line must be closed. The option to close the line after A is printed must be valid.

CASE #1–A printed, no zero printed, line closed.
Case #2–A printed, print zero, line closed.

The simplest way to handle both cases is:

1. PRINT FN A(A);–semicolon leaves the line open.
2. THEN PRINT "0";–semicolon leaves the line open.
3. PRINT–on a separate line number after the PRINT "0";. This satisfies CASE #1–the number is printed, no zero, the PRINT "0"; is false, and a default to the PRINT occurs.

   CASE #2–the number is printed, zero suppressed, THEN PRINT "0";, prints the zero, and a default to the PRINT closes the line.

Lines 50 to 90 demonstrate how decision statements and HTABs can right justify (see Fig. 20-2).

SECTION II

Programming

LESSON 21

Approaching the Problem

Programming is the process by which a set of instructions is produced for the computer to make it perform a specified activity.

Before programming, there is preprogramming. Preprogramming is the ability to understand the problem and work the problem. This point cannot be emphasized too strongly. To be able to program a problem, the programmer must be able to understand and develop each step of the problem. The variables assigned to the formula must be understood. The steps in computing the solution must be understood. The solution must produce the correct results. If the results are incorrect, the programmer must determine why the results are incorrect and rectify the problem.

If you are an accountant, you must be able to solve the problem on paper before you can program it. This is the most important fact in programming. You must be so adept at solving the problem that you can explain it to the computer. If you cannot solve the problem using a pencil and paper, do not attempt to write a program to solve it.

Think of programming this way. An understudy machine is taught to do something you do not have time to do. The understudy is electronic, not human. This electronic understudy does not understand the English language, so it must be instructed in its own language. This electronic understudy, the computer, does not understand what it is doing. It is processing so fast that it does not have time to care. The speed at which the computer does tedious, repetitious, complex tasks is one of it's great advantages. Another advantage is its great accuracy. Unless there is a hardware malfunction, the answers are accurate as to input and according to programming instructions.

To make use of the advantages, the disadvantages must be overcome. The disadvantages are (1) procedures used in the solutions must be completely specified and (2) conversion of the spoken language to the language of the computer must be performed. This aligns the advantages of speed and accuracy versus the disadvantages of procedure and language.

In Lesson 13, the NAME AND ADDRESS program was written to cause the computer to look through a string of characters in order to recognize special markers, called delimiters. In that case, semicolons were used as delimiters. The program also checked for six input errors.

To begin the learning process, write this string of characters on a piece of paper.

RESIDENT;STREET;CITY STATE ZIP

Now separate the string of characters into different fields when a semicolon is encountered.

RESIDENT;
STREET;
CITY STATE ZIP

What did that accomplish? It accomplished the need to think of the minute steps involved in breaking down information so it can be converted into detailed one step instructions that the computer can process.

The list of characters must have a starting point. The individual may use a finger to point at the starting character, or may put a pencil mark on the first character. The first character is marked as the place to begin, so the field between the first character and the first delimiter can be determined. Each character in the field is checked to see if it is a delimiter. This character checking continues until the first delimiter is discovered. The first field is then separated from the remaining fields by writing down the first character in the field, and each succeeding character in the field is written down until the delimiter is encountered. This process is repeated until the string of characters is separated into three fields.

The programmer must tell the computer each individual step to separate the string of characters. The computer must be told to mark the first character in the string. The computer must be told to look at each character in the string of characters, checking to see if it had encountered a semicolon, and told how to determine when it had reached the end of a field. The first field starts with a special condition, the first character in the string. All other fields start with a semicolon. The last field ends with a special condition, the last character. All other fields end with a semicolon. These are special starting and ending conditions.

These points must be understood in relation to what is necessary to solve the programming problem. The programmer must thoroughly understand all facets of the problem and be able to solve it before the problem can be detailed in computer language. The problem is now approached from the computer's side of the program.

The line of characters is placed in a string variable. The computer marks the first character in the string as 1, the second character as 2, the third character as 3, etc., until it reaches the end of the string. This is a logical assignment of the character position, as a reference for the programmer, and the computer uses a numeric variable to hold a position value. When a loop is used that will increment the numeric variable, one by one, each individual character will be compared to the delimiter. An IF statement is used to test the individual character with the delimiter, to see if the delimiter has been reached. The LEN function (L = LEN(A$)) is used to store the length of the string variable, and this LEN function stores the number of characters in the string that are to be examined. Three delimiters have been discussed, (1) the first or beginning character, (2) the semicolon between the fields, and (3) the ending delimiter.

There are three reasons why the semicolon is used as a delimiter.

1. In Applesoft, a comma is used as a special separator in INPUT, READ, GET, and DATA statements. A comma incorrectly placed causes a ? EXTRA IGNORED. A colon is a special separator used to place multiple statements in a single line number. An incorrect placement of a colon causes a ? EXTRA IGNORED. These are limitations of the language. All languages have some types of limitation.
2. Few addresses display a semicolon as a part of the basic information. A pound sign (#) could be used except apartment numbers are usually designated by the pound sign. Diligent research of the problem will eliminate many programming difficulties. Perhaps there are address formats that use a semicolon as part of the basic format, but it is not frequently seen. One type of research is to write down many varied examples and chart which examples are most used and which are least used.
3. The semicolon is easy for the input operator to produce. It is on the home keys and does not require a shift. A division sign (/) could be used as a delimiter but it is not as easy to produce as a semicolon.

Operator convenience, ease of production, and language compatibility are three points that comprise the major network of logic used to write a program for the computer. To extend a program to the complex task of error checking (similar to the program in Lesson 13), the complete string of information must be checked and tested to ensure correct format before the lines are printed. For each line of output to be printed correctly, the numeric value for the beginning of each field and the end of each field must be stored. An efficient way to mark the beginning and end of each field is to store the numeric value in the position of the semicolon delimiter.

Error detecting routines look for three kinds of errors:

1. Errors that do not "make sense" for purposes of processing data.
2. Errors that cause the program to stop running.
3. Errors that create undesired output.

Errors that do not "make sense" for the purposes of processing involve the length of the field. Fields of zero length must be checked because the print formula would give an ILLEGAL VALUE error. This can be tested by removing from the following program the program lines that check the values of 1 to D1C, D1C to D2C, and D2C to L.

Errors that cause the program to stop running are those lines with less than two delimiters. While this option is not used in the program under discussion, it could be used as a method to stop the execution of the program.

Errors that create undesired output include the use of more than two semicolon delimiters and the improper use of the LEN function. If a semicolon was used to end the third field instead of the LEN function, this would indicate that there are more than two delimiters in the string.

A great deal of discussion has centered on the NAME AND ADDRESS program because it has many features that make it a good learning tool.

As an exercise for logic development a situation that occurs frequently will be discussed. While driving home from work late at night, a thumping sound is heard and the car steering pulls unexpectedly. After the possibility of a flat tire flashes through the driver's mind, the car is stopped for a visual inspection. The possible actions are as shown in Fig. 21-1.

While other options could be cited, the four possible actions from the different situations will be discussed. The actions are reached by using common sense and an understanding of a given situation.

When the situation is examined, the action will be taken according to NO FLAT TIRES, or THE NUMBER OF FLAT TIRES as shown in Chart 21-1. If after observing all tires, the flat count is zero, then the action taken is placed in category I. If the flat count is 1,

Chart 21-1. Flat Tire

Situation	Category	Action
1. No tire flat	I	1. Continue the trip
2. One flat tire—the spare is usable	II	2. Exchange the flat and spare and continue trip
3. One flat tire—the spare is unusable	III	3. Walk for assistance
4. More than one tire flat	IV	4. Walk for assistance

and the spare in the trunk is usable, then the action taken is placed in category II. If the flat count is 1, and the spare is unusable, then the action taken is placed in category III. If the flat count is greater than 1, then the action taken is placed in category IV.

The overall reaction to the thumping sound and car pull is included in a general framework.

1. Stop the car.
2. Shut off the engine.
3. Open the door. Exit the car. Close the door.
4. Initialize the flat count to zero.
5. If the left front tire is flat, increment the flat count.
6. If the left rear tire is flat, increment the flat count.
7. If the right rear tire is flat, increment the flat count.
8. If the right front tire is flat, increment the flat count.
9. If the flat count is zero, then continue the trip home.
10. If the flat count is more than one, then call for assistance.
11. Open the trunk.
12. If the spare is unusable then go to step #20.
13. Exchange the flat tire and the spare.
14. Close the trunk.
15. Open the door on the driver's side of the car.
16. Get in the car. Close the door.
17. Start the engine.
18. Continue on the journey home.
19. End the actions.
20. Walk to a phone and call for assistance.

These are decisions and actions involved in the thought process. Most humans do these actions naturally, but they must be completely detailed to the computer.

The flowchart tests to determine if the flat count is zero or greater than one. Since the flat count starts at zero (through initialization) and there are three situations to check, only two decision statements are necessary (This is the same as cutting a log in three pieces—only two cuts are needed). In the first flat count decision statement in

Fig. 21-1, there are two exit decision paths. If the flat count is zero the statement is true, and the decision is made to continue the trip home. If the flat count is not zero the statement is false, and the exit path goes to a second decision statement. Is the flat count greater than one? This decision statement selects the path to follow if the flat count is one, or if the flat count is greater than one. If the flat count is greater than one the statement is true, the exit path flows to the walk for assistance action. If the flat count is greater than one the statement is false, the exit path flows to the open the trunk action, and to another decision statement. Is the spare tire usable? The flowchart details the conclusion, either walk for assistance or continue the homeward journey.

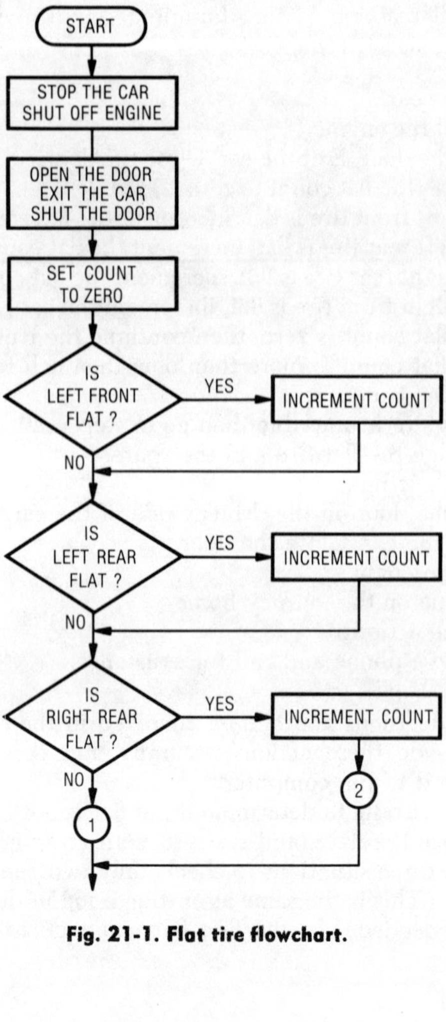

Fig. 21-1. Flat tire flowchart.

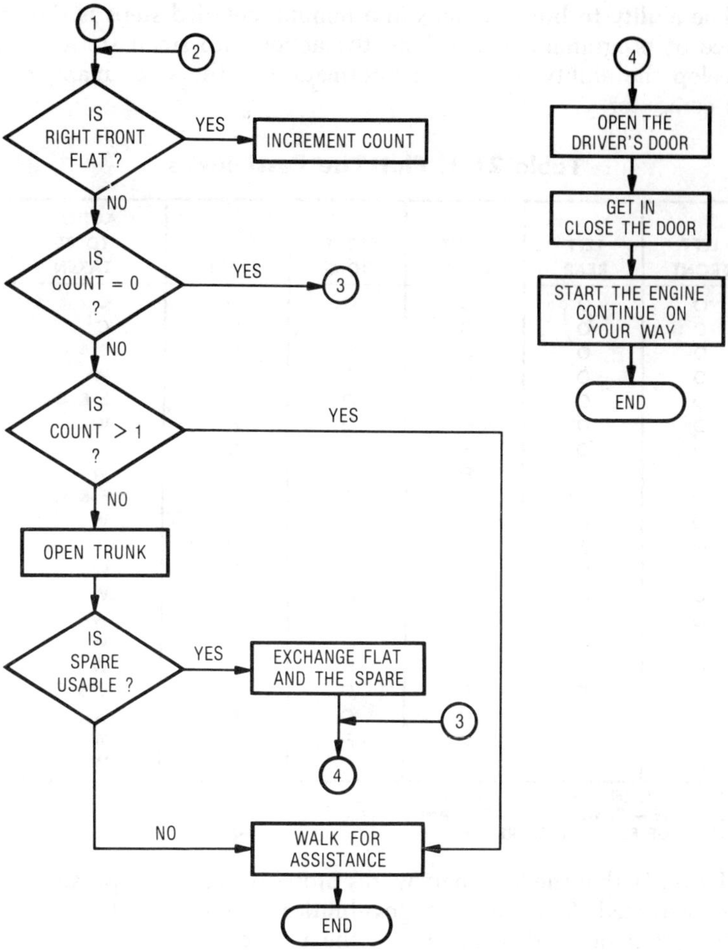

Fig. 21-1. (Cont) Flat tire flowchart.

Flowchart steps can be detailed or general. Fig. 21-1 has both detailed steps (stop the car, shut off the engine, etc.) and general steps (exchange the spare for the flat tire). A flowchart can be on many different levels. It can be a long, complicated written tool to help the programmer keep the action in proper sequence. Or the flowchart can be so simple that the programmer doesn't have to write it down. The flowchart can help to clarify a complex point. It can be a step-by-step set of instructions, complete with line numbers, that will be followed exactly when the program is keypunched. Since the FLAT TIRE is not a programmable problem, the flowchart is used to keep the action in program context.

The ability to break actions into minute, detailed steps is the essence of programming. Breaking the action into small steps helps develop the ability to process information in the same manner as the computer.

Table 21-1. Flat Tire Possibilities

LEFT FRONT	LEFT REAR	RIGHT REAR	RIGHT FRONT	SPARE	ACTION TO BE TAKEN
O	O	O	O	O	C
O	O	O	O	F	C
O	O	O	F	O	E & C
O	O	O	F	F	W
O	O	F	O	O	E & C
O	O	F	O	F	W
O	O	F	F	O	W
O	O	F	F	F	W
O	F	O	O	O	E & C
O	F	O	O	O	W
O	F	O	F	O	W
O	F	O	F	F	W
O	F	F	O	O	W
O	F	F	O	F	W
O	F	F	F	O	W
O	F	F	F	F	W
F	O	O	O	O	E & C
F	O	O	O	F	W
F	O	O	F	O	W
F	O	O	F	F	W

TIRE STATUS (FLAT – F, O – OKAY)
CONTINUE – C, WALK FOR ASSISTANCE – W
EXCHANGE FLAT AND SPARE – E

To verify that the flowchart works properly, a table of possibilities is constructed. The table of possibilities, Table 21-1, follows the flowchart logic to determine that the problem is solved correctly.

Over half of the thirty-two possibilities are listed in Table 21-1. The table shows the status of four tires, the spare, and the course of action to be taken. Table 21-1 was produced by writing down different combinations of tire status and determining the best possible action to take. Common sense was used to confirm the algorithm and produce the table. If the "YES" or "NO" decisions on the flowchart had been switched, the flowchart would give incorrect results even though the logic was correct. For correct results to be produced from the written program, logic, flowcharts, and program coding must be correct.

The first two lines of the table of possibilities show the four tires, the spare, and the action to be taken. Both lines show all four tires are okay, but the first line shows the spare is okay, and the second line shows the spare is flat. According to logic, if all four tires are okay, the spare does not need to be checked.

There is at least one drawback in producing a table of possibilities to check the flowchart logic. On a complex problem, a table of possibilities may have so many entries, it may be unusable. In that case, five or ten comprehensive sample situations are used to try to catch all possible errors.

To sum up, there are three basic steps in programming. The programmer must:

1. Be able to completely describe the situation to be set in basic instructions.
2. Be able to outline the logical progression from one step to another, especially where decisions need to separate actions into different sections.
3. Be able to change instructions from English to equivalent computer form by understanding what the computer can process.

LESSON 22

Program Flexibility

The only thing permanent in life is change. This also applies to programs and programming. The banking industry is highly regulated by the government. Although the regulations are rigid, the bank computer programs change constantly. The bank's needs and equipment are constantly changed and updated. Customer's relations with the bank and customer's situations constantly change. The government regulations constantly change so the bank must revise and check their programs to maintain compliance. This beehive of activity affects the bank's programmers who must constantly revise and rewrite the programs. The programmer also must constantly upgrade his or her education to adapt to new methods and equipment.

In programming, flexibility is a key word. Is the program flexible? Can the program be easily and quickly changed to accommodate a new input situation, a new set of government tables, or a new output format, and produce correct results? Using a programming team, a long complex program may take a year to write. This program should be flexible enough so minor changes do not make the program completely obsolete.

If a mailing list program has a three line input, can a fourth line of input be easily inserted in the program to produce a four line output?

In an inventory program, can data be input both in the alpha and numeric modes?

In an accounts receivable program, can customer information be easily changed without having to rewrite the program and without having to rewrite the whole business program package?

The programs used for this example of flexibility are the computation of federal income tax and net income. The user inputs the adjusted gross income and the program computes the tax due and the net income. The tax table was taken from the 1979 Tax Rate Schedule for married taxpayers filing joint returns and qualifying widows and widowers. For simplicity, only one tax table was used in the program. In reality, the tax rate schedule has four separate tables, (1) for single taxpayers, (2) married filing joint returns, (3) married filing separate returns, and (4) heads of households, etc. The point is that an accountant filing income tax returns for the general public needs all four tables. A flexible program could be easily changed to accept revised tables, while an inflexible program could not accept new tables easily.

The inflexible program in this example is written with IF statements. In this program, it would be difficult to change one table, much less four tables. The flexible program is written with the table inserted in DATA statements. The flexible program would be relatively easy to change or add to by a simple routine.

```
INPUT "ADJUSTED GROSS INCOME ";AGI

MENU
1. SINGLE TAX PAYER
2. MARRIED FILING JOINT RETURN
3. MARRIED FILING SEPARATE RETURN
4. HEAD OF HOUSEHOLD

INPUT "STATUS ";STATUS

ON STATUS GOSUB 2000, 3000, 4000, 5000
```

At 2000, 3000, 4000, and 5000 the tables could be placed in DATA statements similar to the flexible tax computation program.

The variables used for both programs are:

- AGI adjusted gross income.
- UL upper limit.
- BF base figure from which tax is computed. If the base figure is 24,600, the base tax is 3273 plus 28% of everything over 24,600.
- BT base tax is the second number in the table.
- TB tax bracket is the third number in the table.
- TR tax rate is the third number in the table.
- IT income tax.
- RANGE between the base figure and the upper limit.

RESTORE has been previously discussed. RESTORE resets the pointer so the data can be reused. RESTORE-READ-DATA allows data tables to be reused when the program is in constant use. Without the RESTORE, the program would have to be RUN again (started over) if the data were to be reused.

After the adjusted gross income (AGI) is input, it is checked to see if it is less than zero. If the adjusted gross income is less than zero the program ends. The processing starts at the lowest range of base figure values. If the adjusted gross income is greater than the upper limit value for the first range, the adjusted gross income is tested against the next higher upper limit value. The processing continues until the adjusted gross income is less than the upper limit value in the range. The correct range is found when the adjusted gross income is equal to or greater than the base figure, but is less than the upper limit value. The correct range then sets the base tax, tax bracket, and base figure for this range. Both the inflexible and the flexible program process the ranges in approximately the same manner.

The flexible program gets the base figure from the upper limit value of the previous range. If the adjusted gross income is in the first range, zero to 3400, the base figure has been initialized to zero before the processing begins (Line 1040—BF = 0).

If the adjusted gross income is greater than 215,400, the upper limit value of the next range is zero. The zero indicates there is no upper limit to this range. The upper limit value is zero, so that range applies to any amount greater than 215,400.

Line 1060 tests the upper limit value for zero. If line 1060 is true, the program branches to line 1080 to compute the tax. If the upper limit value is zero, the adjusted gross income is greater than 215,400. This sets the base figure as 215,400. Line 1080 computes the income tax.

The inflexible program is shown first, followed by the flexible program.

```
995   REM : INFLEXIBLE TAX PROGRAM
1000  HOME : VTAB 3
1010  INPUT "ENTER ADJUSTED GROSS INCOME ";AGI
1020  IF AGI < 0 THEN END
1030  RESTORE
1040  BF = 0
2000  IF AGI > 3400 THEN 2020
2010  BT = 0:TB = 0:BF = 0: GOTO 7010
2020  IF AGI > 5500 THEN 2040
2030  BT = 0:TB = .14:BF = 3400: GOTO 7010
2040  IF AGI > 7600 THEN 2060
2050  BT = 294:TB = .16:BF = 5500: GOTO 7010
2060  IF AGI > 11900 THEN 2080
2070  BT = 630:TB = .18:BF = 7600: GOTO 7010
2080  IF AGI > 16000 THEN 2100
2090  BT = 1404:TB = .21:BF = 11900: GOTO 7010
```

```
2100  IF AGI > 20200 THEN 2120
2110  BT = 2265:TB = .24:BF = 16000: GOTO 7010
2120  IF AGI > 24600 THEN 2140
2130  BT = 3273:TB = .28:BF = 20200: GOTO 7010
2140  IF AGI > 29900 THEN 2160
2150  BT = 4505:TB = .32:BF = 24600: GOTO 7010
2160  IF AGI > 35200 THEN 2180
2170  BT = 6201:TB = .37:BF = 29900: GOTO 7010
2180  IF AGI > 45800 THEN 2200
2190  BT = 8162:TB = .43:BF = 35200: GOTO 7010
2200  IF AGI > 60000 THEN 2220
2210  BT = 12720:TB = .49:BF = 45800: GOTO 7010
2220  IF AGI > 85600 THEN 2240
2230  BT = 19678:TB = .54:BF = 60000: GOTO 7010
2240  IF AGI > 109400 THEN 2260
2250  BT = 33502:TB = .59:BF = 85600: GOTO 7010
2260  IF AGI > 162400 THEN 2280
2270  BT = 47544:TB = .64:BF = 109400: GOTO 7010
2280  IF AGI > 215400 THEN 2300
2290  BT = 81464:TB = .68:BF = 162400: GOTO 7010
2300  BT = 117504:TB = .7:BF = 215400
7010  IT = BT + (AGI - BF) * TB: PRINT : PRINT "YOUR INCOME TAX IS";IT
7020  PRINT : PRINT "YOUR NET IS";AGI - IT
7030  PRINT : GOTO 1010
7040  END
```

```
995   REM : FLEXIBLE TAX PROGRAM
1000  HOME : VTAB 3
1010  INPUT "ENTER ADJUSTED GROSS INCOME ";AGI
1020  IF AGI < 0 THEN END
1030  RESTORE
1040  BF = 0
1050  READ UL,BT,TB
1060  IF UL = 0 THEN 1080
1070  IF AGI > UL THEN BF = UL: GOTO 1050
1080  IT = BT + (AGI - BF) * TB: PRINT : PRINT "YOUR INCOME TAX IS";IT
1090  PRINT : PRINT "YOUR NET IS";AGI - IT
1100  PRINT : GOTO 1010
1110  END
7100  DATA 3400,0,0
7110  DATA 5500,0,.14
7120  DATA 7600,294,.16
7130  DATA 11900,630,.18
7140  DATA 16000,1404,.21
7150  DATA 20200,2265,.24
7160  DATA 24600,3275,.28
7170  DATA 29900,4505,.32
7180  DATA 35200,6201,.37
7190  DATA 45800,8162,.43
7200  DATA 60000,12720,.49
7210  DATA 85600,19678,.54
7220  DATA 109400,33502,.59
7230  DATA 162400,47544,.64
7240  DATA 215400,81446,.68
7250  DATA 0,117504,.70
```

LESSON 23

Circular Lists, Stacks, & Pointers

Lessons 23 through 26 will deal with specialized methods to aid in solving problems in programming. The lessons deal with (1) circular lists, stacks, and pointers, (2) lists, sorting, searching, and deleting, (3) formulas—how to construct and use them, and (4) double subscripted variables.

A circular list is a list from which all insertions are made at one end and all retrievals are made at the other end (Fig. 23-1). This type of list has several names: circular buffer, queue, and FIFO (first in–first out). FIFO is also applicable to computers, inventory, and science.

The program written for this lesson (Fig. 23-2) uses FIFO in two ways, computer lists and inventory.

A stack is a linear list from which all insertions and all retrievals are made from the top. LIFO (last in–first out) is synonymous with stack (Fig. 23-3). The program written for this lesson uses LIFO in two ways, computer lists and inventory.

A pointer, as shown in Figs. 23-1 and 23-3, is an address location used to designate the location of data contained in a cell of a linear list. A pointer is considered a pointer only if it points at some data within a list. An address location is not considered to be a pointer unless it specifically points to data.

A circular list has two buffer pointers, buffer in (BI) and buffer out (BO). A stack has one buffer pointer (BI).

The program in Fig. 23-2, written to demonstrate a circular list, stack, and pointers, accepts only one inventory item. The fields for

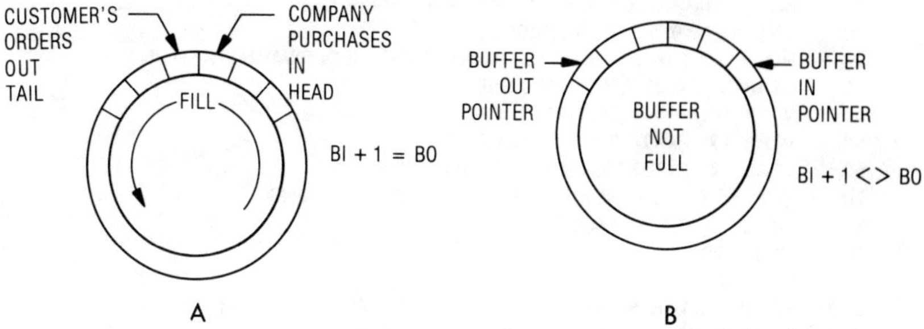

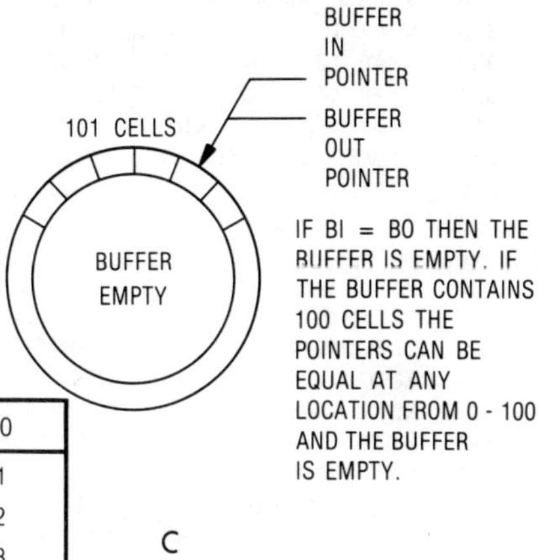

IF BI + 1 - (BI = 100) * 101 = BO

BI	BI + 1 - (BI = 100) * 101		BO
0	1	BI < 100	1
1	2	BI < 100	2
2	3	BI < 100	3
3	4	BI < 100	4
4	5	BI < 100	5
5	6	BI < 100	6
6	7	BI < 100	7
|	|	|	|
100	101	- 100 = 1 * 101	101**

** SPECIAL CASE

Fig. 23-1. Circular list (FIFO).

this one inventory item contain (1) the date the item was purchased by the company, A$(BI), (2) the price of the item, PR(BI), and (3) the number of items the company purchased, AO(BI).

The circular list and the stack contain 101 cells (DIM A$(100), PR(100), AO(100)), into which purchase information is placed and customer orders are taken (Fig. 23-4).

The FIFO (circular list) and the LIFO (stack) give the program flexibility. The program could be used by a company that uses either the FIFO or LIFO inventory method.

```
5     REM : CIRCULAR LISTS, STACKS, AND POINTERS
10    DIM A$(100),PR(100),AO(100)
20    HOME : VTAB 5: HTAB 12: PRINT "FIFO/LIFO DEMONSTRATION"
30    VTAB 8: PRINT SPC( 12);"0.END"
40    VTAB 10: PRINT SPC( 12);"1.FIFO"
50    VTAB 12: PRINT SPC( 12);"2.LIFO"
60    VTAB 14: INPUT "ENTER SELECTION ?";S
70    IF S = 0 THEN HOME : PRINT "THAT'S ALL": END
80    ON S GOSUB 300,600
90    GOTO 20
300   BI = 0:BO = 0:T = 0
310   HOME : VTAB 5: HTAB 12: PRINT "FIFO ENTRY SYSTEM"
320   VTAB 8: PRINT SPC( 12);"0.ENDING REPORT"
330   VTAB 10: PRINT SPC( 12);"1.ENTER PURCHASE"
340   VTAB 12: PRINT SPC( 12);"2.ENTER ORDER"
350   VTAB 14: INPUT "ENTER SELECTION ?";S
360   IF S > 0 THEN 400
370   HOME : VTAB 5: HTAB 12: PRINT "FIFO ENDING REPORT"
380   VTAB 14: GOSUB 1020: GOSUB 1010: RETURN
400   ON S GOTO 420,500
410   GOTO 310
420   HOME : VTAB 5: HTAB 12: PRINT "FIFO PURCHASE HANDLER"
430   IF (BI + 1 - (BI = 100) * 101) = BO THEN VTAB 15: PRINT
      "INVENTORY IS FULL!!!!": PRINT : PRINT "NO PURCHASES PERMITTED
      TODAY": GOSUB 1000: GOTO 310
440   VTAB 8: PRINT "ENTER DATE(MM/DD/YY),PRICE,AMOUNT"
450   VTAB 10: HTAB 11: INPUT A$(BI),PR(BI),AO(BI)
460   N = T:T = AO(BI) + T: IF T < 1 THEN 490
470   IF T < N THEN AO(BI) = T
480   BI = BI + 1 - (BI = 100) * 101
490   VTAB 12: GOSUB 1020: GOSUB 1000: GOTO 310
500   HOME : IF BO = BI THEN VTAB 8: PRINT "THERE IS NO INVENTORY IN
      STOCK": GOSUB 1000: GOTO 310
510   VTAB 4: INPUT "ENTER NUMBER OF ITEMS ORDERED ?";NU: IF NU < 1
      THEN 510
515   T = T - NU
520   IF AO(BO) > NU THEN 560
530   PRINT : PRINT AO(BO);" ITEMS AT $";PR(BO);" PURCHASED ";A$(BO):NU
      = NU - AO(BO):BO = BO + 1 - (BO = 100) * 101: IF NU
      = 0 THEN 570
540   IF BI = BO THEN PRINT : PRINT "WE ARE OUT OF STOCK WITH ";NU;"
      ITEMS": PRINT : PRINT "LEFT ON ORDER": GOSUB 1010: GOTO 310
550   GOTO 520
560   PRINT : PRINT NU;" ITEMS AT $";PR(BO);" PURCHASED ";A$(BO):AO(BO)
      = AO(BO) - NU
570   PRINT : GOSUB 1020: GOSUB 1000: GOTO 310
600   BI = 0:T = 0
610   HOME : VTAB 5: HTAB 12: PRINT "LIFO ENTRY SYSTEM"
620   VTAB 8: PRINT SPC( 12);"0.ENDING REPORT"
630   VTAB 10: PRINT SPC( 12);"1.ENTER PURCHASE"
640   VTAB 12: PRINT SPC( 12);"2.ENTER ORDER"
650   VTAB 14: INPUT "ENTER SELECTION ?";S
660   IF S > 0 THEN 700
670   HOME : VTAB 5: HTAB 12: PRINT "LIFO ENDING REPORT"
```

Fig. 23-2. Circular list, stack and pointers.

```
680   VTAB 14: GOSUB 1020: GOSUB 1010: RETURN
700   ON S GOTO 720,800
710   GOTO 610
720   HOME : VTAB 5: HTAB 12: PRINT "LIFO PURCHASE HANDLER"
730   IF BI = 100 THEN VTAB 15: PRINT "INVENTORY IS FULL!!!!": PRINT :
      PRINT "NO PURCHASES PERMITTED TODAY": GOSUB 1000: GOTO 610
740   VTAB 8: PRINT "ENTER DATE(MM/DD/YY),PRICE,AMOUNT"
750   BI = BI + 1: VTAB 10: HTAB 11: INPUT A$(BI),PR(BI),AO(BI):N = T::T
      = AO(BI) + T: IF T < 1 THEN BI = BI - 1: GOTO 770
760   IF T < N THEN AO(BI) = T
770   VTAB 12: GOSUB 1020: GOSUB 1000: GOTO 610
800   HOME : IF BI = 0 THEN VTAB 8: PRINT "THERE IS NO INVENTORY IN
      STOCK": GOSUB 1000: GOTO 610
810   VTAB 4: INPUT "ENTER NUMBER OF ITEMS ORDERED ?";NU: IF NU < 1
      THEN 810
815   T = T - NU
820   IF AO(BI) > NU THEN 860
830   PRINT : PRINT AO(BI);" ITEMS AT $";PR(BI);" PURCHASED ";A$(BI):NU =
      NU - AO(BI):BI = BI - 1: IF NU = 0 THEN 870
840   IF BI = 0 THEN PRINT : PRINT "WE ARE OUT OF STOCK WITH ";NU;"
      ITEMS": PRINT : PRINT "LEFT ON ORDER": GOSUB 1010: GOTO 610
850   GOTO 820
860   PRINT : PRINT NU;" ITEMS AT $";PR(BI);" PURCHASED ";A$(BI):AO(BI) =
      AO(BI) - NU
870   PRINT : PRINT : GOSUB 1020: GOSUB 1010: GOTO 610
1000  FOR J = 1 TO 1800: NEXT J: RETURN
1010  VTAB 20: PRINT "PRESS RETURN TO CONTINUE!!! ";: GET Q$: RETURN
1020  PRINT "THERE ARE ";T;" ITEMS IN INVENTORY": RETURN
1050  T = 0:PT = BI
1060  FOR J = PT TO 0 STEP - 1
1070  T = T + A0(J): NEXT J: PRINT "THERE ARE ";T;" ITEMS IN INVENTORY":
      RETURN
```

Fig. 23-2. (Cont) Circular list, stack and pointers.

Lines 10 through 80 DIMension the variables and set up the initial menu to select: 0. END THE PROGRAM, 1. FIFO, or 2. LIFO.

Lines 420 through 490 process the purchasing information for the circular list (FIFO). Line 430 detects the buffer full condition (Fig. 23-1, part A).

The buffer is DIMensioned to 101 cells. DIM A$(100) was arbitrarily selected and could have been a smaller number or any number within usable memory limits.

When BO and BI are located in adjacent memory cells there are no empty cells. Therefore, the buffer is full. In line 430, a special case is used when BI = 100 (Fig. 23-1, part D). This special case is used so the circle can continue uninterrupted. The BI = 100 portion of the formula is activated when BI = 100.

Line 440 prints the informational headers, ENTER DATE (MM/DD/YY), PRICE, AMOUNT. Line 450 allows input of the date of purchase, A$(BI), the price of the item, PR(BI), and the number

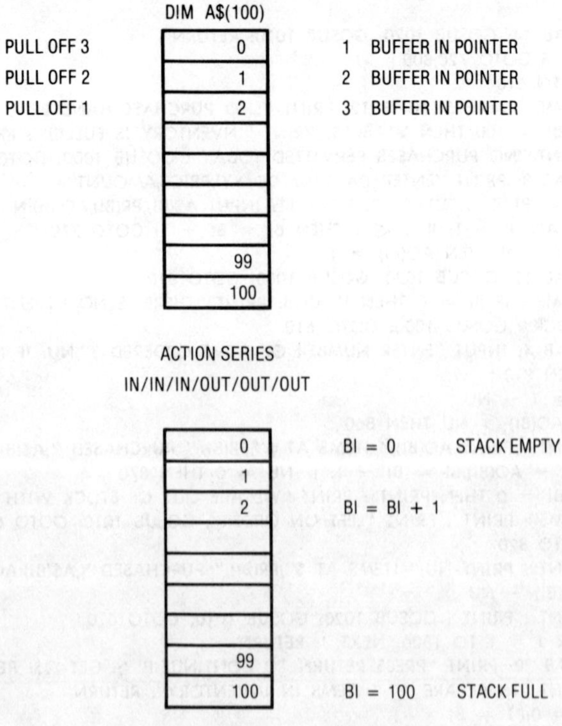

Fig. 23-3. Stack (LIFO) 101 cells.

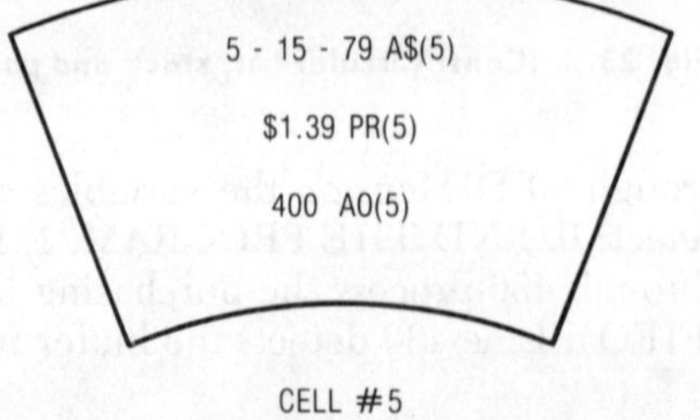

Fig. 23-4. Individual cell and contents.

of items purchased, AO(BI). These items are placed within a specific cell in the circular list (Fig. 23-4).

In line 460, the total number of items purchased is placed in the variable N. N holds the total number of items for comparison purposes in relation to back orders. When N is greater than T, there are not enough items to fill a customer's order and the items have to be back ordered. T = AO(BI) + T holds the total number of items purchased.

A$ = date of purchase of items by company.
AO = number of items purchased by the company.
BI = buffer in pointer.
BO = buffer out pointer.
N = holds total number of items for later comparison to total items (T).
NU = number of items ordered by the customer.
PR = price of the items.
PT = temporary pointer.
T = total number of items.

Fig. 23-5. Variables for circular list, stack, and pointers.

Line 460 IF T < 1 THEN 490. When T is less than 1, there are items back ordered and the subroutine at line 1020 prints out a negative value for the number of items in inventory.

Line 470 IF T < N THEN AO(BI) = T. If there is a back order, the next purchase may not eliminate the back order. When the next purchase does not eliminate the back order, or when the purchase equals the back order, the purchase does not go into the buffer. If the purchase is greater than the back order, the excess is stored in N. The excess in N can then be compared to T, (1) before the purchase order, and (2) after the purchase order. If the total after the order is less than the order, the purchase must be reduced by the number of items in the back order. When the purchase is greater than the back order, the back order is subtracted from the purchase, and the balance of the purchase is stored in a cell in the buffer.

Line 480 increments the buffer in pointer to the next cell in the buffer and line 490 causes the program to jump back to the FIFO menu.

In line 500, when both buffer pointers rest at the same cell in the buffer (Fig. 23-1, part C) the buffer is empty. The buffer has three conditions:

1. BI = BO BUFFER EMPTY—input company purchases only.
2. BI+1 = BO BUFFER FULL—take out customer's orders only.
3. BI+1<>BO company purchases can be placed in the buffer and customer's orders can be taken from the buffer.

Line 510 checks if an order of less than one has been input. If it has, the statement branches back to itself.

Line 515 subtracts the number of items ordered from the total number of items.

In line 520, if the number of items of a particular purchase in the buffer is greater than the number of items ordered, the program branches to line 560 to process the order.

If the statement in line 520 is false, the program defaults to line 530 to print out the number of items purchased and updates the buffer as necessary to complete the order. The order is processed against inventory buffers until the order is filled. If there are not sufficient items in inventory to fill the order, the inventory buffers are depleted and the balance is back ordered, making T a negative number. AO(BO) is printed each time the inventory is reduced by the order. NU = NU – AO(BO) updates the number of items left on the order that need to be filled. If NU is greater than AO(BO), the first buffer cell is emptied, and each following buffer cell is emptied until all buffer cells are empty, or until the order is completely filled. If the order is not completely filled, and there is no remaining inventory, the balance of the items is back ordered. This logic is implemented in lines 520 through 550.

The reduction in inventory is contained in the statement NU = NU – AO(BO). The buffer out cell is computed in the statement BO = BO + 1 – (BO = 100)*101. IF NU = 0 THEN 570 takes care of the condition when the number of items ordered comes out even, with BO entry on the buffer empty.

Line 560 prints out the number of items purchased, the price, and the date of purchase.

The statement AO(BO) = AO(BO) – NU in line 560 computes the number of items that remain in a specific cell in the inventory buffer.

When the transactions are completed, the FIFO menu is displayed. Zero selection prints out an ending report of the number of items remaining in inventory (GOSUB 1020). GOSUB 1000 causes PRESS RETURN TO CONTINUE!!! to be printed below the ending report. When RETURN is pressed, the program returns to line 90—GOTO 20, and the FIFO/LIFO DEMONSTRATION menu is displayed on the screen. Selection zero from the FIFO/LIFO DEMONSTRATION menu causes the program to end.

Selection #2 from the FIFO/LIFO DEMONSTRATION menu causes the program to GOSUB 600 to the LIFO (stack) section of the program.

Line 600 BI = 0 : T = 0 initializes the buffer in pointer and the total to zero. The stack has only one pointer, the buffer in pointer. The LIFO ENTRY SYSTEM menu is printed and there are three selections available, 0. ENDING REPORT, 1. ENTER PURCHASE, and 2. ENTER ORDER.

If 1. ENTER ORDER is selected the program branches to line 720, to print out LIFO PURCHASE HANDLER.

Line 730 IF BI = 100 the program prints out INVENTORY IS FULL.

The stack has three conditions (Fig. 23-3).

1. BI = 100 STACK IS FULL—customer orders can be filled.
2. BI = 0 STACK IS EMPTY—company purchases can be placed in the stack.
3. BI = BI + 1 company purchases may be inserted, and customer's orders may be processed.

Line 750 BI = BI + 1 increments the pointer, and purchasing information is input into an array. A$(BI) is the date of purchase, PR(BI) is the price of the item, and AO(BI) is the number of items purchased.

Line 750 N = T places the total number of items in a variable to be used in comparison later in the program. T = AO(BI) + T totals the number of items in inventory. IF T < 1 THEN BI = BI − 1. If there are items on back order T is less than one and the buffer in pointer is decremented. This means that any purchase received goes first to fill the back orders.

Line 760 IF T < N THEN AO(BI) = T. If the total number of items in inventory is less than the number ordered, the purchases go to eliminate the back order. If the purchases are less than, or equal to the back order, the purchases do not go to inventory. If the purchases are greater than the back order, the excess purchases are stored in N. The excess in N is compared to T before, and T after the purchase. If T after the purchase is greater than N, the back order is eliminated and the excess purchases go into a cell in the buffer.

Line 800 IF BI = 0 THEN PRINT "THERE IS NO INVENTORY IN STOCK". The BI pointer is set to the top cell in the stack (Fig. 23-3). Cell number 100 is the bottom cell in the stack. The top and the bottom of the stack is a matter of semantics. The important aspect is how the stack is filled and emptied.

Line 800 allows the user to enter the number of items ordered by the customer.

Line 820 IF AO(BI) > NU THEN 860. If the number of items in inventory is greater than the number of items ordered by the customer, the program branches to line 860 to process the order and only this cell in the stack is reduced.

If line 820 is false, the program defaults to line 830 to print out the number of items purchased, subtract the number from inventory (NU = NU − AO(BI)), decrement the stack pointer, BI = BI − 1, and go to the next cell to try to complete the order. The order is processed against inventory buffer cells until the order is filled. If there is not sufficient inventory to fill the order, all inventory buffer cells are depleted and the balance is back ordered. T is a negative number. Line 815 T = T − NU. AO(BI) is printed out each time the inventory is reduced by the order. NU = NU − AO(BI) updates the number of items left on order that need to be filled. If NU is greater than AO(BI), this cell is emptied, and adjacent cells are emptied, until the order is filled. If the order is not completely filled, and there is no remaining inventory, the remaining items are back ordered. The logic is implemented in lines 820 through 850.

Line 830 IF NU = 0 THEN 870 is true the program prints an inventory status report of zero items.

When all purchases and orders have been completed, the program returns to line 610 to print out the LIFO ENTRY SYSTEM. Zero selection from this menu prints out an ending inventory report, and press RETURN returns the program to the FIFO/LIFO DEMONSTRATION menu. A zero selection from this menu ends the program.

LESSON 24

Sorting, Searching, & Deleting

The program written for Lesson 24 (Fig. 24-1) prepares a list of names and telephone numbers. The list is sorted and SAVEd to tape. The list may be loaded from tape into the program, searched

```
1       DIM CA(45),CH(1),DA$(1000),CL(1000) : REM : PHONE LIST
10      SP$ = "          ":SP$ = SP$ + SP$ + SP$
15      DC$ = "713"
20      HOME : VTAB 4: HTAB 12: PRINT "PHONE LISTING"
30      VTAB 10: HTAB 8: PRINT "1.ENTER"
40      VTAB 12: HTAB 8: PRINT "2.MODIFY/DELETE"
50      VTAB 14: HTAB 8: PRINT "3.LIST/SEARCH"
60      VTAB 16: HTAB 8: PRINT "4.SAVE LIST AND END"
70      VTAB 18: HTAB 8: INPUT "ENTER SELECTION ?";MS
80      ON MS GOTO 1000,2000,3000,4000
90      GOTO 20
1000    HOME : VTAB 4: HTAB 12: PRINT "FILE MAINTENANCE"
1010    VTAB 10: HTAB 8: PRINT "1.LOAD TAPE FILE"
1020    VTAB 12: HTAB 8: PRINT "2.ENTER NEW ITEMS"
1030    VTAB 14: HTAB 8: PRINT "3.RETURN TO MAIN MENU"
1040    VTAB 16: HTAB 8: INPUT "ENTER SELECTION ?";MS
1050    ON MS GOTO 1100,1200,1400
1060    GOTO 1000
1100    HOME : VTAB 4: HTAB 4: INPUT "READY CASSETTE AND PRESS RETURN
        ! ";Q$
1110    RECALL CH
1120    IF CH(0) = 0 THEN PRINT "THERE IS NO ARRAY ON TAPE": GOTO 1000
1130    FOR J = 1 TO CH(0)
1140    RECALL CA
```

Fig. 24-1. Program written for Lesson 24.

```
1150  DA$(J) = "": FOR K = 1 TO 44:DA$(J) = DA$(J) + CHR$ (CA(K)):
      NEXT K:CL(J) = CA(45):NEXT J
1160  GOTO 1000
1200  HOME :VT = 6: GOSUB 10010
1210  IF CL(CH(0) + 1) = 0 THEN 1000
1260  VT = 12: GOSUB 10080
1310  DA$(CH(0) + 1) = DA$(CH(0) + 1) +
      "(" + TC$ + ")-" + LEFT$(PT$,3)
      + "-" + RIGHT$ (PT$,4)
1320  PRINT : GOSUB 10000
1330  PRINT : INPUT "ENTER 'R' TO REENTER ELSE 'RETURN' ?";Q$ : IF Q$
      < > "R" THEN CH(0) = CH(0) + 1
1340  GOTO 1200
1400  GOSUB 1410: GOTO 20
1410  IF CH(0) < 2 THEN RETURN
1420  FOR J = 1 TO CH(0) - 1
1430  M = J: FOR K = J + 1 TO CH(0)
1440  IF LEFT$ (DA$(K),30) < LEFT$ (DA$(M),30) THEN M = K
1450  NEXT K
1460  IF M = J THEN 1480
1470  TC$ = DA$(M):DA$(M) = DA$(J):DA$(J) = TC$:CL(0)
      = CL(M):CL(M) = CL(J):CL(J) = CL(0)
1480  NEXT J
1490  RETURN
2000  HOME : VTAB 4: IF CH(0) = 0 THEN PRINT "THERE IS NO LIST ";
      CHR$ (7): FOR J = 1 TO 2000: NEXT J: GOTO 20
2010  PRINT "ENTER NAME TO BE CHANGED": PRINT : INPUT NA$
2020  IF LEN (NA$) = 0 THEN 20
2030  FOR K = 1 TO CH(0)
2040  IF NA$ < > LEFT$ (DA$(K),CL(K)) THEN 2060
2050  GOTO 2100
2060  NEXT K: VTAB 10: HTAB 6: PRINT "THIS NAME NOT ON LIST": PRINT
      CHR$ (7): FOR J = 1 TO 1000 : NEXT J: GOTO 2000
2100  CH(1) = CH(0):CH(0) = K - 1:VTAB 6: PRINT "CURRENT RECORD IS ":
      PRINT
2110  VTAB 8: GOSUB 10000: PRINT : PRINT "ENTER 'C' TO CHANGE, 'D' TO
      DELETE": PRINT : INPUT "ELSE 'RETURN' ?";Q$
2120  IF Q$ < > "C" AND Q$ < > "D" THEN 2240
2125  IF Q$ = "D" THEN DA$(K) = "DELETE" + LEFT$ (SP$,24) + "(000)-
      000-0000": GOTO 2230
2130  VTAB 12: CALL - 958: VTAB 12: PRINT "ENTER 'N'-NAME, 'P'-PHONE#,
      'B'-BOTH" : PRINT

2140  T$ = RIGHT$ (DA$(K),14): INPUT "LETTER PLEASE ?";C$: IF C$ < >
      "N" AND C$ < > "P" AND C$ < > "B" THEN 2130
2150  IF C$ = "P" THEN 2170
2160  VT = 14: GOSUB 10010
2170  IF C$ = "N" THEN 2190
2180  VT = 16: GOSUB 10080
2190  IF C$ = "N" THEN DA$(K) = DA$(K) + T$: GOTO 2230
2200  IF C$ = "P" THEN DA$(K) = LEFT$(DA$(K),30)
2220  DA$(K) = DA$(K) + "(" + TC$ + ")-"
      + LEFT$ (PT$,3) + "-" + RIGHT$ (PT$,4)
```

Fig. 24-1. (Cont) Program written for Lesson 24.

```
2230   CH(0) = CH(1): PRINT : INPUT "ANY MORE CORRECTIONS (Y OR N)
       ?";Q$: IF Q$ = "Y" THEN 2000
2240   K = 0: FOR J = 1 TO CH(0)
2250   IF LEFT$ (DA$(J),6) = "DELETE" THEN 2280
2260   K = K + 1: IF K = J THEN 2280
2270   DA$(K) = DA$(J):CL(K) = CL(J)
2280   NEXT J
2290   CH(0) = K
2300   GOSUB 1410: GOTO 20
3000   HOME : VTAB 3: INPUT "ENTER 'S' TO SEARCH OR 'L' TO LIST ?";Q$:
       IF Q$ < > "L" AND Q$ < > "S" THEN 3000
3010   IF Q$ = "S" THEN 3100
3030   FOR J = 1 TO CH(0)
3040   IF J < > INT ((J - 1) / 5) * 5 + 1 THEN 3070
3050   IF J < > 1 THEN PRINT : INPUT "!";Q$
3060   HOME : VTAB 3
3070   PRINT "NAME = "; LEFT$ (DA$(J),30): PRINT SPC( 7);"PHONE # = ";
       RIGHT$ (DA$(J),14): PRINT
3080   NEXT J
3090   PRINT : INPUT "!";Q$: GOTO 20
3100   HOME : VTAB 3: HTAB 12: PRINT "SEARCH SELECTION": PRINT
3110   HTAB 12: PRINT "1.NAME SEARCH": PRINT : HTAB 12: PRINT "2.NUMBER
       SEARCH": PRINT : HTAB 12: PRINT "3.RETURN TO MAIN MENU": PRINT
3120   INPUT "ENTER SEARCH KEY ?"; MS
3130   ON MS GOTO 3150,3250,20
3140   GOTO 3100
3150   HOME : VTAB 4: PRINT "ENTER NAME OR FRAGMENT ?": PRINT :
       INPUT NA$:L = LEN (NA$): IF L = 0 THEN 3100
3160   CO = 0: FOR J = 1 TO CH(0): IF L > CL(J) THEN 3220
3170   FOR K = 1 TO CL(J) - L + 1
3180   IF NA$ < > MID$ (DA$(J),K,L) THEN 3210
3190   CH(1) = CH(0):CH(0) = J - 1: PRINT : GOSUB 10000: PRINT :
       INPUT Q$
3200   CH(0) = CH(1):CO = CO + 1: GOTO 3220
3210   NEXT K
3220   NEXT J: IF CO > 0 THEN 3100

3230   PRINT : PRINT "THIS WORD IS NOT ON FILE": FOR J = 1 TO 1000:
       NEXT J: PRINT CHR$ (7): GOTO 3100
3250   HOME : VTAB 6: HTAB 6: INPUT "ENTER AREA CODE,PHONE # ?";
       AC$,PN$
3260   IF LEN (AC$) = 0 THEN AC$ = DC$
3270   TC$ = "(" + AC$ + ")-" + LEFT$(PN$,3)
       + "-" + RIGHT$ (PN$,4)
3280   FOR J = 1 TO CH(0)
3290   IF TC$ < > RIGHT$ (DA$(J),14) THEN 3310
3300   CH(1) = CH(0):CH(0) = J - 1: GOSUB 10000: PRINT :CH(0) = CH(1):
       INPUT Q$: PRINT
3310   NEXT J
3320   GOTO 3100
4000   HOME : VTAB 6: HTAB 10: INPUT "READY CASSETTE TO SAVE FILE !";Q$
4010   STORE CH
4020   FOR J = 1 TO CH(0)
```

Fig. 24-1. (Cont) Program written for Lesson 24.

```
4030   FOR K = 1 TO 44
4040   CA(K) = ASC ( MID$ (DA$(J),K,1))
4050   NEXT K
4060   CA(45) = CL(J)
4070   STORE CA
4080   NEXT J
4090   PRINT CHR$ (7); CHR$ (7)
4100   HTAB 10: PRINT "PHONE SYSTEM IS ENDED"
4110   END
10000  PRINT "NAME = "; LEFT$ (DA$(CH(0) + 1),30): PRINT : PRINT "PHONE
       #= "; RIGHT$ (DA$(CH(0) + 1),14): RETURN
10010  VTAB VT: CALL - 958: VTAB VT: PRINT "ENTER NAME(LESS THAN 31
       CHARACTERS)"
10020  PRINT : INPUT DA$(CH(0) + 1)
10030  CL(CH(0) + 1 = LEN (DA$(CH(0) + 1)): IF CL(CH(0) + 1) = 0 THEN
       RETURN
10040  IF CL(CH(0) + 1) > 30 THEN PRINT : PRINT "NAME IS TOO LONG";
       CHR$ (7): FOR J = 1 TO 1000: NEXT J: GOTO 10010
10050  IF CL(CH(0) + 1) = 30 THEN RETURN
10060  DA$(CH(0) + 1) = DA$(CH(0) + 1) + LEFT$ (SP$,30 - CL(CH(0)
       + 1))
10070  RETURN
10080  VTAB VT: PRINT "ENTER AREA CODE,PHONE NO."
10090  PRINT : PRINT : INPUT AC$, PN$
10100  IF LEN (AC$) = 0 THEN AC$ = DC$
10110  IF LEN (AC$) < > 3 OR LEN (PN$) < > 7 THEN 10080
10120  TC$ = STR$ ( VAL (AC$)):PT$ = STR$ ( VAL (PN$)): IF TC$ < > AC$
       OR PT$ < > PN$ THEN PRINT : PRINT "PLEASE USE NUMERICS"; CHR$
       (7): FOR J = 1 TO 1000: NEXT J: GOTO 10080
10130  RETURN
```

Fig. 24-1. (Cont) Program written for Lesson 24.

for a name or fragment of a name, and searched for an area code and a phone number. Items on the list may be deleted. There are many techniques to sort, search, and delete items on a list. The techniques introduced in this lesson are a basis for further study. The variables, as they appear in the program, are shown in Fig. 24-2. The variables are given in Fig. 24-3 in alphabetical order.

Sorting is the act of placing information in a predetermined sequence. Sorting depends on sequencing items according to a key word. Lists of names are usually keyed or sorted alphabetically on the first letters of the last name. Telephone numbers are usually keyed or sorted on the area code. Mailing lists may be sorted according to the zip code. Lists can be sorted in any manner that meets the needs of the user.

Lists are sorted to increase the speed and efficiency of the search and delete functions. From the human point of view, a list is sorted because we expect to see lists in proper order.

The correct time to sort the list is after file maintenance is complete and before the list is SAVEd to tape, disk, or paper. File main-

CA	Array used to store to, and retrieve from, tape. AS language cannot store string arrays directly. The string arrays are converted to the numbered equivalent to store the number. CA(K) = ASC(MID$(DA$ (J),K,1)). Lines 4010-4050. STORE CA saves the file. RECALL CA loads the file. The file is converted into a string — DA$ = DA$ + CHR$ (CA(K)) in lines 1110 — 1150.
CH	CH(0) holds the number or records in the record count.
CH(1)	Temporary storage for the record count.
DA$	String in which the name, area code, and phone number are held.
CL	Length of the name string before it is padded to exactly 30 characters.
SP$	Padding string that contains 30 blank spaces.
DC$	713. Default string holds the area code. A comma input places 713 in the area code. A different area code can be inserted by typing in the numbers.
MS	Menu selection.
Q$	String that holds "Y" for yes, "N" for no, or "R" for return.
RECALL CA	Retrieves a real or integer array that has been STOREd on tape. The array must be DIMensioned in the program. Subscripts are not used when storing or recalling arrays. CA(0), CA(1), CA(2), etc., are stored and recalled as CA. CA(45) contains 45 characters including the padded spaces. 44 CHARACTERS NAME STRING PADDED TO 30 CHARACTERS (713) — 688 — 1212 = 44 + CL = 45 1 3 1 1 3 1 4 1 + 30 = 45
J,K	Loop variables used throughout the program.
VT	Sets up VTAB VT to VTAB to different rows according to program structure.
CL(CH(0)+1)	Holds the length of the name being input before padding in relation to the length of DA$ before it was padded.
GOSUB 10010	Inputs name into the 1st part of DA$ and pads the 1st part of the string to 30 characters.
GOSUB 10080	Inputs area code and phone number into the last 14 characters of DA$. PT$ = STR$(VAL(PN$)) — checks that all phone numbers are numeric characters and not alpha characters.
PN$	Phone number string.
TC$	Temporary area code string to check numeric character input into area code. TC$ = STR$(VAL(AC$)).
PT$	Temporary phone number string to check numeric character input into the phone number string. PT$ = STR$(VAL(PN$)).

Fig. 24-2. Variables as they appear in the program.

AC$	Area code string. A comma defaults to DC$ = 713.
M	Minimum.
NA$	Name to be changed.
GOSUB 10000	Prints out name, area code, and telephone number before it is changed.
STORE CA	Stores real or integer numbers on tape. SEE RECALL CA.
2125	Delete line—see Fig. 24-4.
CHR$(7)	PRINT CHR$(7) rings the bell on the computer—CONTROL G.
CH(0)=J−1	The name and phone number are placed in CH(0)+1. Subroutines 10010 and 10080 input name and phone number.
CO	Count of the number of times a match is found on the list.

Fig. 24-2. (Cont) Variables as they appear in the program.

tenance includes all changes to the list, all updates to the list, and all deletions from the list.

The sort is set up inside double nested loops so the items on the list can be compared and ordered (Fig. 24-4). Each comparison is called a pass. The items on the list are compared to each other during the passes and items on the list are swapped to place them in the correct order.

There are several types of sorts used in programming. Ripple, modified ripple, bubble, and Shell-Metzner are some of the better known sorts. Shell-Metzner is the most efficient sort of this group. A detailed discussion of sorts is out of the scope of this book.

A search is the act of examining items in the list to discover whether the key being searched for is on the list. All items related to that key are then displayed. A search aids the user in discovering all items on a list related to a key. A key can be a name or fragment of a name or a phone number. How often do you remember the last name of a person but not his first name? If the name is on the list a search will reveal it. A search allows the user to pull one record off the list by using a keyword with which to search.

A search can be made anytime the user needs information from the records on the list.

Deletion is the act of removing a record or records from the list (Fig. 24-5). Deleting is used to keep the file as small as possible to use the least memory and to keep the file current. A list containing unneeded names is nonproductive and costly to most users.

Deletions should be made anytime names on the list become of no use to the user. If the list is for subscriptions, each name on the list costs money in production costs, mailing costs, and labor. Nonsubscribers' names on the list should be deleted.

Line 1 DIMensions the variables. CA(45) is the array used to

AC$	Area code string.
CA	Array used to store to, and retrieve from, tape. AS language cannot store string arrays directly. The string arrays are converted to the numbered equivalent to store the number. CA(K) = ASC(MID$(DA$(J),K,1)). Lines 4010 — 4050. STORE CA saves the file. RECALL CA loads the file. The file is converted into a string — DA$ = DA$ + CHR$(CA(K)) in lines 1110 — 1150.
CH	CH(0) holds the number of records in the record count.
CH(0)=J−1	The name, area code, and the phone number are placed in CH(0) +1. Subroutines 10010 and 10080 input the name, area code, and the phone number. In order to print the list CH(0) must be decremented (jump out of the loop) to the correct end of the list. J+1 and J−1 must be offset so CH(0) is the one name on the list to be printed out.
CH(1)	Temporary storage for the record count.
CHR$(7)	PRINT CHR$(7) rings the bell on the computer—CONTROL G.
CL	Length of the name string before it is padded to exactly 30 characters.
CL(CH(0)+1)	Holds the length of the name being input before padding.
CO	Count of the number of times a match is found on the list.
DA$	String in which the name, area code, and phone number are held.
DC$	713. Default string holds the area code. A comma input places 713 in the area code. A different area code can be inserted by typing in the numbers.
GOSUB 10000	Prints out the name, area code, and telephone number before it is changed.
GOSUB 10010	Inputs name into the 1st part of DA$ and pads the 1st part of the string to 30 characters.
GOSUB 10080	Inputs area code and phone number into the last 14 characters of DA$. PT$ = STR$(VAL(PN$))—checks that all phone numbers are numeric characters and not alpha characters.
J,K	Loop variables used throughout the program.
M	Minimum.
MS	Menu selection.
NA$	Name to be changed.
PN$	Phone number string.
PT$	Temporary phone number string to check numeric character input into the phone number string. PT$ = STR$(VAL(PN$)).
Q$	String that holds "Y" for yes, "N" for no, or "R" for return.

Fig. 24-3. Variables in alphabetical order.

RECALL CA	Retrieves a real or integer array that has been STOREd on tape. The array must be DIMensioned in the program. Subscripts are not used when storing or recalling arrays. CA(0), CA(1), CA(2), etc., are stored and recalled as CA. CA(45) contains 45 characters including the padded spaces. 44 CHARACTERS NAME STRING PADDED TO 30 CHARACTERS. (713) – 688 – 1212 = 44 + CL = 45 1 3 1 1 3 1 4 1 + 30 = 45
SP$	Padding string that contains ten blank spaces.
STORE CA	Stores real or integers on tape. SEE RECALL CA.
TC$	Temporary area code string to check numeric character input into area code. TC$ = STR$(VAL(AC$)).
VT	Sets up VTAB VT to VTAB to different rows according to program structure.
2125	Delete line—see Fig. 24-4.

Fig. 24-3. (Cont) Variables in alphabetical order.

store to and retrieve from tape. The record (name and telephone number) is input as a string array. Each record is stored as 45 numbers because the store and recall commands do not store string arrays. The conversion is shown in lines 4010 through 4070 in Fig. 24-1.

```
4010  STORE CH
```

Line 4010 stores the number of records to be placed on the tape. In this case, CH(0) = 5 (5 is an arbitrary number).

```
4020  FOR J = 1 TO CH(0)
```

Line 4020 sets the beginning of the loop that stores five records on tape (CH(0) = 5).

```
4030  FOR K = 1 TO 44
```

Line 4030 states there are 44 characters in each record plus CL = 1. CL stores the length of DA$ before it is padded. Thirty charac-

NUMBER OF ITEMS IN THE LIST—5
ORIGINAL ORDER OF THE LIST

DA$(1)	DA$(2)	DA$(3)	DA$(4)	DA$(5)
E	D	C	B	A

DA$(K)	CONTAINS NAME AND TELEPHONE NUMBER
FOR J=1 TO CH(0)−1 (FOR J= 1 TO 4)	NUMBER OF PASSES IS ONE LESS THAN THE # OF ITEMS IN THE LIST
FOR K= J+1 TO CH(0) (FOR K= 2 TO 5) (1st pass only)	IF K STARTED AT #1 THE SAME ITEM WOULD BE COMPARED TO ITSELF

(A) *Information for sort.*

Fig. 24-4. Sorting a list.

PASS	J	Ms	J+1	K	DA$(1)	DA$(2)	DA$(3)	DA$(4)	DA$(5)	LINE #	CONDITION	Ma
0	1	1			E	D	C	B	A	1430-1470		
1	1	1	2	2		D				1440	TRUE	2
				3			C			1440	TRUE	3
				4				B		1440	TRUE	4
				5					A	1440	TRUE	5
M=5, J=1					A	D	C	B	E	1460	FALSE	
2	2	2	3	3			C			1440	TRUE	3
				4				B		1440	TRUE	4
				5					E	1440	FALSE	4
M=4, J=2					A	B	C	D	E	1460	FALSE	
3	3	3	4	4	A	B	C	D	E	1440	FALSE	3
				5						1440	FALSE	
NO EXCHANGE M = J												
4	4	4	5	5	A	B	C	D	E	1440	FALSE	4
NO EXCHANGE M = J												

Ms—M AT SORT PASS
Ma—M AFTER CHANGE

1st PASS EXCHANGE M = 5(A), J = 1(E)
2nd PASS EXCHANGE M = 4(B), J = 2(D)
3rd PASS NO EXCHANGE 3rd ITEM IN THE LIST IS IN THE CORRECT ORDER
4th PASS NO EXCHANGE 4th ITEM IN THE LIST IS IN THE CORRECT ORDER

(B) Computer sort.

1470 T$ = DA$(M) : DA$(M) = DA$(J) : DA$(J) = T$CL(0) = CL(M) : CL(M) = CL(J) : CL(J) = CL(0)

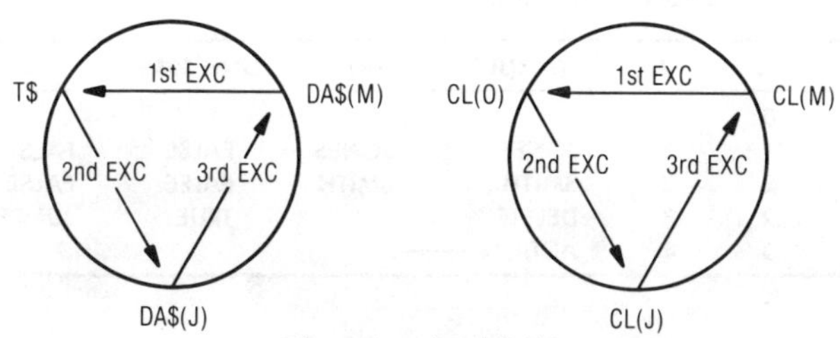

CL = length of DA$
before it is padded.
In this example, CL
is always 1 character.

(C) Exchange routine.

Fig. 24-4. (Cont) Sorting a list.

		T$	DA$(M)	DA$(J)	
ORIGINAL			E	A	
1st PASS	1st EXC	E	E	A	T$ = DA$(5)
	2nd EXC	E	A	A	DA$(5) = DA$(1)
	3rd EXC	A	A	E	DA$(1) = T$
2nd PASS	1st EXC	D	D	B	T$ = DA$(4)
	2nd EXC	D	B	B	DA$(4) = DA$(2)
	3rd EXC	B	B	D	T$ = DA$(2)
3rd PASS	NO EXCHANGE—3rd ITEM IS IN THE CORRECT POSITION				
4th PASS	NO EXCHANGE—4th ITEM IS IN THE CORRECT POSITION				

(D) Table of passes and exchanges.

Fig. 24-4. (Cont) Sorting a list.

ters are in the name string, including padded characters (spaces) produced by SP$.

(713) – 688 – 1212

There are 1 + 3 + 1 + 1 + 3 + 1 + 4 + 30 = 44 characters in DA$. CL = 1. CL is the length of DA$ before it is padded.

30 characters in DA$
14 characters in area code (AC$) and phone number (PN$)
1 character for CL = length of DA$ before padding.
45 = CA(45)

FILE:
DA$(1) = "JONES (713)-688-1212"
DA$(2) = "SMITH (713)-688-1213"
DA$(3) ="DELETE (000)-000-0000"
DA$(4) = "ACTION (713)-688-1214"

CH(0) = 4

PASS	K	J	DA$(J)	DA$(K)	LINE 2250	K = J
	0					
1	1	1	JONES	JONES	FALSE	FALSE
2	2	2	SMITH	SMITH	FALSE	FALSE
3	2	3	DELETE		TRUE	JUMPS OVER
4	3	4	ACTION ⟶			

FILE:
DA$(1) = "JONES (713)-688-1212"
DA$(2) = "SMITH (713)-688-1213"
DA$(3) = "ACTION (713)-688-1214"
DA$(4) = "ACTION (713)-688-1214"
2290 CH(0) = K (K = 3)—LAST RECORD DA$(4) IS REMOVED

Fig. 24-5. Delete routine.

```
4040  CA(K) = ASC(MID$(CA$(J),K,1))
```

RELATES TO RECORD NUMBER

RELATES TO CHARACTER NUMBER K IN RECORD J

CONVERTS ONE CHARACTER FOR EACH EXECUTION OF THE LOOP

Line 4040 converts the string array, DA$, into ASCII characters and places it in CA numeric array to be stored on tape.

```
4050  NEXT K
```

Line 4050 completes the conversion of one record.

```
4060  CA(45) = CL(J)
```

In line 4060, CL is the length of DA$ before it is padded and stored in CA(45). CL(J) is one number. One added to the 44 characters produced in line 4020 equals 45 numbers, thus, CA(45).

```
4070  STORE CA
```

Line 4070 stores the real array, CA, on tape. The subscript of the array is not indicated when STORE is used. This stores all 45 values from each record.

```
4080  NEXT J
```

Line 4080 ends the J loop. In this loop, when one record is converted to a numeric array and stored, the next record is processed. This processing continues until all five records have been stored.

But returning to line 1, we see that CL holds the length of DA$ (name) before it is padded. DA$(1000) can contain 1000 records stored in DA$.

```
10 SP$ = "          " : SP$= SP$ + SP$ + SP$ - SP$
```

Line 10 contains the string that pads DA$ (name) to 30 characters. SP$ originally contained 10 blank spaces. SP$ concatenated contains 30 blank spaces. SP$ is used in the subroutine 10010 through 10070, partially shown below.

```
10060  DA$(CH(0)+1) = DA$(CH(0)+1)+LEFT$(SP$, 30-CL(CH(0)+1))
```

30 SPACES

LENGTH OF DA$ (name) RECORD BEING BUILT

```
10070  RETURN
```

Going back to line 15, we see

```
15 DC$ = "713"
```

which is the area code of Beaumont, Texas. The default area code is used to save input time. The area code can be input directly, or the default area code can be input by typing a comma followed by the phone number. The default area code can be easily changed to any area code.

```
10100  IF LEN (AC$) = 0 THEN AC$ = DC$
```

In line 10100, we see that the comma input works successfully because everything before the comma is put in AC$ and everything after the comma goes into PN$.

Lines 20 through 90 present the PHONE LISTING menu that asks the user to make a selection before proceeding. Based on that selection, the computer goes to different parts of the program. Line 80 tells the computer to where it must branch: to line 1000 if item 1 (line 30) is selected, to line 2000 if item 2 (line 40) is selected, to line 3000 if item 3 (line 50) is selected, and to line 4000 if item 4 (line 60) is selected.

Lines 1000 through 1060, selected by item 1 of the PHONE LISTING menu, make up the FILE MAINTENANCE menu. If item 1 of the *new* menu is selected (items from the FILE MAINTENANCE menu are selected when the computer reaches line 1040), the program jumps to line 1100 to load tape into memory. We assume for the purposes of this explanation that the user has prepared a tape containing names and phone numbers.

Let's follow this path of the program to line 1100. After the tape is loaded, line 1110, RECALL CH, obtains however many records from tape that CH designates. We set that number to 5 earlier in line 4010.

```
1120  IF CH(0) = 0 THEN PRINT "THERE IS NO ARRAY ON TAPE" : GOTO 1000
```

Line 1120 tells us if there are no records on the tape to be recalled.

```
1130  FOR J = 1 TO CH(0)
```

Line 1130 is the beginning of the loop to load the records into memory.

```
1140  RECALL CA
```

In Line 1140, RECALL CA retrieves a real array which has been stored on tape. Subscripts are not used with STORE or RECALL.

```
1150  DA$ = " " : FOR K = 1 TO 44 : DA$(J) = DA$(J) + CHR$(CA(K)) :
      NEXT K : CL(J) = CA(45) : NEXT J
```

DA$ = " " sets DA$ to a null value. There are no characters in DA$. It is just initialized for later use. FOR K = 1 TO 44 sets the number of characters to be retrieved and converted from a numeric array to a string array.

DA$ = DA$ + CHR$(CA(K)) converts the numeric arrays stored on tape to string arrays used within the program.

NEXT K completes the loop and CL(J) = CA(45) completes the transfer from tape to RAM by adding the length of DA$ before it is padded with spaces.

NEXT J is the end of the loop and processes until all five records have been loaded into memory.

If we had picked item 2 of the FILE MAINTENANCE menu (line 1020), the program would have branched to line 1200.

```
1200  HOME : VT = 6; GOSUB 10010
```

In line 1200, HOME clears the screen. VT = 6 sets the vertical tab value that is used in the subroutine beginning at 10010.

```
10010  VTAB VT : CALL -958 : VTAB VT : PRINT "ENTER NAME (LESS THAN 31
       CHARACTERS)"
```

In line 10010, VTAB VT (tabs to line 6 on the screen). CALL −958 is a machine language call that clears the screen below the cursor.

```
10020  INPUT DA$(CH(0)+1)
```

Line 10020 allows the name to be input into a specific record number.

```
10030  CL(CH(0)+1) = LEN(DA$(CH(0)+1)) : IF CL(CH(0)+1) = 0 THEN RETURN
```

Line 10030 stores the length of DA$ for the current record being built. This is held in CL array of the next position available (indicated by the +1 added to CH(0)). The second part of line 10030, IF CL(CH(0)+1) = 0 THEN 1000, checks to see if no record is input. If there is no record input, the program branches to line 1000. Line 10020 is related to line 10030.

```
10040  IF CL(CH(0)+1) > 30 THEN PRINT : PRINT "NAME IS TOO LONG"
       CHR$(7) : FOR J = 1 TO 1000 : GOTO 10010
```

DA$ (name) can be a total of 30 characters. If the length of the name string is over 30 characters it is disallowed because the file is not designed to hold over 30 characters in the name part of DA$.

The pause loop FOR J = 1 TO 1000 delays for the count of 1000. CHR$(7) rings a bell on the computer to attract the user's attention and GOTO 10010 causes the program to jump to 10010 to input a name of 30 characters or less. If the DA$ is a correct entry, the program RETURNS to line 1260, which merely changes the value of VT and begins another subroutine.

```
1260   VT = 12 : GOSUB 10080
10080  VTAB VT : PRINT "ENTER AREA CODE, PHONE NO."
10090  INPUT AC$, PN$
```

Line 10090 allows the area code and the phone number to be input.

```
10100  IF LEN(AC$) = 0 THEN AC$ = DC$
```

The input format is AC$,PN$. If there is no input into AC$ (a comma is the first character typed), line 10100 is true and the AC$ = DC$, which is the area code 713.

```
10110  IF LEN(AC$)<>3 OR LEN(PN$)<>7 THEN 10080
```

In line 10110, if the area code is not three characters or the phone number is not seven characters, then the computer goes to line 10080 for the correct input.

```
10120  TC$ = STR$ (VAL(AC$)):PT$ = STR$(VAL(PN$)); IF T C$<>AC$ OR PT$
       <>PN$ THEN PRINT : PRINT "PLEASE USE NUMERICS"; CHR$(7): FOR J
       = 1 TO 1000: NEXT J: GOTO 10080
```

Line 10120 converts the string arrays to numeric arrays as a further check that the area code and the phone number are numerics. TC$ = STR$(VAL(AC$)) converts the area code string to a numeric value and that value is reconverted to a string. PT$ = STR$(VAL (PN$)) converts the phone number string to a numeric value and that value is reconverted to a string. IF TC$<>AC$ OR PT$<>PN$ THEN PRINT : PRINT "PLEASE USE NUMERICS" is a check to determine that the area code string and the phone number string have been input incorrectly. CHR$(7) rings the bell. The pause loop is activated and the program branches to line 10080 for the correct input. If the input is correct, the program returns to line 1310 to concatenate the name, area code, and phone number into a single string array, DA$.

```
1310  DA$(CH(0)+1) = DA$(CH(0)+1)+"(" + TC$ + ") − " + LEFT$(PT$,3)
      + "−" + RIGHT$(PT$,4).
```

This translates to:

```
JOHN SMITHXXXXXXXXXXXXXXXXXXXX          30 CHARACTERS
(713) − 688 − 1212                      14 CHARACTERS.
```

```
1320  PRINT : GOSUB 10000
```

Line 1320 causes the record entered to be printed on the screen by the subroutine at line 10000. A sample output is shown below:

```
NAMEX=XXJOHN SMITH
PHONEX#=X(713) - 688 - 1212
```

```
1330  PRINT : INPUT "ENTER 'R' TO REENTER ELSE 'RETURN' ";Q$: IF Q$<>"R"
      THEN CH(0) = CH(0)+1.
```

In line 1330, IF Q$<>"R", then the record count is incremented and a new record may be entered. IF "R" has been input, the next record input is placed over the last record entered. The program then goes to line 1200.

```
1210  IF CL(CH(0)+1) = 0 THEN 1000
```

In line 1210, if no record is input and RETURN is pressed in the subroutine at 10010, line 1210 is true and the program branches to line 1000, the FILE MAINTENANCE menu.

If selection #3 is chosen in the menu, the program jumps to line 1400 to sort the list in alphabetical order using the full name as the key.

```
1410  IF CH(0) < 2 THEN RETURN
```

Line 1410 says, if there is only one record, there is no need to sort the list.

Lines 1420 through 1480 perform the sort routine. In this example, there are five records in the list (Fig. 24-4A). The five records E, D, C, B, A represent a list of names, area codes, and telephone numbers. Fig. 24-4B shows the details of program lines 1420, 1430, 1440, 1450, 1460, and 1480. The details of the exchange produced by line 1470 are shown in Fig. 24-4D. The number of records in the list is CH(0) = 5.

```
1420  FOR J = 1 TO CH(0) -1
```

Line 1420 determines the maximum number of passes through five records to order the list. This list took only two passes to order.

```
1430  M = J : FOR K = J+1 TO CH(0)
```

In line 1430, the K variable begins at the second record in the list. If J and K both started at the same record, the same record would be compared to itself and this would be a useless comparison.

```
1440  IF LEFT$(DA$(K), 30) < LEFT$(DA$(M), 30) THEN M = K
```

Line 1440 compares the position of the records in the list. If record K is less than record M, then the value of K is stored in M (Fig. 24-4B). This comparison continues K times.

```
1460  IF M = J THEN 1480
```

If 1460 is true, the records for a specific pass in the list are in the correct order and no exchange is made. If 1460 is false, the program defaults to line 1470 to exchange the records on the list. In a sort, all items out of order must be exchanged. The DA$'s are ordered by exchanging records that are out of position.

```
1480   NEXT J
```

Line 1480 processes the next record on the list.

```
1490   RETURN
```

Line 1490 returns the program to the second statement in line 1400, which is GOTO 20. GOTO 20 causes the program to jump to the PHONE LISTING main menu.

```
40   VTAB 12 : HTAB 8 : PRINT "2.MODIFY/DELETE"
```

Selection #2 of the main menu (line 40) causes a jump to line 2000 to modify or delete records in the list.

```
2000   HOME : VTAB 4 : IF CH(0) = 0 THEN PRINT "THERE IS NO LIST";
       CHR$(7) : FOR J = 1 TO 2000 : NEXT J : GOTO 20
```

If CH(0) = 0, there are zero records in the list and there is no list.

```
2010   PRINT "ENTER NAME TO BE CHANGED" : PRINT : INPUT NA$
2020   IF LEN(NA$) = 0 THEN 20
```

If the length of the name string is zero, the program branches to the main menu.

```
2030   FOR K = 1 TO CH(0)
```

Line 2030 sets the beginning of the loop to process each record on the list.

```
2040   IF NA$<>LEFT$(DA$(K), CL(K)) THEN 2060
```

If the name string that was input does not match any name on the list then the computer goes to line 2060.

```
2060   NEXT K : VTAB 10: HTAB 6 : PRINT "THIS NAME IS NOT ON THE LIST" :
       PRINT CHR$(7) : FOR J = 1 TO 1000 : NEXT J : GOTO 2000
```

If line 2040 is false, the program defaults to line 2100.

```
2100   CH(1) = CH(0) : CH(0) = K -1: VTAB 6 : PRINT "CURRENT RECORD IS "
       : PRINT
```

CH(1) = CH(0) stores the value of the 5 records in the list in CH(1) for temporary storage. CH(0) = K −1 stores the value of the record to be changed. Each time the loop executes, it is incremented by one greater than the loop value. K −1 decrements the loop value to correspond to the number of records on the list.

GOSUB 10000 prints the current record on the screen.

```
2110  VTAB 8 : GOSUB 10000 : PRINT : "ENTER 'C' TO CHANGE, 'D' TO
      DELETE" : PRINT : INPUT "ELSE 'RETURN' ?";Q$
```

Line 2110 sets up the record to be modified, prints the heading to change or delete the record, and requests the user input.

```
2120  IF Q$<>"C" AND Q$<>"D" THEN 2240
```

If "C" is not pressed, and "D" is not pressed, and RETURN is pressed, the program branches to line 2240 to reestablish the list in the correct order. Line 2300 causes the list to be sorted in alphabetical order and then makes the program jump to line 20 of the PHONE LISTING menu.

```
2125  IF Q$ = "D" THEN DA$(K) = "DELETE" + LEFT$(SP$,24) + "(000) - 000
      - 0000" : GOTO 2230
```

If "D" is entered, the program jumps to line 2230 to reset the value of the list into CH(0), and print "ANY MORE CORRECTIONS (Y OR N) ?".

```
2230  CH(0) = CH(1) : PRINT : INPUT "ANY MORE CORRECTIONS (Y OR N)
      ?" ;Q$ : IF Q$ = "Y" THEN 2000
```

If there are no more corrections, the program defaults to line 2240 to the delete routine (Fig. 24-5).

```
2240  K = 0 : FOR J = 1 TO CH(0)
2250  IF LEFT$(DA$(J),6) = "DELETE" THEN 2280
2260  K = K + 1 : IF K = J THEN 2280
```

If 2250 is false, line 2260, K = K + 1, increments the value of K to accommodate the record. IF K = J THEN 2280 is false, the record is stored in DA$(K), (DA$(K) = DA$(J) and the length of the record CL(K) is also stored (CL(K) = CL(J). This transfer places the record in K.

Records are taken from DA$(J) and placed in DA$(K) unless they are equal to "DELETE". If K = J, no action is taken because the record DA$(J) = DA$(K) and the records are not moved. Each time a DELETE record is encountered, J is incremented but K remains the same. As an example (Fig. 24-5), if the third record is DELETE, then when the fourth record is processed, K is still equal to 3, but J = 4. DA$(4) is then moved into DA$(3). If 2250 is true, K remains the same value for the next loop execution. The next record is placed over the deleted record.

```
2230  GOSUB 1410 : GOTO 20
```

Line 2230 causes the program to sort the list and jump to the PHONE LISTING menu.

Going back to line 2120, if the statement IF Q$<>"C" is true, the program defaults to line 2130.

```
2130  VTAB 12 : CALL -958 : VTAB 12 : PRINT "ENTER 'N'-NAME, 'P'-PHONE#,
      'B'-BOTH" : PRINT
```

CALL −958 is a machine call that clears the screen below the cursor at VTAB 12. The name and phone number headings are printed, and remain on the screen as a prompt during the changes. The program defaults to line 2140 to store the area code and phone number in T$, and requests a letter input from the user.

```
2140  T$ = RIGHT$(DA$(K),14) : INPUT "LETTER PLEASE ?;C$ : IF C$<>"N"
      AND C$<>"P" AND C$<>"B" THEN 2130
```

If the letter input is "B", the program defaults to line 2150, which is, IF C$ = "P" THEN 2170. Since the letter "B" is input, this makes line 2150 false, and the program defaults to line 2160.

```
2160  VT = 14 : GOSUB 10010
```

Line 2160 sets the VTAB variable to line 14 and the subroutine at 10010 asks for the name change to be input. The subroutine returns to line 2170.

```
2170  IF C$ = "N" THEN 2190
```

The letter "B" was input and this makes line 2170 false, and the program defaults to line 2180.

```
2180  VT = 16 : GOSUB 10080
```

The subroutine at 10080 asks the user to input the new telephone number.

The "B" for both name and phone number is not written into the program routine. "B" is a default when "N" or "P" is not input. Remember the cliche about cutting a log in two places to get three sticks of wood? This example demonstrates the use of the default value in programming. "B" was the selection, but "B" was not written into the program. Another point to be reenforced is, when an IF statement is true, all following statements on that line are executed. When an IF statement is false, no following statements on that line are executed.

In line 2140, the user inputs the letter "N" for a name change. The program defaults to line 2150.

```
2150  IF C$ = "P" THEN 2170
```

The letter "N" was input, so line 2150 is false and the program defaults to line 2160.

```
2160  VT = 14 : GOSUB 10010
```

The subroutine at 10010 asks for the name change to be input.

The subroutine at 10010 returns to line 2170.

```
2170  IF C$ = "N" THEN DA$(K) = DA$(K) + T$ : GOTO 2230
```

The name change is concatenated to the area code and the phone number stored in T$. Line 2230 sets CH(0) = CH(1) and asks for more corrections. If there are no more corrections, the number of records in the list is stored in CH(0), the list is sorted, and the program jumps to the PHONE LISTING menu.

If the user inputs the letter "P" in line 2140, the program defaults to line 2150.

```
2150  IF C$ = "P" THEN 2170
```

The letter "P" is input. Line 2150 is true, so the program branches to line 2170.

```
2170  IF C$ = "N" THEN 2190
```

The letter "P" was input. Line 2170 is false. The program defaults to line 2180.

```
2180  VT = 16 : GOSUB 10080
```

GOSUB 10080 allows input of the phone number to be changed and returns to line 2190.

```
2190  IF C$ = "N" THEN DA$(K) = DA$(K) + T$ : GOTO 2230
```

The letter "P" was input, so line 2190 is false and the statement GOTO 2230 is not executed. The program defaults to line 2200.

```
2200  IF C$ = "P" THEN DA$(K) = LEFT$(DA$(K),30)
```

Line 2200 is true and sets up DA$(K) so it contains the name in the specific record. The program defaults to line 2220 to concatenate the name and new phone number into DA$(K).

```
2220  DA$(K) = DA$(K) + "(" + TC$ + ")-"
      + LEFT$(PT$,3) + RIGHT$(PT$,4)
```

The program defaults to line 2230 to ask for more corrections. If there are no more corrections, the program defaults to line 2300.

```
2300  GOSUB 1410 : GOTO 20
```

GOSUB 1410 sorts the list, and GOTO 20 causes the program to jump to the PHONE LISTING menu.

Entry 3 in the PHONE LISTING menu is "3.LIST/SEARCH". This selection causes the program to jump to line 3000.

```
3000  HOME : VTAB 3 : INPUT "ENTER 'S' TO SEARCH OR 'L' TO LIST ?";Q$ :
      IF Q$<>"L" AND Q$<>"S" THEN 3000.
3010  IF Q$ = "S" THEN 3100
```

The user typed in the letter "L" to list the records. Line 3010 is false, so the program defaults to line 3030, the next line.

```
3030  FOR J = 1 TO CH(0)
```

Line 3030 is the beginning of a loop to process the records in the list.

```
3040  IF J<>INT((J-1)/5)*5+1 THEN 3070
3050  IF J<>1 THEN PRINT : INPUT "!";Q$
```

Lines 3040 and 3050 use negative logic and are both related (Fig. 24-6). On the first pass of the loop, line 3040 is false and the program

```
3040  IF J<>INT((J-1)/5)*5+1 THEN 3070
3050  IF J<>1 THEN PRINT : INPUT "!";Q$
```

J	J−1	INT((J−1)/5)	INT((J−1)/5)*5+1	3040	GOES TO	3050	ACTION OF 3050
1	0	0	1	FALSE	3050	FALSE	GOES TO 3060 PRINTS RECORD #1
2	1	0	1	TRUE	3070		PRINTS RECORD #2
3	2	0	1	TRUE	3070		PRINTS RECORD #3
4	3	0	1	TRUE	3070		PRINTS RECORD #4
5	4	0	1	TRUE	3070		PRINTS RECORD #5
6	5	1	6	FALSE	3050	TRUE	INPUTS "!";Q$ PRESS RETURN TO CONTINUE PRINTS RECORD #6
7	6	1	6	TRUE	3070		PRINTS RECORD #7
8	7	1	6	TRUE	3070		PRINTS RECORD #8
9	8	1	6	TRUE	3070		PRINTS RECORD #9

Fig. 24-6. Relationship of lines 3040 and 3050.

defaults to line 3050. On the first loop pass J = 1, so line 3050 is false and defaults to line 3060, to clear the screen and VTAB 3.

```
3060  HOME : VTAB 3

3070  PRINT "NAME" = ";LEFT$(DA$(J),30) : PRINT SPC(7);"PHONE # = ";
      RIGHT$(DA$(J),14) : PRINT
```

Line 3070 is executed and prints the first record. On loop executions 2, 3, 4, and 5, line 3040 is true, so the program branches to line 3070 to print records 2, 3, 4, and 5.

On the sixth loop execution line 3040 is false (6 = 6). The program defaults to line 3050 IF J<>1 THEN PRINT : INPUT "!"; Q$. On the sixth execution (6<>1), and line 3050 is true. The loop execution stops, "!" is printed, and the computer waits for the user to press RETURN to continue printing the list.

```
3080  NEXT J
```

Line 3080 completes the loop execution.

```
3090  PRINT: INPUT "!" ;Q$ : GOTO 20
```

Line 3090 stops the program. When the user presses RETURN, the program jumps to line 20, the PHONE LISTING menu.

Selection 3 on the PHONE LISTING menu "3.LIST/SEARCH" causes the program to jump to line 3000. If "S" for search is typed at line 3000, the program branches to line 3100 to begin the search.

```
3100  HOME : VTAB 3 : PRINT "SEARCH SELECTION" : PRINT
```

Line 3110 prints out the three selections.

```
1.NAME SEARCH
2.NUMBER SEARCH
3.RETURN TO MAIN MENU
```

Selection 1 causes the program to jump to line 3150 to begin the NAME search.

```
3150  HOME : VTAB 4 : PRINT "ENTER NAME OR FRAGMENT ?" : PRINT :
      INPUT NA$ : L = LEN(NA$) : IF L = 0 THEN 3100
```

The name search is processed in lines 3160 through 3220. For this example, variables are given specific values to make the learning easier.

NA$	"ABC"–SEARCH FOR ABC
L	LEN(NA$) = 3
DA$(J)	"EDABC"–THIS NAME IS SEARCHED
CL(J)	LENGTH OF DA$(J) IS 5 CHARACTERS
CO	COUNTING VARIABLE TO COUNT THE NUMBER OF MATCHES FOUND IN THE LIST
CH(0)	CH(0) = 7–THERE ARE 7 RECORDS IN THE LIST
FOR J = 1	TO CH(0) – FOR J = 1 TO 7
FOR K = 1	TO CL(J) – L + 1 – FOR K = 1 TO 3

Lines 3160 through 3220, using variables with specific values, are detailed in Fig. 24-7. Fig. 24-7 should be studied in detail to learn the name search routine. The record count is stored in a temporary location, CH(1). In line 3200, CH(0) = CH(1), the record count is

SPECIFIC VARIABLES USED FOR THE NAME SEARCH

NA$	**LEN(NA$)**	**DA$(J)**	**LEN(DA$(J))**	**# OF RECORDS**	**CL(J) − L + 1**
ABC	3	EDABC	5	7	3
				FOR J = 1 TO 7	FOR K = 1 TO 3

```
PROGRAM LINES 3160 - 3220 FOR NAME SEARCH
3160  CO = 0 : COUNTS THE NUMBER OF MATCHES IN THE LIST.
      FOR J = 1 TO CH(0) - FOR J = 1 TO 7
3170  FOR K = 1 TO CL(J) - L + 1 - FOR K = 1 TO 3
                IF NA$ < > MID$(DA$(J),    K, L)  THEN      3210
                    ABC                EDABC
          1st  PASS  ABC (TRUE)  < > EDA     1, 3 K=1, L=3  3210
          2nd  PASS  ABC (TRUE)  < > DAB     2, 3 K=2, L=3  3210
          3rd  PASS  ABC (FALSE) < > ABC     3, 3 K=3, L=3  3190
3190  CH(1) = CH(0)  7 = 7 - THE RECORD COUNT MUST BE STORED BEFORE
      THE GOSUB 10000 OR RECORD COUNT WILL BE WIPED OUT
      CH(0) = J - 1 - SEE Fig. 24-2 OR Fig. 24-3
      GOSUB 10000 - PRINTS OUT THE RECORD
      INPUT Q$ - STOPS THE PROGRAM - PRESS RETURN TO CONTINUE
3200  CH(0) = CH(1) 7 = 7 - CH(1) RESTORES THE RECORD COUNT TO CH(0)
      CO = CO + 1 - INCREMENTS THE COUNT TO DETERMINE IF A MATCH
      OCCURS MORE THAN ONCE IN THE LIST
      GOTO 3220 - PREVENTS THE SAME ITEM ON THE LIST FROM BEING
      MATCHED TWICE
3210  NEXT K
3220  NEXT J - SEARCHES THE NEXT RECORD
```

Fig. 24-7. Name search.

stored in CH(0). This step is necessary to preserve the record count. This storage process occurs before the GOSUB 10000, and after the GOSUB 10000. Fig. 24-7 should be more explanatory than comment.

If at line 3100, the user had input 2, "2.NUMBER SEARCH", the program would jump to line 3250 to search for a specific phone number.

```
3250  HOME : VTAB 6 : HTAB 6 : INPUT "ENTER AREA CODE,PHONE#
      ?";AC$,PN$
3260  IF LEN(AC$) = 0 THEN AC$ = DC$
```

Line 3260 allows the user to enter a comma for the area code, if the user wants the default area code of 713. The area code and the phone number are always the last 14 characters of DA$. The phone number for a specific record is RIGHT$(DA$(J),14).

```
3270  TC$ = "(" + AC$ + ")-" + LEFT$(PN$,3)
      + "-" + RIGHT$(PN$,4)
```

Line 3270 concatenates the area code and phone number in the proper format and stores it in the temporary string variable, TC$.

```
3280  FOR J = 1 TO CH(0)
```

Line 3280 sets up the loop that will list the area codes and phone numbers on the list.

```
3290  IF TC$<>RIGHT$(DA$(J),14) THEN 3310
```

All phone numbers are composed of 14 numeric characters located in the last 14 places in DA$. The TC$ was formatted in the same places in DA$ as RIGHT$(DA$(J),14), so the comparison is relatively simple. It is much simpler than the name search, though not nearly as flexible.

```
3300  CH(1) = CH(0) : CH(0) = J -1: GOSUB 10000 : PRINT : CH(0) = CH(1) :
      INPUT Q$ : PRINT
```

The record count is again stored in a temporary location, CH(1), so it will not be lost during the execution of the subroutine at line 10000. The subroutine prints out both the name, area code, and telephone number produced from the number search. On returning from the subroutine, the record count is again stored in CH(0) (CH(0) = CH(1)).

```
3310  NEXT J
```

Each record on the list is searched for the phone number in question and line 3320, GOTO 3100, causes the program to jump to the SEARCH SELECTION menu. Selection 3, "3.RETURN TO MAIN MENU", causes a jump to line 20, the PHONE LISTING menu. Selection 4, "4. SAVE LIST AND END", from the PHONE LISTING menu causes the program to end.

LESSON 25

Formulas

Lesson 25 contains three programs dealing with formulas for (1) decimal to hexadecimal conversion (Fig. 25-1), (2) hexadecimal to decimal conversion (Fig. 25-6), and (3) systematic and efficient output (Fig. 25-9).

"Formula" has many different meanings but a good definition is "the rule for doing something." A formula is a recipe or a prescription. Formulas have been used and demonstrated in almost every lesson of this book.

The computer, which understands only binary (1 and 0), must use a formula to convert binary input and output, which are in deci-

```
5    REM : DECIMAL TO HEXADECIMAL
10   HOME : VTAB 6
20   INPUT "ENTER DECIMAL INTEGER ?";DEC
30   IF DEC < 1 THEN END
40   DEC =  INT (DEC)
50   HEX = 0:HX$ = " "
60   FOR J = 0 TO 15: IF DEC < 16 ↑ J THEN 80
70   NEXT J: PRINT "THE NUMBER IS TOO LARGE" : PRINT : GOTO 20
80   FOR K = J - 1 TO 0 STEP  - 1
90   HEX =  INT (DEC / 16 ↑ K)
100  HX$ = HX$ +  CHR$ (HEX + 48 + (HEX > 9) * 7)
110  DEC = DEC - HEX * 16 ↑ K
120  NEXT K
130  PRINT : HTAB 9: PRINT "HEX DISPLAY IS ";HX$
140  PRINT : GOTO 20

]RUN
ENTER DECIMAL INTEGER ?863
HEX DISPLAY IS 35F
```

Fig. 25-1. Decimal to hexadecimal conversion program.

mal form. This formula is invisible to you because you won't see it on your program listing. The visible ones are the formulas *you* write. The invisible ones are the formulas that your computer needs to interpret your program. The invisible formulas reside in the Applesoft interpreter.

The most efficient way to use a formula in programming is to input the data in a variable. The variable or variables in the formula compute the data and output the information in a variable. In this way, the input data and the output information can be easily changed, and the program remains relatively constant.

In the first program (Fig. 25-1) decimal is converted to hexadecimal. In the second program, hexadecimal is converted to decimal. The conversion formulas encompass two important aspects of the Apple computer: (1) humans speak decimal and computers speak hexadecimal, before it is converted to binary, and (2) decimal contains numeric characters and hexadecimal contains alpha and numeric characters. In the conversion process, decimal is input as numerics and converted to string arrays. In converting hexadecimal to decimal, the hexadecimal is input as a string array and converted to numerics.

The decimal system uses a base of 10. The hexadecimal system uses a base of 16. The decimal figure 312 means

$$\begin{array}{rcr} 3 * 10^2 &=& 300 \\ +\ 1 * 10^1 &=& 10 \\ +\ 2 * 10^0 &=& \underline{2} \\ && 312 \end{array}$$

The hexadecimal system uses the decimal numbers from 0 to 9 as its first ten digits, and uses A = 10, B = 11, C = 12, D = 13, E = 14, and F = 15 as its last 5 digits (Fig. 25-2). The hexadecimal number 35F means

$$\begin{array}{rcr} 3 * 16^2 &=& 768 \\ +\ 5 * 16^1 &=& 80 \\ +\ F * 16^0 &=& \underline{15} \\ && 863 \end{array}$$

Fig. 25-3 shows the manual system for converting decimal to hexadecimal. Fig. 25-4 details the decimal to hex conversion program statements in relation to the manual conversion to hex. Figs. 25-2 and 25-3 should be studied closely before going to the conversion program.

Fig. 25-2 presents the relationship between the first 15 decimal numbers and the first 15 hexadecimal numbers.

Fig. 25-3 shows the ASCII numerics and the character strings they represent. Conversion of string arrays to numeric arrays and conver-

HEXADECIMAL	DECIMAL
0	0
1	1
2	2
3	3
4	4
5	5
6	6
7	7
8	8
9	9
A	10
B	11
C	12
D	13
E	14
F	15

Fig. 25-2. Comparing first sixteen hexadecimal and decimal digits.

ASC	CHR$
48	0
49	1
50	2
51	3
52	4
53	5
54	6
55	7
56	8
57	9
58	:
59	;
60	<
61	=
62	>
63	?
64	@
65	A
66	B
67	C
68	D
69	E
70	F
90	Z

CONVERSION OF A NUMERIC ARRAY TO A STRING ARRAY
ASC(65) = A

CONVERSION OF A NUMERIC ARRAY TO A STRING ARRAY
CHR$(A) = 65

Fig. 25-3. ASCII characters.

sion of numeric arrays to string arrays were discussed in Lesson 5. The sequence of ASCII characters for ten numerics and 26 alpha characters goes from 48 through 90. The character strings represented by the ASCII characters run from zero to zerba (Z). Between the numeric and the alpha characters is an intervening group of

NUMBER IN DECIMAL	DIVIDE BY	QUOTIENT	REMAINDER IN DECIMAL	REMAINDER IN HEXADECIMAL
863	863/16	53	15	F
	53/16	3	5	5
	3/16	0	3	3

3 5 F

Fig. 25-4. Manual system for decimal to hexadecimal conversion.

characters (58 – 64) that interrupt the chain of continuity. This interruption is very important to understand. It is programmed in line 100 of Fig. 25-1. The hexadecimal number is converted into a string array to accommodate both the alpha and numeric characters.

```
100  HX$ = HX$ + CHR$(HEX + 48 + (HEX > 9)*7)
```

The ASCII number 48 represents the string character zero (0).

If the ASCII characters were set so 48 through 59 represented zero to 9, and ASCII 60 through 86 represented A through Z, there would be no need for the logical expression, (HEX > 9)*7), in line 100. Since ASCII 59 through 64 interrupt the continuity of the numeric and alpha characters, "+48" is necessary to establish base zero for the character string. The "+48" corrects for the offset of the ASCII values.

Line 100 converts in this manner: (HEX > 9)*7) is a logical expression used as a bridge between ASCII 48 to 59 (0 – 9), and ASCII 65 to 90 (A to Z). When HEX is less than 9, the expression is false or zero. Zero times 7 = 0. If HEX is greater than 9, the expression is true or 1. One times 7 = 7. The following example shows how line 100 works:

```
HEX = 6
HX$ = HX$ + CHR$(6 + 48 + 0) = CHR$(54)
CHR$(54) = "6"

HEX = 14
HX$ = HX$ + CHR$(14 + 48 + (1*7)) = CHR$(69)
CHR$(69) = "E"
```

In line 50 we see HX$ = " ". This means HX$ is initialized as a null string.

Fig. 25-5 shows three loop executions by each program statement involved in converting decimal 863 to hexadecimal 35F. This was done to show how the individual loop executions compared with the manual conversion.

The formulas in program 2 (Fig. 25-6) convert hexadecimal to decimal. Since hexadecimal may contain both alpha and numeric characters (Fig. 25-2), it is input in a string array. The string array

20	INPUT "ENTER DECIMAL INTEGER ?";DEC	863
30	IF DEC < 1 THEN END	
40	DEC = INT(DEC)	If a real number is input, this statement converts it to an integer.
50	HEX = 0 : HX$ = " "	Initializes variables. HX$ is a null string with no characters.
60	FOR J = 0 TO 15 : IF DEC < 16 ∧ J THEN 80	Numbers larger than $1.15*10^{18}$ will not be accepted.
70	NEXT J : PRINT " THE NUMBER IS TOO LARGE"	Sets up the position of DEC − 863 = 16^3
80	FOR K = J−1 TO 0 STEP −1	The largest power is divided 1st. When the J loop checks the size of DEC, J is 1 more than the greatest power when J jumps out of the loop. J−1 is the offset for the correct power. K sets up positional values.
90	HEX = INT(DEC/16 ∧ K)	Divides DEC by the positional value to give the HEX value. 1. INT(DEC/16^2) = 863/16^2 = HEX 3 R95 2. INT(DEC/16^1) = 95/16^1 = HEX 5 R15 3. INT(DEC/16^0) = 15/16^0 = HEX F (15)
100	HX$ = HX$+CHR$(HEX+48+(HEX > 9) *7)	1. 15+48+(1*7)=70 ASC(70) = F 2. 5+48+(0*7)=53 ASC(53) = 5 3. 3+48+(0*7)=51 ASC(51) = 3
110	DEC = DEC − HEX*16∧ K	1. DEC = 863 − HEX(3)*16^2 = 768 2. DEC = 95 − HEX(5)*16^1 = 80 3. DEC = 15 − HEX(15)*16^0= 15
120	NEXT K	
130	PRINT "HEX DISPLAY IS ";HX$	35F

Fig. 25-5. Decimal to hex conversion program statements as related to manual conversion to hex.

is converted into a numeric variable to print out the decimal number. The hexadecimal number, 35F, is input and converted to decimal 863. The program statements and manual conversion comparisons are detailed in Fig. 25-8. The three loop executions are included with each involved program statement to view the change in computation.

The hexadecimal value is input as a string array in line 10.

```
10    INPUT "ENTER HEX VALUE ?";Q$
```

Line 40 converts the hex input string array (Q$) into a numeric variable by the ASC function. In conjunction with the loop beginning at line 30, line 40 processes the characters one at a time.

J = 1 : HEX = 3 CHR$(51)
J = 2 : HEX = 5 CHR$(53)
J = 3 : HEX = F CHR$(70)

```
1    REM : HEXADECIMAL TO DECIMAL
5    HOME : VTAB 6
10   INPUT "ENTER HEX VALUE T";Q$
20   IF LEN (Q$) = 0 THEN END
30   DEC = 0: FOR J = 1 TO LEN (Q$)
40   HX = ASC ( MID$ (Q$,J,1)): IF (HX > 47 AND HX < 58) OR (HX > 64
     AND HX < 71) THEN DEC = DEC * 16 + HX - 48 - (HX > 58) * 7
50   NEXT J
60   PRINT : PRINT "DEC = ";DEC: PRINT
70   GOTO 10

]RUN
ENTER HEX VALUE ?35F
DEC = 863
```

Fig. 25-6. Hexadecimal to decimal conversion program.

HEXADECIMAL NUMBER	POSITIONAL VALUE	MULTIPLY BY
35F	F * 16^0	F * 1 = 15
	5 * 16^1	5 * 16 = 80
	3 * 16^2	3 * 256 = 768
		863

Fig. 25-7. Manual system for hexadecimal to decimal conversion.

If the hexadecimal character is a numeric it must be between 48 and 58. If the hexadecimal character is an alpha character it must be between 65 and 70.

The statement THEN DEC = DEC * 16 + HX − 48 − (HX > 58) * 7) is similar to the summing statement DEC = DEC + HX. This statement converts from hexadecimal display input to an actual numeric number (Fig. 25-8) in that it takes the sum of the computed DEC and adds it to DEC on each loop execution. An input display string can be converted to an actual numeric number and display the numeric number because of machine design or configuration.

Line 50 is the end of the loop, and line 60 displays the numeric number that has been converted from hexadecimal input.

```
60   PRINT "DEC = ";DEC
```

Line 70 gives the user a chance to input another hexadecimal number.

The formulas in program number three (Fig. 25-9) produce systematic and efficient output and are applied to a statistical problem.

The statistical problem inputs student grades. The grades are output in seventeen different ranges. The grades are used to produce an ogive of cumulative distribution.

The definition of cumulative distribution is "heaped up," or "growing in amount."

Program statement	Manual conversion
5 HOME : VTAB 5	
10 INPUT "ENTER HEX VALUE ?";Q$	35F — HEX is input in a string array. It may contain alpha and numeric characters.
20 IF LEN(Q$) = 0 THEN END	
30 DEC = 0 : FOR J = 1 TO LEN(Q$)	Initialized DEC to zero. Sets up loop to check each character.
40 HX = ASC(MID$(Q$,J,1)) : IF (HX > 47 AND HX < 58) OR (HX > 64 AND HX < 71) THEN DEC = DEC*16+HX−48−(HX > 58)*7 1. DEC=0*16+51−48−(51 > 58) =3 DEC=3 (0 * 7) 2. DEC=3*16+48−53−(53 > 58) =53 DEC=53 (0 * 7) 3. DEC=53*16=848+70−48− (70 > 58) **DEC = 863** (1 * 7)	Converts the string array to a numeric array one character at the time. Picks off the 1st, 2nd, and 3rd character. ASC numerics 48 — 58 represent the numbers zero to 9. ASC numbers 64 — 71 represent the letters A — F, Fig. 25-3. Positional value 35F 16^0 * 15 = 15 16^1 * 5 = 80 16^2 * 3 = 768 863
50 NEXT J	
60 PRINT : PRINT "DEC = ";DEC	DEC = 863
70 GOTO 10	

Fig. 25-8. Comparing program statements and manual conversion.

Ogive is a distribution curve or graph in which the frequencies are cumulative.

The educator takes the 80 student grades, places them in 17 ranges of varying widths, adds the number of grades in each range, and plots them on a graph (Fig. 25-10).

The program in Fig. 25-9 uses a RND function to produce the 80 grades. The grades are placed in ranges by a formula and the ranges are computed by a formula. A formula is used to break the printout into a heading and five ranges, then the printout continues. The ogive is produced by hand to demonstrate the use of the output. In Lesson 27, LOW RESOLUTION GRAPHICS, the ogive is produced by a graphics program. One point to note—since the grades are produced by the RND function, *NO TWO PROGRAM RUNS OR GRAPHS WILL BE THE SAME*. The ogive does not pattern itself in the manner of the standard distribution curve.

Line 10 provides dimensions for 17 grade ranges.

```
5    REM : OGIVE PROGRAM
10   HOME
20   DIM CG(17)
30   GOSUB 800
40   T = 0: FOR J = 1 TO 17
50   IF J < > INT ((J - 1) / 5) * 5 + 1 THEN 80
60   IF J < > 1 THEN PRINT "OGIVE COUNT=";T;" OF 80 =";T / 80;"%":
     INPUT "!";Q$
70   PRINT "RANGE #  BASE  TOP  COUNT"
80   R = J: GOSUB 900:UL = RL:R = J - 1: GOSUB 900:LL
     = RL + 1: IF LL = 1 THEN LL = 0
90   PRINT SPC( 3);J;: HTAB 13: PRINT LL;: HTAB 20: PRINT UL;: HTAB 30:
     PRINT CG(J)
100  T = T + CG(J): NEXT J
110  PRINT "OGIVE COUNT=";T;" OF 80 =";T / 80;"%"
120  END
800  FOR J = 1 TO 80:SG = INT ( RND(1.0) * 101): IF SG = 0 THEN
     SG = 1
810  IF SG > 32 THEN 830
820  CG((SG - 1) / 16 + 1) = CG((SG - 1) / 16 + 1) + 1: GOTO 880
830  IF SG > 64 THEN 850
840  CG(3 + (SG - 33) / 8) = CG(3 + (SG - 33) / 8) + 1:: GOTO 880
850  IF SG > 92 THEN 870
860  CG(7 + (SG - 65) / 4) = CG(7 + (SG - 65) / 4) + 1:: GOTO 880
870  CG(14 + (SG - 93) / 2) = CG(14 + (SG - 93) / 2) + 1
880  NEXT J: RETURN
900  RL = R * 16 - (R > 2) * (R - 2) * 8 - (R > 6)
     * (R - 6) * 4 - (R > 13) * (R - 13)
     * 2
910  RETURN

]RUN
RANGE #      BASE     TOP     COUNT
   1           0       16       11
   2          17       32       11
   3          33       40        4
   4          41       48        9
   5          49       56        5
OGIVE COUNT=40 OF 80 =.5%
!
RANGE #      BASE     TOP     COUNT
   6          57       64        6
   7          65       68        3
   8          69       72        3
   9          73       76        5
   10         77       80        3
OGIVE COUNT=60 OF 80 =.75%
!
RANGE #      BASE     TOP     COUNT
   11         81       84        4
   12         85       88        2
   13         89       92        7
   14         93       94        2
```

Fig. 25-9. OGIVE program.

```
    15           95          96          1
OGIVE COUNT=76 OF 80 =.95%
I
RANGE #         BASE        TOP        COUNT
    16           97          98          2
    17           99          100         2
OGIVE COUNT=80 OF 80 =1%
```

Fig. 25-9. (Cont) OGIVE program.

Line 30 branches to the subroutine at 800, which produces the 80 student grades. Lines 810 through 880 place them in the proper range.

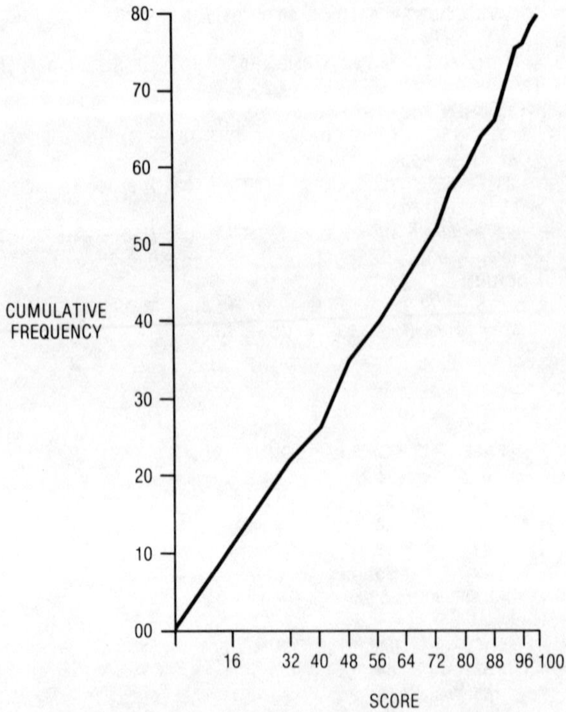

Fig. 25-10. Ogive of the distribution of 80 scores.

In line 800, FOR J = 1 TO 80 is the beginning of a loop to produce the 80 student grades. SG = INT (RND(1.0) * 101) produces student grades from 0 to 100. The purpose of IF SG = 0 THEN SG = 1 is as follows: If the RND function produces a student grade of zero, the grade has to be modified to fit the program pattern. The grade ranges have no place for a grade of zero, so a zero grade is replaced with a grade of one.

Lines 810, 830, and 850 set up to divide the ranges into four divisions, (1) two ranges containing 16 score points each, (2) four ranges containing 8 score points each, (3) six ranges containing 4 score points each, and (4) four ranges containing 2 score points each (Figs. 25-11 and 25-12).

J	LL(BASE)	UL(TOP)	SPREAD	NO. OF RANGES
1	0	16	16	2
2	17	32	16	
3	33	40	8	4
4	41	48	8	
5	49	56	8	
6	57	64	8	
7	65	68	4	7
8	69	72	4	
9	73	76	4	
10	77	80	4	
11	81	84	4	
12	85	88	4	
13	89	92	4	
14	93	94	2	4
15	95	96	2	
16	97	98	2	
17	99	100	2	

Fig. 25-11. Ranges and score points.

```
810  IF SG > 32 THEN 830    (handles grades from 1 to 32)
830  IF SG > 64 THEN 850    (handles grades from 33 to 64)
850  IF SG > 92 THEN 870    (handles grades from 65 to 92 if the statement is false,
                            and grades from 93 to 100 if the statement is true)
```

If line 810, IF SG > 32 THEN 830, is false the program defaults to line 820 to tabulate the grades in the first two grade ranges from zero to 32.

```
820  CG((SG-1)/16 + 1) = CG((SG-1)/16 + 1) + 1 : GOTO 880
```

The summing statement in line 820, CG((SG–1)/16 + 1) = CG((SG–1)/16 + 1) + 1, sums the number of student grades in each of the first two grade ranges (Fig. 25-12).

There are statements similar to the statement in line 820 at lines 840, 860, and 870. These statements compute and total the number of student grades in each grade range (Fig. 25-12).

```
830  IF SG > 64 THEN 850
```

If line 830 is false, line 840 increments the number of grades in the proper grade range from 33 to 64 (Fig. 25-12).

```
850  IF SG > 92 THEN 870
```

```
810  IF SG > 32 THEN 830
820  CG((SG-1)/16+1) = CG((SG-1)/16+1)+1 : GOTO 880
            GRADE    (SG-?)    CG((SG-?)/ ?+?
              1         0             1
             17        16             2
             32        31             2
830  IF SG > 64 THEN 850
840  CG(3+(SG-33)/8) = CG(3+(SG-33)/8)+1 : GOTO 880
             33         0             3
             41         8             4
             49        16             5
             57        24             6
             64        31             6
850  IF SG > 92 THEN 870
860  CG(7+(SG-65)/4) = CG(7+(SG-65)/4+1 : GOTO 880
             65         0             7
             69         4             8
             73         8             9
             77        12            10
             81        16            11
             85        20            12
             89        24            13
             92        27            13
870  CG(14+(SG-93)/2) = CG(14+(SG-93)/2+1
             93         0            14
             95         2            15
             97         4            16
             99         6            17
            100         7            17
```

Fig. 25-12. Grades and ranges.

If line 850 is false, line 860 increments the number of grades in the proper grade range from 65 to 92. If line 850 is true, line 870 increments the number of grades in the proper grade range from 93 to 100 (Fig. 25-12).

```
880  NEXT J : RETURN
```

NEXT J completes the loop to input 80 student grades and to place them in the proper range limit, and RETURN causes the subroutine to return to line 40.

```
40   T = 0 : FOR J = 1 TO 17
```

The totaling variable is initialized to zero, and the 17 grade ranges are placed in a loop structure for processing.

```
50   IF J <> INT((J-1)/5)*5 + 1 THEN 80
60   IF J <> 1 THEN PRINT "OGIVE COUNT = ";T/80; "%" : INPUT Q$
```

Lines 50 and 60 control the printout. The printout changes its routine after every 5 lines. The details of the printout can be viewed in the RUN section of Fig. 25-9. Similar operational details of lines

```
40  FOR J = 1 TO 17
80  R = J : GOSUB 900 : UL = RL : R = J - 1
```

RL =	UL = RL	R = J − 1
R ∗ 16 − (R > 2)		
1 ∗ 16 = 16	16	1
2 ∗ 16 = 32	32	2
RL = (R − 2) ∗ 8 − (R > 6)		
3 − 2= 1 ∗ 8 = 8	40	3
4 − 2= 2 ∗ 8 = 16	48	4
5 − 2= 3 ∗ 8 = 24	56	5
6 − 2= 4 ∗ 8 = 32	64	6
RL = (R − 6) ∗ 4 − (R > 13)		
7 − 6= 1 ∗ 4 = 4	68	7
8 − 6= 2 ∗ 4 = 8	72	8
9 − 6= 3 ∗ 4 = 12	76	9
10 − 6= 4 ∗ 4 = 16	80	10
11 − 6= 5 ∗ 4 = 20	84	11
12 − 6= 6 ∗ 4 = 24	88	12
13 − 6= 7 ∗ 4 = 28	92	13
RL = (R −13) ∗ 2		
14 −13= 1 ∗ 2 = 2	94	14
15 −13= 2 ∗ 2 = 4	96	15
16 −13= 3 ∗ 2 = 6	98	16
17 −13= 4 ∗ 2 = 8	100	17

Fig. 25-13. Computer upper limit range.

50 and 60 may be seen in Fig. 24-6. Statements similar to the statements in lines 50 and 60 are routinely used formulas to control printouts to the screen.

```
70  PRINT "RANGE#  BASE  TOP  COUNT"
```

Line 70 prints the heading for each column in the printout.

```
80  R = J : GOSUB 900 : UL = RL : R = J - 1 : GOSUB 900 :
    LL = RL + 1 : IF LL = 1 THEN LL = 0
```

R = J is used as a temporary storage for the range loop J. If J is not stored, it will be lost during the jump to, and return from, the subroutine.

The branch to line 900 computes the range level (RL) by using a logical comparison for all ranges (Fig. 25-14).

```
900 RL = R * 16 - (R > 2) * (R - 2) * 8 - (R > 6)
    * (R - 6) * 4 - (R > 13) * (R - 13)
    * 2
```

R ∗ 16 − (R > 2), the range number times 16 (# of grade points in the first two ranges), separates the first two ranges. The logical expression, (− (R > 2)), separates the first two grade ranges based on a spread of 16 points. If R is less than 2, the statement is true, or 1. When the logical expression is true, it is activated for the first two

```
40  FOR J = 1 TO 17
80  R = J : GOSUB 900 : UL = RL : R = J − 1 : GOSUB 900 :
    LL = RL + 1 : IF LL = 1 THEN LL = 0
```

RL = R * 16 − (R > 2)	IF LL = 1 THEN LL = 0 LL = RL + 1	J − 1
		0
1 * 16 = 16	0	1
2 * 16 = 32	17	2
RL = (R − 2) * 8 − (R > 6)		
3 − 2 = 1 * 8 = 8	33	3
4 − 2 = 2 * 8 = 16	41	4
5 − 2 = 3 * 8 = 24	49	5
6 − 2 = 4 * 8 = 32	57	6
RL = (R − 6) * 4 − (R > 13)		
7 − 6 = 1 * 4 = 4	65	7
8 − 6 = 2 * 4 = 8	69	8
9 − 6 = 3 * 4 = 12	73	9
10 − 6 = 4 * 4 = 16	77	10
11 − 6 = 5 * 4 = 20	81	11
12 − 6 = 6 * 4 = 24	85	12
13 − 6 = 7 * 4 = 28	89	13
RL = (R −13) * 2		
14 −13 = 1 * 2 = 2	93	14
15 −13 = 2 * 2 = 4	95	15
16 −13 = 3 * 2 = 6	97	16
17 −13 = 4 * 2 = 8	99	17

Fig. 25-14. Compute lower limit range.

loop values (R = J). If R is greater than 2, the logical expression is false, or zero. When the expression is false (0), zero times 16 = 0, and the logical expression is not included in any other computation (Fig. 25-13). Line 900 processes the range levels from 1 through 17. This is the power of formulas in programming.

Lines 80 and 900 work in conjunction to produce the upper level (TOP), UL = RL, of the range, and the lower level (BASE), LL = RL + 1, of the range.

When the subroutine at line 900 has completed processing each range level, it returns to line 80, UL = RL, to store the range level computed into the upper level variable.

R = J −1 decrements the value of the loop variable stored in R, so the upper level and the lower level will remain at the same value. The program jumps to line 900 (GOSUB 900) to process the range level again. When the subroutine at line 900 returns to line 80, the range limit is incremented by 1 (LL = RL + 1), to produce the lower limit (BASE) of the grade range. Line 80 and the formula at line 900 have now produced the upper and lower limits of the grade range from 1 to 100. The grade ranges run from one to 100, so a special case must be accommodated to produce a grade range from zero to 100.

IF LL = 1 THEN LL = 0 converts the lower level of the first grade range from one to zero.

```
90   PRINT SPC(3); J : HTAB 13 : PRINT LL; : HTAB 20 : PRINT UL; :
     HTAB 30 : PRINT CG(J)
```

Line 90 prints the output information under the proper headings.

```
100  T = T + CG(J) : NEXT J
```

T = T + CG(J) totals the number of grades in each grade range, and NEXT J completes the loop structure, so all 17 grade ranges are produced.

```
110  PRINT "OGIVE COUNT = ";T; " OF 80 = "; T/80; "%"
```

Line 110 prints out the final OGIVE count as a check to determine if all 80 student grades have been input and processed. The ogive count was printed for each five ranges by line 60.

```
120  END
```

Formulas produce fast, efficient, orderly output. This program, written without formulas, would take approximately six times the number of program statements to solve the same problem. When possible, use formulas to save memory space, increase speed and efficiency, and to systematize output.

LESSON 26

Double Subscripted Arrays

Double subscripted arrays were introduced in Lesson 13. In that lesson, a business program was presented that accepted inputs of gross income and expenses and produced outputs of net income and totals for all columns.

Double subscripted arrays may be thought of as an arrangement of numbers in rows and columns. Numbers in the array may be accessed by specifying the row and column of the array. For instance, CF(2,3) calls the number in the array named CF (cash flow). The number is located in the row numbered 2 and in the column numbered 3. Double subscripted arrays permit great flexibility. The size may be determined exactly. The array serves as a storage area for large amounts of data or information. The contents of an array can be processed and the results entered in other parts of the same array with tremendous maneuverability.

The cash flow program (Fig. 26-1) does an analysis of an investment in income producing property to assist the potential buyer to determine if the purchase will be profitable. Information concerning the loan, depreciation, and investors' income is input (Fig. 26-2). The input information is processed by the program (Fig. 26-3). The output is a summary of cash benefits, tax benefits, and yields on which to aid the purchase decision (Fig. 26-4).

The cash flow program was written to be used as an investment tool, and is being used to evaluate income situations.

The cash flow program demonstrates the power of the double subscripted array by producing 25 rows (the length of the loan) and

```
10    REM : CASH FLOW PROGRAM TO
20    REM : DETERMINE INVESTMENT
30    REM : YIELDS ON INCOME PROP-
40    REM : ERTY:::COPYWRITED 1980
50    REM : BRIAN D. BLACKWOOD AND
60    REM : GEORGE H. BLACKWOOD
70    REM : 7020 BURLINGTON
80    REM : BEAUMONT, TEXAS 77706
90    REM : 713-866-6141
140   DEF FN R(Z) = ( INT (Z * 1000 + .5) / 1000)
145   DEF FN A(X) = INT ((X) + .5)
150   DIM H1$(15),NUM(2),H4(15,1)
160   HOME : VTAB 3
200   H1$ = "NET OP INC  LOAN VAL INT RATE  LOAN LEN"
210   PRINT H1$
220   VTAB 4: INPUT " ";NOI: VTAB 4: HTAB 12: INPUT " ";PV: VTAB 4:
      HTAB 23: INPUT " ";I: VTAB 4: HTAB 33: INPUT " ";LL
240   H2$ = "ASSET COST  ASSET LIFE SALVAGE VALUE": VTAB 5: PRINT H2$
245   VTAB 6: HTAB 1: INPUT " ";CA
250   VTAB 6: HTAB 15: INPUT " ";LA: VTAB 6: HTAB 26: INPUT " ";SV
255   DIM CF(LL + 1,14)
260   H3$ = "RATE OF DEP  YRLY INCOME CASH EQUITY"
270   VTAB 7: PRINT H3$
280   VTAB 8: HTAB 4: INPUT " ";RD : VTAB 8: HTAB 14: INPUT " ";YI:
      VTAB 8: HTAB 26: INPUT " ";CE
290   IF I > = 1 THEN I = I / 100 : GOTO 290
292   IF RD < 1 THEN RD = 100
310   GOSUB 8000
320   DP = 1 / LA:DEP = (RD / 100) * DP:BV = CA - SV:TB = BV
360   CF(1,8) = 0:CF(1,9) = 0:NE = YI:CF(0,14) = 0:J = 1: GOSUB 7000
365   CF(0,14) = IRS
370   GOSUB 9000
380   AN = PV / DF: FOR J = 1 TO LL

385   CF(J,2) = NOI
390   I1 = PV * I:CF(J,3) = I1
395   CF(LL + 1,3) = CF(LL + 1,3) + CF(J,3)
410   PR = AN - I1:CF(J,4) = PR
415   CF(LL + 1,4) = CF(LL + 1,4) + CF(J,4)
420   BR = PV - PR:PV = BR
425   REM : COMPUTE CASH FLOW
430   CF(J,5) = CF(J,2) - (CF(J,3) + CF(J,4))
435   CF(LL + 1,5) = CF(LL + 1,5) + CF(J,5)
462   D1 = TB * DEP
464   CF(J,6) = D1
466   CF(LL + 1,6) = CF(LL + 1,6) + CF(J,6)
470   TB = TB - D1
500   CF(J,7) = CF(J,3) + CF(J,6)
505   CF(LL + 1,7) = CF(LL + 1,7) + CF(J,7)
520   CF(J,8) = CF(J,2) - CF(J,7)
523   IF CF(J,8) < 0 THEN CF(J,8) = 0
525   CF(LL + 1,8) = CF(LL + 1,8) + CF(J,8)
540   CF(J,9) = CF(J,2) - CF(J,7)
545   CF(J,9)= ( SGN (CF(J,9)) - 1) * CF(J,9) / 2
```

Fig. 26-1. Cash flow program.

```
547  CF(LL + 1,9) = CF(LL + 1,9) + CF(J,9)
560  CF(J,10) = CF(J,8) * CF(J - 1,14)
565  CF(LL + 1,10) = CF(LL + 1,10) + CF(J,10)
580  CF(J,11) = CF(J,9) * CF(J - 1,14)
585  CF(LL + 1,11) = CF(LL + 1,11) + CF(J,11)
590  CF(J,0) = YI + CF(J,10) - CF(J,11)
595  NE = YI + CF(J,10) - CF(J,11) : GOSUB 7000:CF(J,14) = IRS
600  CF(J,12) = CF(J,5) + CF(J,11) - CF(J,10)
610  CF(LL + 1,12) = CF(LL + 1,12) + CF(J,12)
660  CF(J,13) = CF(J,12) + CF(J,4)
670  CF(LL + 1,13) = CF(LL + 1,13) + CF(J,13): NEXT J:CF(LL + 1,2) =
     CF(1,2) * LL
675  CF(J,14) = IRS
680  VTAB 9: INPUT "YRS OWNED=";YO
690  IF YO = 0 THEN 900
695  IF YO < 1 OR YO > LL THEN 680
697  VTAB 9: CALL -958
700  FOR K = 3 TO 13
710  CF(0,K) = 0
720  FOR J = 1 TO YO
730  CF(0,K) = CF(0,K) + CF(J,K)
740  NEXT J,K
750  CF(0,2) = YO * CF(1,2)
760  IRS = CF(YO,14)
770  NE = CF(YO,0)
780  VTAB 9: PRINT "YRS OWNED=";YO; TAB( 16);"END INC=";
     FN A(CF(YO,0));"(";IRS;")"
810  VTAB 11: HTAB 16: PRINT YO;" YR TOT ";YO;" YR AV"; TAB( 35);"YIELD"
820  VTAB 12: PRINT "CASH FLOW"; TAB(18); FN A(CF(0,5)); TAB ( 28);
     FN A(CF(0,5) / YO); TAB( 35); FN R(CF(0,5) / (YO * CE)
830  VTAB 14: PRINT "TAX SAV'S"; TAB( 11); FN A(CF(0,11))
840  VTAB 16: PRINT "TAX PAY"; TAB( 11); FN A(CF(0,10)); TAB( 19);
     FN A(CF(0,11) - CF(0,10))

850  VTAB 18: PRINT "CASH BENEFITS"; TAB( 18); FN A(CF(0,12)); TAB( 28);
     FN A(CF(0,12) / YO); TAB( 35); FN R(CF(0,12) / (YO * CE))
860  VTAB 19: PRINT "ADD:PRINCIPAL"; TAB( 18); FN A(CF(0,4))
870  VTAB 21: PRINT "TOTAL CASH AND"
880  VTAB 22: PRINT "AMORTIZATION"; TAB( 18); FN A(CF(0,13)); TAB( 28);
     FN A(CF(0,13) / YO); TAB( 35); FN R(CF(0,13) / (YO * CE))
890  GOTO 680
900  H1$(0) = " 0.INCOME":H4(0,0) = 6:H4(0,1) = 0:H1$(1) = " 1.TAX
     PAYABLE":H4(1,0) = 3:H4(1,1) = 7
910  H1$(2) = " 2.NET OP INCOME":H4(2,0) = 6:H4(2,1) = 6:H1$(3) =
     " 3.INTEREST":H4(3,0) = 8:H4(3,1) = 0
920  H1$(4) = " 4.PRINCIPAL":H4(4,0) = 9:H4(4,1) = 0:H1$(5) = " 5.CASH
     FLOW":H4(5,0) = 4:H4(5,1) = 4
930  H1$(6) = 6.TOT DEPRECIATION ":H4(6,0) = 9:H4(6,1) = 7:H1$(7) =
     " 7.INC TAX DEDUCTS":H4(7,0) = 7:H4(7,1) = 7
940  H1$(8) = 8.TAXABLE INC.":H4(8,0) = 7:H4(8,1) = 4:H1$(9) = "
     9.TAXABLE LOSS":H4(9,0) = 7:H4(9,1) = 4
950  H1$(10) = "10.TAX PAYABLE":H4(10,0) = 3:H4(10,1) = 7:H1$(11) =
     "11.TAX SAVINGS":H4(11,0) = 3:H4(11,1) = 7
```

Fig. 26-1. (Cont) Cash flow program.

```
960  H1$(12) = "12.CASH AVAILABLE":H4(12,0) = 4:H4(12,1) = 9:H1$(13) =
     "13.TOTAL BENEFITS":H4(13,0) = 5:H4(13,1) = 8
965  H1$(14) = "14.TAX BRACKET":H4(14,0) = 3:H4(14,1) = 7:H1$(15) =
     "15.ANNUAL PAYMENT":H4(15,0) = 6:H4(15,1) = 7
970  CALL - 936: HTAB 14: PRINT "TABLE LISTING": PRINT : PRINT "ENTER 3
     COLUMN VALUES FOR TABLE PRINT"
980  FOR J = 0 TO 14 STEP 2: PRINT H1$(J); TAB( 19);H1$(J + 1): NEXT J:
     PRINT
990  FOR N = 0 TO 2: PRINT "COLUMN ";N + 1;" = ";: INPUT NUM(N):
     IF NUM(N) < 0 OR NUM(N) > 15 THEN 1010
1000 NEXT N
1010 N = N - 1: IF N < 0 THEN 3000
1020 FOR L = 1 TO LL
1030 IF L < > INT ((L - 1) / 15) * 15 + 1 THEN 1080
1040 IF L < > 1 THEN INPUT "!";A$
1050 CALL - 936: PRINT "YEARS";: FOR J = 0 TO N: HTAB (J + 1) * 10:M
     = NUM(J): PRINT MID$(H1$(M),4,H4(M,0));: NEXT J: PRINT
1060 FOR J = 0 TO N: HTAB (J + 1) * 10:M = NUM(J): IF H4(M,1) > 0
     THEN PRINT RIGHT$ (H1$(M),H4(M,1));
1070 NEXT J: PRINT : PRINT
1080 PRINT L;: FOR J = 0 TO N
1090 HTAB (J + 1) * 10:M = NUM(J): IF M = 14 THEN 1110
1095 IF M < > 15 THEN 1100
1096 PRINT FN A(AN);: GOTO 1120

1100 PRINT FN A(CF(L,M));: GOTO 1120
1110 PRINT FN R(CF(L,M));
1120 NEXT J: PRINT : NEXT L
1130 INPUT "!";A$: GOTO 970
3000 END
7000 RESTORE
7010 BS = 0
7020 READ UL,BF,IRS
7030 IF NE > = UL AND UL < > 0 THEN BS = UL: GOTO 7020
7040 CF(J,14) = IRS
7050 CF(J,1) = BF + CF(J - 1,14) * (CF(J,0) - BS)
7100 DATA 3400,0,0
7110 DATA 5500,0,.14
7120 DATA 7600,294,.16
7130 DATA 11900,630,.18
7140 DATA 16000,1404,.21
7150 DATA 20200,2265,.24
7160 DATA 24600,3273,.28
7170 DATA 29900,4505,.32
7180 DATA 35200,6201,.37
7190 DATA 45800,8162,.43
7200 DATA 60000,12720,.49
7210 DATA 85600,19678,.54
7220 DATA 109400,33502,.59
7230 DATA 162400,47544,.64
7240 DATA 215400,81464,.68
7250 DATA 0,117504,.70
7900 RETURN
8000 FOR J = 3 TO 13
```

Fig. 26-1. (Cont) Cash flow program.

```
8010  CF(LL + 1,J) = 0
8020  NEXT J
8030  RETURN
9000  FOR J = 1 TO LL
9010  DF = DF + 1 / (1 + I) ↑ J
9020  NEXT J
9030  RETURN
```

Fig. 26-1. (Cont) Cash flow program.

PURCHASE PRICE		
LAND	50,000	
BUILDING	750,000	
TOTAL PURCHASE PRICE	800,000	
SALVAGE VALUE	50,000	
CASH EQUITY	200,000	
NET OPERATING INCOME	80,000	per year
OUTSIDE INCOME	40,000	per year
MORTGAGE		
LIFE OF THE LOAN	25	years
INTEREST RATE	12	%
ANNUAL PAYMENTS (INTEREST & PRINCIPAL)	76,500	
DEPRECIATION		
LIFE OF THE BUILDING	40	years
DEPRECIATION METHOD	200	% double declining balance

Fig. 26-2. Cash flow and tax benefits of investment property ownership.

YEAR	NET OPERATING INCOME J,2	INTEREST J,3	AMORTIZATION PRINCIPAL J,4	CASH FLOW J,5	TOTAL DEPRECIAT. J,6	TOTAL DEDUCTIONS J,7
1	8,000	72,000	4,500	3,500	35,000	107,000
2	8,000	71,460	5,040	3,500	33,250	104,710
3	8,000	70,855	5,645	3,500	31,588	102,443
4	8,000	70,178	6,322	3,500	30,008	100,186
5	8,000	69,419	7,081	3,500	28,508	97,927
TOTALS	400,000	353,912	28,588	28,558	158,354	512,266

TAXABLE INCOME J,8	TAX LOSS J,9	TAX PAYABLE J,10	TAX SAVINGS J,11	CASH AVAILABLE AFTER MORTGAGE & TAX BENEFIT J,12	TOTAL CASH & AMORTIZAT. BENEFITS J,13	TAX BRACKET J,14
0	27,000	0	11,610	15,110	19,610	.32
0	24,710	0	7,907	11,407	16,447	.37
0	22,443	0	8,304	11,804	17,449	.37
0	20,186	0	7,469	10,969	17,291	.37
0	17,927	0	6,633	10,133	17,214	.37
0	122,266	0	41,923	59,423	88,011	

Fig. 26-3. Input information.

14 columns. Fig. 26-3 shows 5 rows and 14 columns of the cash flow problem. The columns are J, 1 through J,14. Columns within the array are operated on to produce other columns. The cash flow col-

SUMMARY OF CASH & BENEFITS		10 YR. TOTAL	10 YR. AVG.	YIELD
CASH FLOW (BEFORE INCOME TAX EFFECT)		35,000	3,500	.018
TAX SAVINGS	+63,023			
TAX PAYABLE	− 0			
SUB TOTAL		63,023		
TOTAL CASH BENEFITS AFTER TAXES		98,023	9,802	.049
ADD PRINCIPAL PAID ON MORTGAGE		78,969		
TOTAL CASH & AMORTIZATION BENEFITS AFTER TAXES		176,992	17,699	.088

Fig. 26-4. Summary of cash and tax benefits.

umn (J,5) is produced by subtracting the principal (J,4) and the interest (J,3) from the net operating income (J,2). CF(J,5) = CF(J,2) − (CF(J,3) + CF(J,4)). Net operating income is input as NOI, and a replacement statement is used to place NOI into CF(J,2). CF(J,2) = NOI.

The variables used in the program are shown in Fig. 26-5, as they appear in the program. The variables in Fig. 26-6 are placed in alphabetical order.

The double declining balance depreciation constant is computed in line 320, and applied to the remaining depreciation (line 462) as each year is incremented during the life of the loan loop.

```
310  GOSUB 8000
```

Line 310 initializes the columns that hold the totals to zero.

Line 360 sets up the investors' tax information contained in the table at lines 7000 to 7900.

Lines 380 to 670 are the life of the loan loop that computes all the rows and columns in the cash flow array.

After the rows and columns are generated, which takes about 60 seconds on a 25 year loan, the program defaults to line 780. Line 780 requests the user to input the YEARS OWNED. This input allows the user to view the cash and tax benefits and yields for periods from one year to the life of the loan. This output helps the user to determine which period of holding time results in the greatest profit.

If zero is input in YEARS OWNED, the program branches to the menu at line 900 to print out the individual tables in the array.

The menu selections and headings for the tables are set up in lines 900 through 965. This ingenious method uses single subscripted string arrays to hold the header and double subscripted numeric arrays to hold the number of spaces in the first and second lines of the headers (Figs. 26-7 and 26-8). H1$(O-15) holds the menu selection headings of each table. The string arrays and the numeric arrays are related. The first subscript in the numeric array relates to the string array, and the second subscript relates to the line of the header. Some of the two line headers are incorrectly separated, as in

H1$	= Header.
H2$	= Header.
H3$	= Header.
NOI	= Net operating income.
PV	= Loan amount
I	= Interest rate.
LL	= Life of the loan.
CA	= Cost of the asset.
LA	= Life of the asset.
SV	= Salvage value.
CF	= Cash flow array.
CF(LL + 1,?)	= Holds totals for the individual column.
RD	= Rate of depreciation — 200% double declining balance.
YI	= Your personal yearly income.
CE	= Cash equity.
DP	= 1/LA — depreciation factor.
DEP	= (RD/100)*DP — depreciation per year.
BV	= Book value.
TB	= Total book value.
NE	= Net income.
IRS	= Tax bracket — CF(J,14) = IRS
AN	= Annual payment on the loan.
CF(J,2)	= NOI — net operating income.
I1	= Yearly interest.
CF(J,3)	= I1
CF(LL + 1,3)	= Total interest paid for the period of analysis.
PR	= Principal remaining.
CF(J,4)	= PR
CF(LL + 1,4)	= Total principal paid for the period analyzed.
BR	= Balance remaining.
CF	= Cash flow.
CF(J,5)	= CF
D1	= Total depreciation for one year.
CF(J,6)	= D1
CF(LL + 1,6)	= Total depreciation for the period analyzed.
TB	= Total book value.
CF(J,7)	= Total deductions — interest and depreciation.
CF(LL + 1,7)	= Total deductions for the period of analysis.
CF(J,8)	= Taxable income.
CF(LL + 1,8)	= Total taxable income for the period of analysis.
CF(J,9)	= Tax loss.
CF(LL + 1,9)	= Total tax loss for the period analyzed.
CF(J,10)	= Tax payable.
CF(LL + 1,10)	= Tax payable for the period analyzed.
CF(J,11)	= Tax savings.
CF(LL + 1,11)	= Total tax savings for the period analyzed.
CF(J,0)	= Yearly income and tax payable — CF(J,10)−CF(J,11)
CF(J,12)	= Cash available after mortgage payments and payment of income tax effect.
CF(LL + 1,12)	= Total of cash available after mortgage payments and income tax effect for period analyzed.
CF(J,13)	= Total cash and amortization benefits after taxes.
CF(LL + 1,13)	= Total of cash and amortization benefits after taxes for the period analyzed.

Fig. 26-5. Variables as they appear in the program.

YO	= Years owned.
H1$(0)	= See Fig. 26-7
H1$(15)	= See Fig. 26-7
H4(0,0)	= See Fig. 26-7
H4(15,1)	= See Fig. 26-7
NUM(N)	= Number of column to be printed.
N	= Number of the column.
M = NUM(J)	= Loop variable J, placed in column array NUM, stored in the variable M.

Fig. 26-5. (Cont) Variables as they appear in the program.

AN	= Annual payment on the loan.
BR	= Balance remaining.
BV	= Book value.
CA	= Cost of the asset.
CE	= Cash equity.
CF	= Cash flow.
CF(J,0)	= Yearly income and tax payable − CF(J,10)−CF(J,11)
CF(J,2)	= Net operating income.
CF(LL + 1,2)	= Total net operating income for the period analyzed.
CF(J,3)	= I1 − yearly interest.
CF(LL + 1,3)	= Total interest for the period analyzed.
CF(J,4)	= PR = principal remaining.
CF(LL + 1,4)	= Total principal for the period analyzed.
CF(J,5)	= CF = cash flow.
CF(LL + 1,5)	= Total cash flow for the period analyzed.
CF(J,6)	= D1 = depreciation for one year.
CF(LL + 1,6)	= Total depreciation for the period analyzed.
CF(J,7)	= Total deductions − interest and depreciation.
CF(LL + 1,7)	= Total deductions for the period analyzed.
CF(J,8)	= Taxable income.
CF(LL + 1.8)	= Total taxable income for the period analyzed.
CF(J,9)	= Tax loss.
CF(LL + 1,9)	= Total tax loss for the period analyzed.
CF(J,10)	= Tax payable.
CF(LL + 1,10)	= Total tax payable for the period analyzed.
CF(J,11)	= Tax savings.
CF(LL + 1,11)	= Total tax savings for the period analyzed.
CF(J,12)	= Cash available after mortgage payments and payment of income tax effect.
CF(LL + 1,12)	= Total of cash available after mortgage payments and income tax effect for period analyzed.
CF(J,13)	= Total cash and amortization benefits after taxes.
CF(LL + 1,13)	= Total of cash and amortization benefits after taxes for the period analyzed.
CF(J,14)	= IRS = tax bracket.
DEP	= (RD/100)*DP − depreciation for one year.
DP	= 1/LA − depreciation factor.
D1	= Total depreciation for one year.
H1$	= Header.
H2$	= Header.
H3$	= Header.
H1$(?)	= See Fig. 26-7.

Fig. 26-6. Variables in alphabetical order.

H4(0,0) = See Fig. 26-7.
J = Loop variable — FOR J = 1 TO N
LA = Life of the asset.
LL = Life of the loan.
M = NUM(J) = Loop variable J, placed in array column NUM, stored in the variable M.
N = Number of the column.
NOI = Net operating income.
NUM(N) = Number of the column to be printed.
PR = Principal remaining.
PV = Loan amount.
RD = Rate of depreciation — 200% double declining balance.
SV = Salvage value.
TB = Total book value.
YI = Your personal yearly income.
YO = Years owned.

Fig. 26-6. (Cont) Variables in alphabetical order.

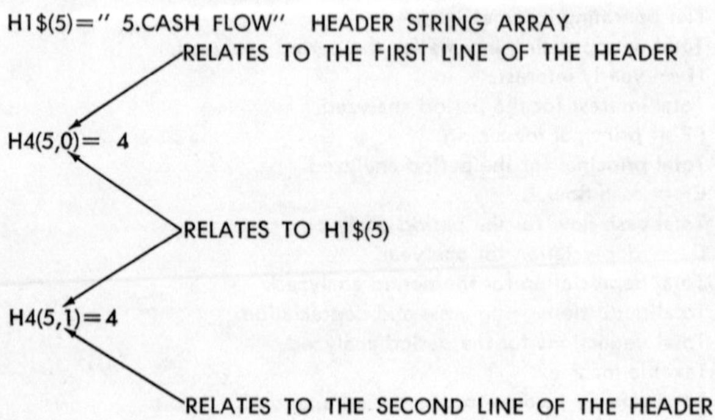

(H1$(6) — TOT. DEPRE---CIATION), but the technique produces the correct results.

The logic of the algorithm stores the values to indicate a one line header (H4(0,0)=6 — H4(0,1)=0) or a two line header (H4(5,0)=4 — H4(5,1)=4), and indicates how many characters are contained in the first line and how many characters are contained in the second line.

```
H1$(0)=" 0.INCOME" ————————HEADER STRING ARRAY
H4(0,0)=6 ————————————————SIX CHARACTERS IN THE FIRST LINE
H4(0,1)=0 ————————————————ZERO CHARACTERS IN THE SECOND LINE
```

After all fifteen values are set, line 970 clears the screen and prints TABLE LISTING and ENTER 3 VALUES FOR TABLE PRINT.

Line 980 prints the menu selection.

Line 990 sets up a loop to output to the screen three columns (0 to 2). The user inputs the number of the column in a single subscripted array and the array is checked to determine if it is between 1 and 15. If the column number is not between 1 and 15, the program jumps out of the loop to line 1010.

H1$	1st LINE	2nd LINE	LENGTH OF 1st LINE	LENGTH OF 2nd LINE
H1$(0)=" 0.INCOME"	INCOME	NONE	H4(0,0)=6	H4(0,1)=0
H1$(1)=" 1.TAX PAYABLE"	TAX	PAYABLE	H4(1,0)=3	H4(1,1)=7
H1$(2)=" 2.NET OP INCOME"	NET OP	INCOME	H4(2,0)=6	H4(2,1)=6
H1$(3)=" 3.INTEREST"	INTEREST	NONE	H4(3,0)=8	H4(3,1)=0
H1$(4)=" 4.PRINCIPAL"	PRINCIPAL	NONE	H4(4,0)=9	H4(4,1)=0
H1$(5)=" 5.CASH FLOW	CASH	FLOW	H4(5,0)=4	H4(5,1)=4
H1$(6)=" 6.TOT DEPRECIATION"	TOT DEPRE	CIATION	H4(6,0)=9	H4(6,1)=7
H1$(7)=" 7.INC TAX DEDUCTS"	INC TAX	DEDUCTS	H4(7,0)=7	H4(7,1)=7
H1$(8)=" 8.TAXABLE INC."	TAXABLE	INC.	H4(8,0)=7	H4(8,1)=4
H1$(9)=" 9.TAXABLE LOSS"	TAXABLE	LOSS	H4(9,0)=7	H4(9,1)=4
H1$(10)="10.TAX PAYABLE"	TAX	PAYABLE	H4(10,0)=3	H4(10,0)=7
H1$(11)="11.TAX SAVINGS	TAX	SAVINGS	H4(11,0)=3	H4(11,1)=7
H1$(12)="12.CASH AVAILABLE"	CASH	AVAILABLE	H4(12,0)=4	H4(12,1)=9
H1$(13)="13.TOTAL BENEFITS"	TOTAL	BENEFITS	H4(13,0)=5	H4(13,1)=8
H1$(14)="14.TAX BRACKET	TAX	BRACKET	H4(14,0)=3	H4(14,1)=7
H1$(15)="15.ANNUAL PAYMENT"	ANNUAL	PAYMENT	H4(15,0)=6	H4(15,1)=7

THE 1st ALPHA CHARACTER OF H1$(?) IS ALWAYS THE 4th CHARACTER OF THE HEADER

Fig. 26-7. Header construction.

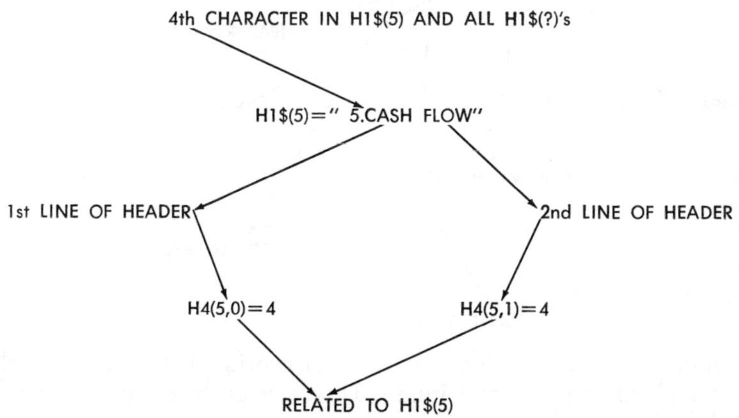

Fig. 26-8. Header detail.

In line 1010, N = N − 1 decrements the column number to produce the correct value of N. When the program jumps out of the loop, the loop value is one more than the correct value. To produce the correct value of N, one must be subtracted. This was discussed in Lesson 6.

IF N < 0 THEN 3000. When the user is through working with the program, an input of −1 (less than zero) causes a branch to line 3000 to end the program.

Line 1020 is the beginning of the loop to compute the values in the tables. LL is the variable used to hold the life of the loan value.

Program statements similar to lines 1030 and 1040 are detailed in Fig. 24-6 in Lesson 24. Line 1030 computes when 15 years of the table have been printed on the screen.

The only function of line 1040 is to stop the program. On the first loop pass L = 1. The program defaults through 1030, 1040, and prints the headings in 1050 and 1060. On each subsequent loop pass, the program branches from 1030 to 1080. When line 1030 is false the program defaults to line 1040. If L is not one (L = 16) the program inputs "!" and stops. This allows the user to view and study the 15 rows of the tables printed on the screen. When the user is ready for the program to resume, RETURN is pressed.

Line 1050 prints the first line of the column header on the screen and clears the screen. In line 1050, N is the variable that holds the number of columns, and HTAB (J + 1)*10 sets the column in the correct position on the screen. The column value is stored in the variable M.

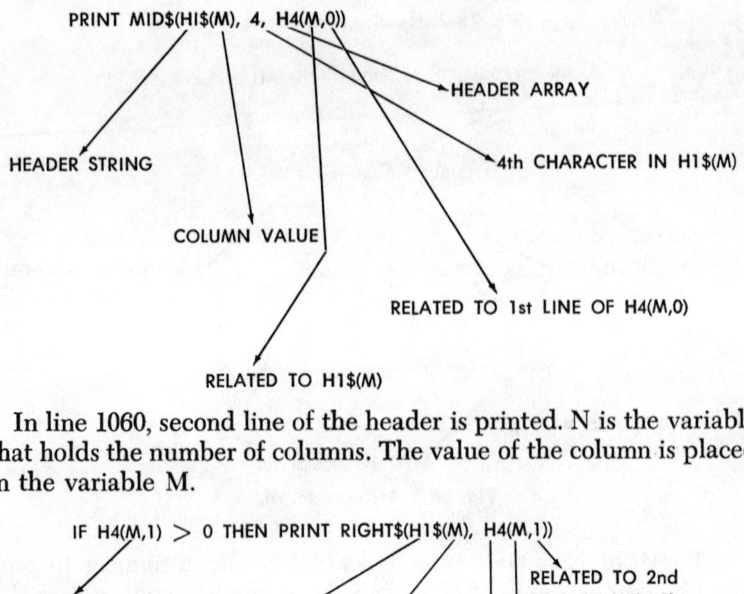

In line 1060, second line of the header is printed. N is the variable that holds the number of columns. The value of the column is placed in the variable M.

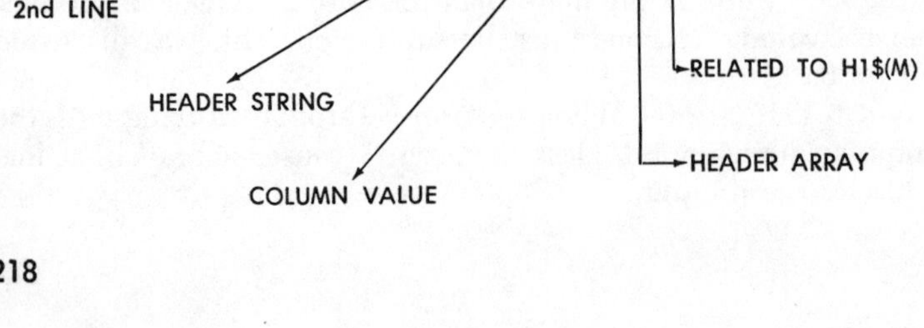

When the column headings have been printed, the program defaults to line 1080 to print L, which represents the year. The second statement in line 1080, FOR J = 0 TO N, is the beginning of a loop that controls the number of columns to be printed. Line 1090 tabs to the proper location on the screen to print the columns. M = NUM(J) stores the number of the column to be printed in the variable M.

If line 1090 is true the program branches to line 1110 to print out the rounded (line 140) cash flow array values for row L, column M. If M = 14 is false, the program defaults to line 1095. If line 1095 is true, the program branches to line 1100 to print out the integer function (line 145) of the cash flow array, row L, column M. If M<>15 is false, the program defaults to line 1096. FNA (AN) is the integer (line 145) cash flow array of the annual payment. The annual payment on the loan is computed by dividing the loan value by the discount factor (line 380), and is not computed by the loop execution and placed in the table.

```
SGN FUNCTION MAKES ALL NEGATIVE NUMBERS—POSITIVE
SGN FUNCTION MAKES ALL ZERO NUMBERS ———————ZERO
SGN FUNCTION MAKES ALL POSITIVE NUMBERS —ZERO

TAXABLE LOSS    NET OPERATING INCOME    DEDUCTIONS
CF(J,9)         = CF(J,2)               − CF(J,7)

CF(J,9) = (SGN(CF(J,9)) −1)*CF(J,9)/2

IF CF(J,9) < 0 THEN SGN IS −1
    IF CF(J,9) = −2000
        (SGN(CF(J,9)) −1)*CF(J,9)/2
         (SGN(−2000) −1)* −2000/2
           (−1 −1)* −2000/2
                −2* −2000/2
                  +4000/2
                   = 2000

    IF CF(J,9) = 0 THEN SGN = 0
        (0 −1)* 0/2 = 0

    IF CF(J,9) = + 2000 THEN SGN = +1
        (SGN(CF(J,9)) −1)* CF(J,9)/2
            (+1 −1)* 2000/2
                0 * 2000/2
                  = 0
```

Fig. 26-9. Sign (SGN) function.

The SGN function (Fig. 26-9) is used in line 545. The SGN function returns only three values +1, 0, and −1. These values relate to greater than zero, zero, or less than zero. In this case, if the tax loss is a positive number, SGN(CF(J,9)) = +1, (SGN(CF(J,9)) −1)

= 0, and zero times CF(J,9)/2 = zero. When the tax loss is a negative number, (SGN(CF(J,9)) −1) = −2. When −2 is multiplied by a negative CF(J,9)/2, the factor (−2/+2) divides out leaving a negative value. A negative times a negative is a positive value. The purpose of the SGN function is to make all negative numbers positive, leave zero numbers zero, and make all positive numbers zero. The SGN function is used so a tax loss, which is a negative number, can be converted into a positive number. The positive number is then multiplied by the previous year's tax rate, (CF(J−1, 14)), and the results are placed in the tax savings column, CF(J,11).

CF(J−1, 14) gives the tax rate for the previous year which is used to compute this year's taxes. CF(J, 14) gives the tax rate for the present year.

The cash flow program outputs the cash flow, tax benefits, and yields for a single year or a number of years. This information assists the prospective buyer in determining how the purchase will affect his cash flow and future net worth. This information will aid with the decision to buy the property or not to buy the property.

SECTION III

Supplement

LESSON 27

Graphics

Lesson 27 contains two programs. The first program, LO – RES EXPLAINER, explains the details of low resolution graphics. The second program, OGIVE, uses the program in Lesson 25 to generate a graph of cumulative distribution of student grades.

Graphics is the art or science of drawing, especially by mechanical principles, as in mechanical drawing. It is also the science of calculating by means of graphics, diagrams, etc.

The Apple II computer has three modes of screen display: (1) full text, (2) split screen graphics with four lines of text at the bottom of the screen, and (3) full screen graphics (Figs. 27-1 and 27-2).

The full text mode has 24 rows, 1 to 24, and 40 columns, 0 to 39, to display text on the screen.

The split screen graphics mode contains 40 X positions, 0 to 39, and 40 Y positions, 0 to 39, leaving four rows for text. The text rows are 21, 22, 23, and 24. Each two rows of graphics equals one row of text.

The full screen graphics mode contains 40 X positions, 0 to 39, and 48 Y positions, 0 to 47. In the full screen graphics mode, one X position is the same width as one column of text, but one Y position is equal to one-half row of text, Fig. 27-1, and Fig. 27-2.

Fig. 27-3 lists the low resolution graphics commands and statements.

Fig. 27-4 lists the color names and related values used in low graphics.

The LO – RES EXPLAINER program (Fig. 27-5) was written to explain and demonstrate the use of low resolution graphics.

When the Apple computer is turned on, it comes up in the text mode. To change the TEXT mode, GR is typed on the screen as an

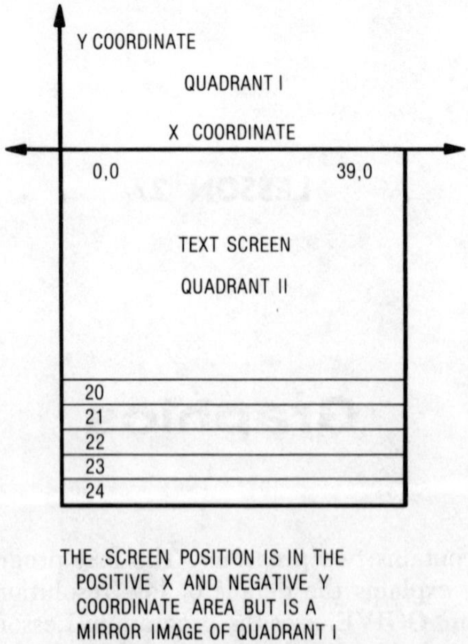

Fig. 27-1. Text screen.

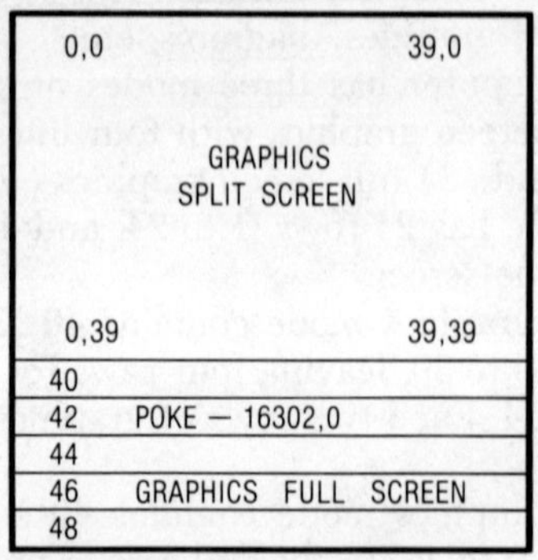

Fig. 27-2. Graphics screen.

immediate execution, or GR is placed in a program statement to be executed in the deferred mode. GR mode comes up with COLOR = 0 (black). The color must be changed before a PLOT, VLIN, or HLIN execution. If the color is not designated, it remains the same color as previously set.

Line 10 clears the screen and VTAB's to row 10 on the screen.

COLOR = 8	Sets color for lo — resolution graphics. 8 = pink.
GR	Sets lo — resolution graphics mode of screen. 40 rows by 40 columns. Sets COLOR = 0 (black). POKE – 16301,0 = GR.
HLIN 1, 39 AT 20	Draws a horizontal line from column 1 to column 39 at row 20.
PLOT 5,10	Places a square on the screen at X coordinate 5, and Y coordinate 10. COLOR must be set to other than zero or the square will be black on a black screen.
SCRN 5,10	Returns the color value of the square at location 5, 10.
TEXT	Sets the screen to the full screen TEXT mode.
VLIN 10,20 AT 20	Draws a line from row 10 to row 20 at column 20.

Fig. 27-3. Low resolution graphics commands and statements.

Line 20 indicates the program content.

Line 40 is a pause loop to allow the user time to view the printout. GOSUB 1000 is used throughout the program, and will not be mentioned again during the discussion.

0	BLACK	8	BROWN
1	MAGENTA	9	ORANGE
2	DARK BLUE	10	GREY
3	PURPLE	11	PINK
4	DARK GREEN	12	GREEN
5	GREY	13	YELLOW
6	MEDIUM BLUE	14	AQUA
7	LIGHT BLUE	15	WHITE

Fig. 27-4. Low resolution graphics color names and related numbers.

Line 50 sets the graphics mode and VTAB's to line 21, which is the first usable line in the TEXT portion of the screen, and prints the line in the print statement. This line remains on the screen as a reminder of the beginning of the first portion of usable text, in split screen graphics.

Line 70 places the screen in the text mode and returns it to the GRaphics mode to demonstrate what a graph looks like when the screen is changed back to text.

In line 80, COLOR = 15 sets the color to white before the square is colored. The computer retains the color designation in memory and sets all lines and squares to that color, until the color designation is changed (Fig. 27-4).

PLOT 0,0 in line 80 sets the square at column 0, row 0 to white. The column value is the first digit or digits, and the row value is the second digit or digits (Fig. 27-6). PLOT 0,0 and PLOT 39,0 cause two white squares to be placed at the outermost positions on the top row (Fig. 27-6).

In line 90, the color is changed to magenta (COLOR = 1), and PLOT 0,39 and PLOT 39,39 place two magenta squares on the outermost position of the split screen graphics.

```
10    HOME : VTAB 10
20    HTAB 12: PRINT "LO-RES EXPLAINER"
30    PRINT : PRINT
40    GOSUB 1000
50    GR : VTAB 21: PRINT " ———————— THIS IS THE BOTTOM
      EDGE—————————"
60    GOSUB 1000
70    TEXT : GOSUB 1000: GR
80    COLOR= 15: PLOT 0,0: PLOT 39, 0: GOSUB 1000
90    COLOR= 1: PLOT 0,39: PLOT 39, 39: GOSUB 1000
100   COLOR= 11: HLIN 2,37 AT 0: GOSUB 1000
110   HLIN 2,37 AT 39: GOSUB 1000
120   COLOR= 12: VLIN 2,37 AT 0: GOSUB 1000
130   VLIN 2,37 AT 39: GOSUB 1000
140   FOR K = 1 TO 4: GOSUB 1000: NEXT K
150   FOR X = 2 TO 36: COLOR= X - INT (X / 16) * 16
160   PLOT X,(37 - .122 * (X - 19)↑ 2)
170   NEXT X: VTAB 22: HTAB 2: PRINT "GRAPH OF Y = -.122 * (X-19) ↑
      2 + 37": GOSUB 1000: GOSUB 1000: GOSUB 1000
180   PLOT 15,47: GOSUB 1000
190   POKE - 16302,0: GOSUB 1000
200   COLOR= 0
210   FOR K = 40 TO 47: HLIN 0,39 AT K: NEXT K: GOSUB 1000
220   COLOR= 1: VLIN 42,46 AT 0: HLIN 1,2 AT 41: HLIN 1,2 AT 47: VLIN
      45,46 AT 3: PLOT 3,42: PLOT 2,44
240   COLOR= 3: VLIN 42,47 AT 5: HLIN 6,7 AT 41: VLIN 42,43 AT 8: HLIN
      6,7 AT 44: PLOT 6,45: PLOT 7,46: PLOT 8,47
260   COLOR= 5: VLIN 42,47 AT 10: HLIN 11,12 AT 41: VLIN 42,47 AT 13:
      HLIN 11,12 AT 44
280   COLOR= 7: VLIN 42,47 AT 15: HLIN 16,17 AT 41: VLIN 42,43 AT 18:
      HLIN 16,17 AT 44
300   COLOR= 9: VLIN 41,47 AT 20: HLIN 21,22 AT 44: VLIN 41,47 AT 23
320   COLOR= 11: HLIN 25,27 AT 41: VLIN 42,47 AT 26: HLIN 25,27 AT 47
340   COLOR= 13: VLIN 42,46 AT 29: HLIN 30,31 AT 41: PLOT 32,42: VLIN
      45,46 AT 32: HLIN 30,31 AT 47
360   COLOR= 15: HLIN 35,37 AT 41: HLIN 35,37 AT 47: PLOT 34,46: PLOT
      38,46: PLOT 37,45: PLOT 36,44: PLOT 35,43: PLOT 34,42: PLOT 38,42
950   FOR K = 1 TO 30: GOSUB 1000: NEXT K
960   POKE - 16301,0: HOME : VTAB 22: PRINT "THAT'S ALL"
970   GOSUB 1000: GOSUB 1000: GOSUB 1000
980   TEXT : HOME
999   END
1000  FOR J = 1 TO 1800: NEXT J: RETURN
```

Fig. 27-5. LO-RES EXPLAINER program.

In line 100, the color is changed to pink and a horizontal line is drawn from column 2 to column 37 at row 0, across the top of the screen (Fig. 27-6). HLIN is the statement for a horizontal line.

Line 110 draws a horizontal line at row 39, across the bottom of the screen. The line is pink.

In line 120, the color is changed to green, and a vertical line is drawn from row 2 to row 37 at column zero. VLIN sets the column

COLOR = 15 WHITE	PLOT 0,0 (A) PLOT 39,0 (B)
COLOR = 1 MAGENTA	PLOT 0, 39 (C) PLOT 39, 39 (D)
COLOR = 11 PINK	HLIN 2, 37 AT 0 (E) HLIN 2, 37 AT 39 (F)
COLOR = 12 GREEN	VLIN 2, 37 AT 0 (G) VLIN 2, 37 AT 39 (H)

POKE −16302,0 GOES TO FULL SCREEN GRAPHICS

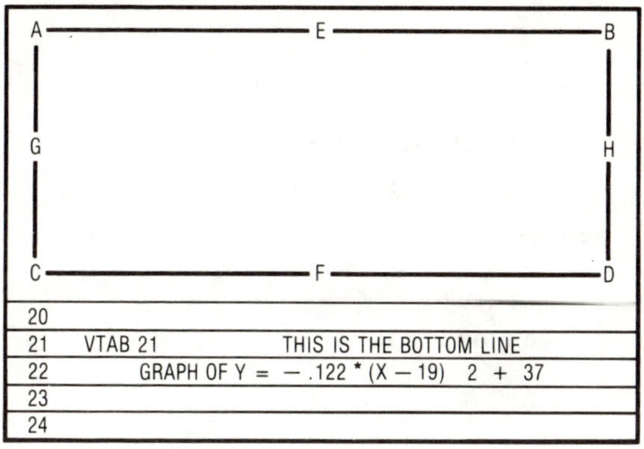

Fig. 27-6 LO-RES EXPLAINER

value to color the squares. The "AT 0" designates the column in which to draw the line (Fig. 27-6).

In line 130, a green vertical line is drawn on the right side of the screen. The screen now has four colored squares at each corner and a colored line on each side of the screen. The lines are separated from the squares by a single space.

Line 140 is a pause loop that is four times as long as the normal pause loop at GOSUB 1000.

In line 150, FOR X = 2 TO 36 is the beginning of a loop used to plot a parabola on the screen starting at column 2. The loop has a second function, to set the color value for the squares to be plotted. COLOR = X − INT(X/16) * 16 in line 150 subtracts color values over 15. If the color value went over 15 the program would stop running. The values input to the computer must be in the legal range (0 to 15) or a processing error will occur.

Line 160 plots the parabola.

The standard X, Y axes are the basis of the screen display (Fig. 27-7). In the standard graph, the value of X increases from left to right. The value of Y increases from bottom to top. The two axes cross at the 0,0 position. There are four quadrants on the graph. Quadrant I is positive X, positive Y. Quadrant II is positive X, negative Y. Quadrant III is negative X, negative Y. Quadrant IV is negative X, positive Y.

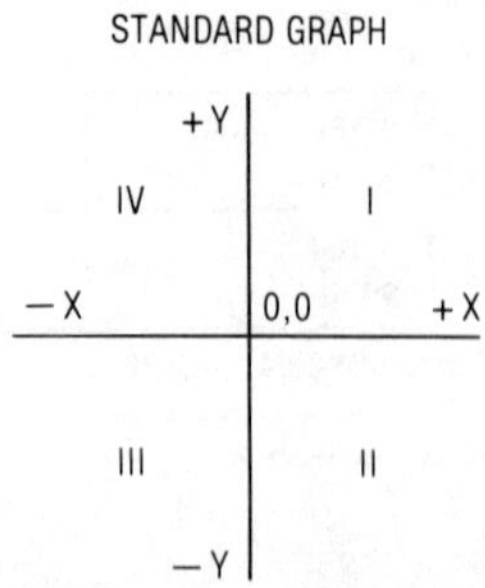

Fig. 27-7. Standard graph.

The Apple screen is located in quadrant I of the graph. However, the negative Y and positive Y axes are reversed. This causes the Apple screen to be a mirror image of quadrant I (Fig. 27-8).

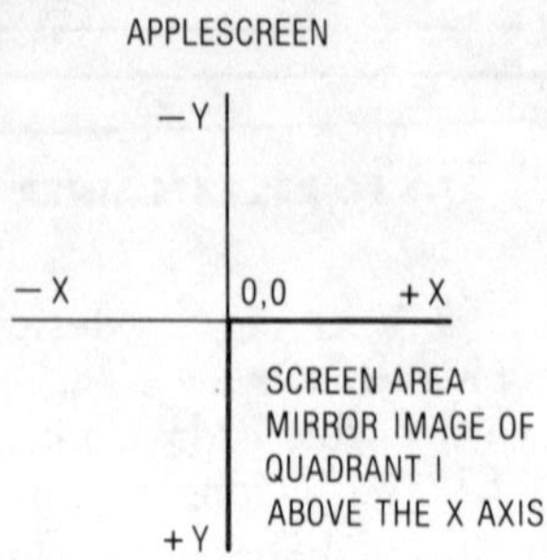

Fig. 27-8. Apple screen.

The problem to be solved in the graphics demonstration is to plot the graph of a parabola with its apex pointing toward the bottom of the display screen. Figs. 27-9, 27-10, 27-11, 27-12, 27-13, and 27-14 show the formula graph display as it appears on the screen.

The formula for a parabola is $Y = AX^2 + B$. Variations of this formula are used to plot the parabola. Lines 150, 160, and 170 of the program produce the graph of a parabola with its apex pointed toward the bottom of the screen.

Plotting $Y = X^2$ (Fig. 27-9) produces a graph in the proper quadrant. The apex of the graph is pointing up, but only the right half of the graph is displayed on the screen.

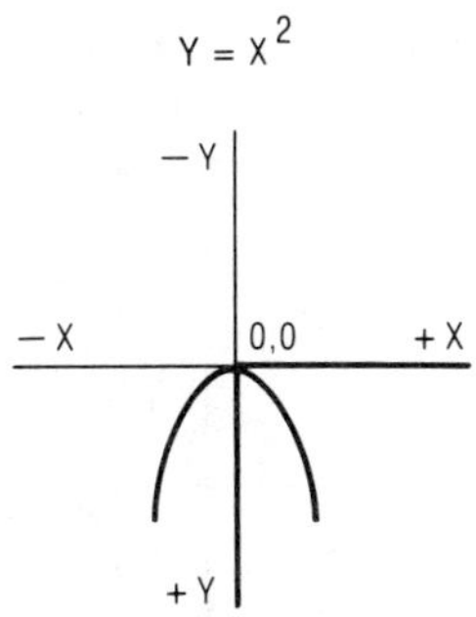

Fig. 27-9. Y = X².

Plotting $Y = (X - 19)^2$ (Fig. 27-10) produces a graph with its apex pointing up, and the graph is centered on the screen. The graph has been moved nineteen X positions to the right on the positive X axis.

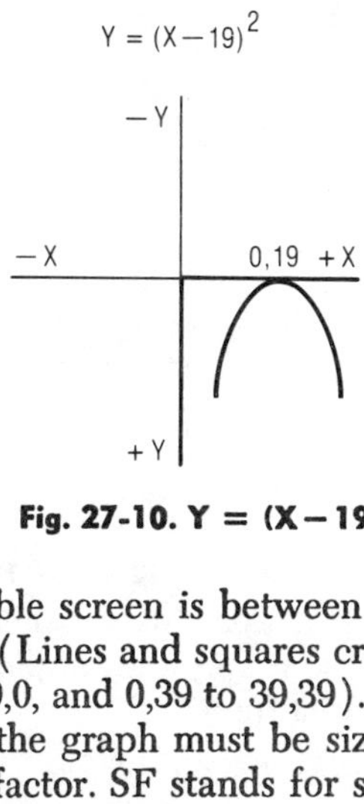

Fig. 27-10. Y = (X − 19)².

The remaining usable screen is between the line 2,0 to 37,0, and the line 2,37 to 37,37 (Lines and squares created by the program fill the screen at 0,0 to 39,0, and 0,39 to 39,39). To fit the graph into the usable screen space, the graph must be sized to the screen. We do this using the sizing factor. SF stands for sizing factor.

LEFT EDGE SIZING FACTOR

$37 = SF * (2 - 19)^2 = 17^2 = 289$
$SF = 37/289 = .128$

RIGHT EDGE SIZING FACTOR

$37 = SF * (37 - 19)^2 = 18^2 = 324$
$SF = 37/324 = .114$

The two sizing factors are averaged, $(.128 + .114)/2 = .122$, and the constant .122 is the figure we use to size the graph vertically.

The formula is changed to include the sizing constant, $Y = .122 * (X - 19)^2$ (Fig. 27-11).

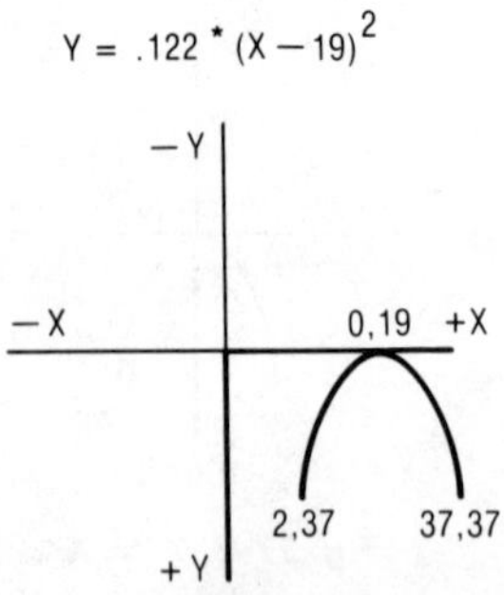

Fig. 27-11. $Y = .122 * (X-19)^2$.

The next step is to place the apex of the parabola towards the bottom of the screen. To invert the graph, a negative sign is placed before .122. The formula, $Y = -.122 * (X - 19)^2$, is shown in Fig.

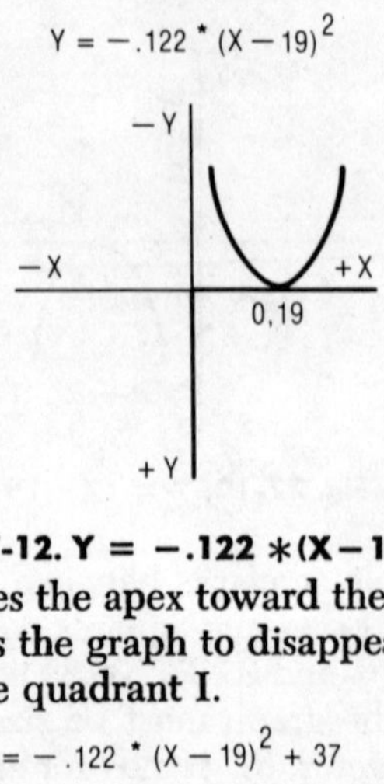

Fig. 27-12. $Y = -.122 * (X-19)^2$.

27-12. The formula places the apex toward the bottom of the screen. The negative sign causes the graph to disappear from the screen because it shifts to the true quadrant I.

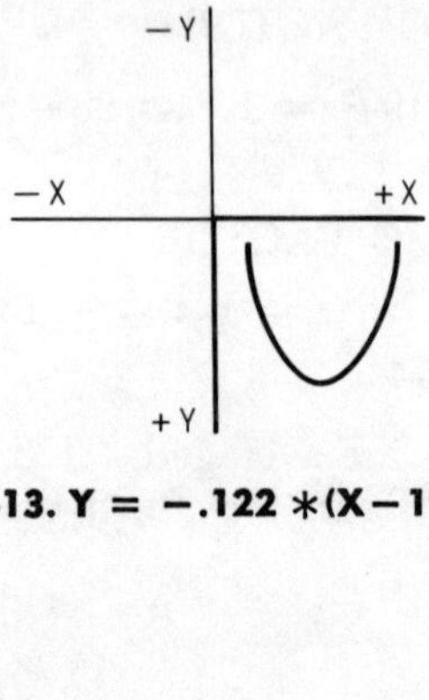

Fig. 27-13. $Y = -.122 * (X-19)^2 + 37$.

To cause the graph to be displayed on the screen, +37 is added to the formula. The formula is, $Y = -.122 * (X - 19)^2 + 37$ (Fig. 27-13). This adjustment to the formula places the graph, apex down, on the viewing screen.

The formula in Fig. 27-14 is coded to plot the graph. The program statement at line 160 causes the parabola to be graphed on the screen with its apex pointing down, thus solving the problem.

Line 170 completes the plot of the graph. VTAB 22 : HTAB 2 sets the location for the print statement. GRAPH OF Y = −.122 * (X − 19) ∧ 2) + 37 is printed on line 22 of the TEXT area of the split screen graph (Fig. 27-6).

PLOT X, (37 — .122 * (X — 19) ∧ 2)

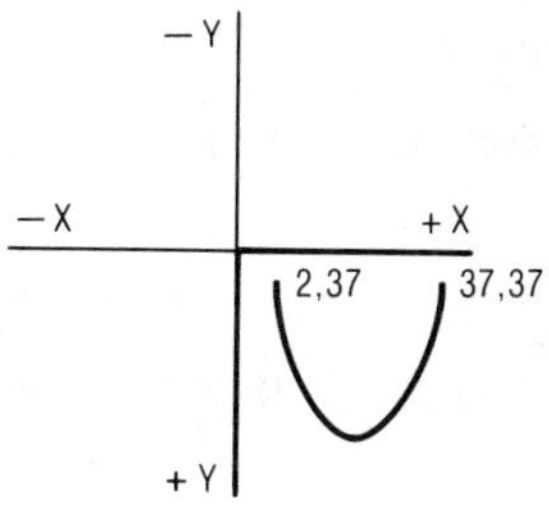

Fig. 27-14. Plot X, (37—.122∗(X—19)∧2).

Line 180 plots the square at 15,47. The square is plotted in the TEXT area of the screen and shows as a light "@".

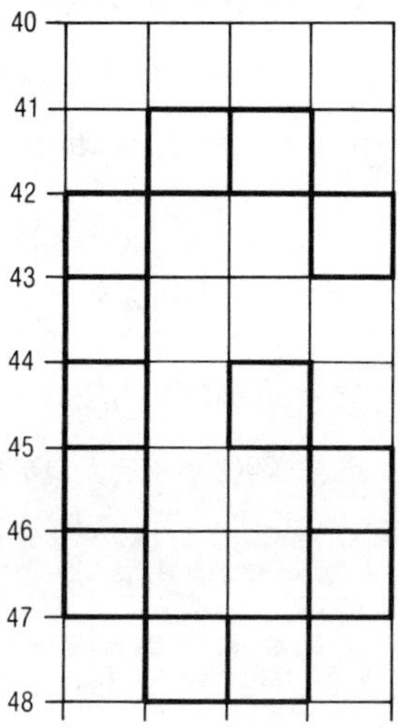

Fig. 27-15. Graphics G.

Line 190 causes the display to go to full screen graphics.

Line 200 sets the color to black.

Line 210 blacks out horizontal lines in the full screen graphics from lines 40 to 47.

Lines 220 through 360 produce the word GRAPHICS, each letter in a different color, at the bottom of the screen in lines 40 to 47 (Fig. 27-15).

Line 950 is a long pause loop. It gives the user time to view the demonstration.

In line 960, POKE −16301,0 switches display from graphics mode

```
5    REM : OGIVE GRAPHICS
10   HOME
20   DIM CG(17)
30   GOSUB 800
40   T = 0: FOR J = 1 TO 17
50   IF J < > INT ((J - 1) / 5) * 5 + 1 THEN 80
60   IF J < > 1 THEN PRINT "OGIVE COUNT=";T;" OF 80 =";T / 80;"%":
     INPUT "!";Q$
70   PRINT "RANGE #       BASE      TOP       COUNT"
80   R = J: GOSUB 900:UL = RL:R = J - 1: GOSUB 900:LL = RL + 1:
     IF LL = 1 THEN LL = 0
90   PRINT SPC( 3);J;: HTAB 13: PRINT LL;: HTAB 20: PRINT UL;: HTAB 30:
     PRINT CG(J)
100  T = T + CG(J): NEXT J
110  PRINT "OGIVE COUNT=";T;" OF 80 = ";T / 80;"%"
120  INPUT "!";Q$
130  GR : HOME : COLOR= 1: VLIN 0,39 AT 0: HLIN 2,39 AT 39
140  T = 0: FOR J = 1 TO 17: COLOR= J - 1 + (J = 1) * 15 -
     (J = 17)
150  VLIN 37 - (CG(J) + T - CG(1)) / (80 - CG(1)) * 37,37 AT J * 2 + 2
160  T = T + CG(J): NEXT J
170  VTAB 21: PRINT " R# ";: FOR J = 1 TO 9: PRINT J;" ";: NEXT J:
     FOR J = 1 TO 8: PRINT "1";: NEXT J
180  VTAB 22: HTAB 23: FOR J = 0 TO 7: PRINT J;" ";: NEXT J
190  PRINT
690  INPUT "!";Q$
700  TEXT : HOME : END
800  FOR J = 1 TO 80:SG = INT ( RND(1.0) * 101): IF SG = 0 THEN
     SG = 1
810  IF SG > 32 THEN 830
820  CG((SG - 1) / 16 + 1) = CG((SG - 1) / 16 + 1) + 1: GOTO 880
830  IF SG > 64 THEN 850
840  CG(3 + (SG - 33) / 8) = CG(3 + (SG - 33) / 8) + 1:: GOTO 880
850  IF SG > 92 THEN 870
860  CG(7 + (SG - 65) / 4) = CG(7 + (SG - 65) / 4) + 1:: GOTO 880
870  CG(14 + (SG - 93) / 2) = CG(14 + (SG - 93) / 2) + 1
880  NEXT J: RETURN
900  RL = R * 16 - (R > 2) * (R - 2) * 8 - (R > 6)
     * (R - 6) * 4 - (R > 13) * (R - 13)
     * 2
910  RETURN
```

Fig. 27-16. OGIVE program.

back to text mode. HOME clears the screen. VTAB 22 tabs to line 22 to print THAT'S ALL.

The second program in Lesson 27 is OGIVE (Fig. 27-16). In Lesson 25, FORMULAS, the OGIVE program was presented. The program randomly input 80 student grades and placed them in 17 ranges. The output was information on which to make an ogive of cumulative distribution. Lesson 27 adds graphics to the original program so the ogive is printed on the screen. Lines 130 through 700 (Fig. 27-16) produce and print the ogive on the screen.

```
RANGE #      BASE      TOP      COUNT
   1           0        16        11
   2          17        32        11
   3          33        40         4
   4          41        48         9
   5          49        56         5
OGIVE COUNT=40 OF 80 =.5%

RANGE #      BASE      TOP      COUNT
   6          57        64         6
   7          65        68         3
   8          69        72         3
   9          73        76         5
  10          77        80         3
OGIVE COUNT=60 OF 80 =.75%

RANGE #      BASE      TOP      COUNT
  11          81        84         4
  12          85        88         2
  13          89        92         7
  14          93        94         2
  15          95        96         1
OGIVE COUNT=76 OF 80 =.95%

RANGE #      BASE      TOP      COUNT
  16          97        98         2
  17          99       100         2
OGIVE COUNT=80 OF 80 =1%
```

Fig. 27-17. OGIVE data.

In line 130 GR sets the split screen graphics mode. HOME clears the screen. COLOR = 1 sets the color to white.

VLIN 0,39 AT 0 draws a vertical line in column zero. HLIN 2,39 AT 39 draws a horizontal line at row 39. These lines highlight the left side and bottom area in which the ogive is placed (Fig. 25-10). The student grades are randomly input, so no two ogives will be the same.

In line 140, T = 0 initializes the totaling variable to zero. FOR J = 1 TO 17 is the beginning of the loop to display the 17 different grade ranges.

COLOR = J − 1 + (J = 1) * 15 − (J = 17) is a formula used to change the color on each loop execution. J = 1 is a logical expression used to eliminate J = 0 (black). J = 17 is a logical expression used to subtract the value of J = 17, and cause the color value to be generated in a circular mode.

The formula at line 150 processes the ogive data generated by the program and graphs the ogive of cumulative distribution.

Fig. 27-18 details the processing action to produce the bar graph.

The value of the loop variable, J, is recorded in column C1. J represents the 17 ranges used in the graph.

	COLUMN4'CG(1)' =11			COLUMN6'80−C4' =69			
J	CG(J)	T	C2+C3−C4	C5/C6	C7*37	37−C8	VLIN C9,37 AT J*2+2
C1	C2	C3	C5	C7	C8	C9	C10
1	11	0	0	0000	0	37	37,37 AT 4
2	11	11	11	.159	5	32	32,37 AT 6
3	4	22	15	.217	8	29	29,37 AT 8
4	9	26	24	.348	12	25	25,37 AT 10
5	5	35	29	.420	15	22	22,37 AT 12
6	6	40	35	.507	18	19	19,37 AT 14
7	3	46	38	.551	20	17	17,37 AT 16
8	3	49	41	.594	21	16	16,37 AT 18
9	5	52	46	.667	24	13	13,37 AT 20
10	3	57	49	.710	26	11	11,37 AT 22
11	4	60	53	.768	28	9	9,37 AT 24
12	2	64	55	.797	29	8	8,37 AT 26
13	7	66	62	.899	33	4	4,37 AT 28
14	2	73	64	.928	34	3	3,37 AT 30
15	1	75	65	.942	34	3	3,37 AT 32
16	2	76	67	.971	35	2	2,37 AT 34
17	2	78	69	1000	37	0	0,37 AT 36

Fig. 27-18. OGIVE graph information.

Column C2 holds the value of the number of grades in grade range CG(J). These are the same values generated by the program and listed in Fig. 27-17.

Column C3 holds the total number of grades and is computed by the formula in line 160, T = T + CG(J).

Column C4 is a constant, whose value is 11 . Eleven is the number of grades in the first grade range.

Column C5, C2 + C3 − C4, computes the number of grades in each grade range less the number of grades in the first grade range (11). This causes range 1 to be printed as one instead of 11. The 11 is subtracted out of the number of grades in each grade range. Subtracting the 11 from all range values expands the rest of the ranges to accurately relate how many students are in each range. It expands the graph to give better definition without distorting the truth.

Column C6 is a constant to reflect the total number of grades less the grades in range 1. Total grades = 80, less the 11 grades in range 1, leaves the constant with a value of 69.

Column C7, C5/C6, divides the total grades less the grades in range 1, by the constant 69. Column C7 produces a percentage of the total grades in each range.

The maximum length of any bar in the graph is 37. Column C8, C7*37, takes the percentage of grades and multiplies by 37 to get the number of squares to be subtracted from the bar in the graph.

Column C9, 37 − C8, subtracts the value computed in C8 from 37 (maximum length of the bar), so that the bar extends from the bottom line upwards.

Column C10, VLIN C9,37 AT J * 2 + 2, produces the vertical line to be printed in the proper column on the ogive.

The column at which the bar is printed is computed by the formula J * 2 + 2.

Careful study of Figs. 27-17 and 27-18 shows the power and beauty of formulas, and how they produce speed and efficiency.

Lines 170 and 180 produce the range labels, below the ogive.

```
VTAB 21   R#  1 2 3 4 5 6 7 8 9 1 1 1 1 1 1 1
VTAB 22 : HTAB 23                 0 1 2 3 4 5 6 7
```

The range labels are tied with the formula in line 150, so J * 2 + 2 prints the bar in the properly labeled column.

Line 190 causes a line to be skipped between the lowest label in the ogive and the input at line 690.

Line 690 causes an exclamation mark to be placed at line 24, column 1, and allows the user time to study the ogive. When the user has completed his study of the ogive, RETURN is pressed. Pressing RETURN places the screen in the TEXT mode. HOME clears the screen and the program ends.

LESSON 28

High Resolution Graphics

High resolution graphics is very similar to low resolution graphics in Lesson 27. High resolution graphics will not run with Applesoft on tape or disk. *HGR WILL ONLY RUN WITH APPLESOFT IN ROM.*

High resolution graphics has two modes: (1) split screen graphics, with the four bottom lines for text, and (2) full screen graphics.

The split screen mode (Fig. 28-1) divides the screen into 280

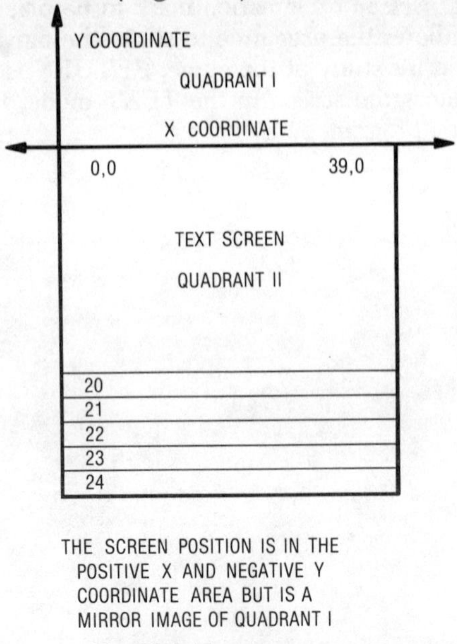

Fig. 28-1. Text screen.

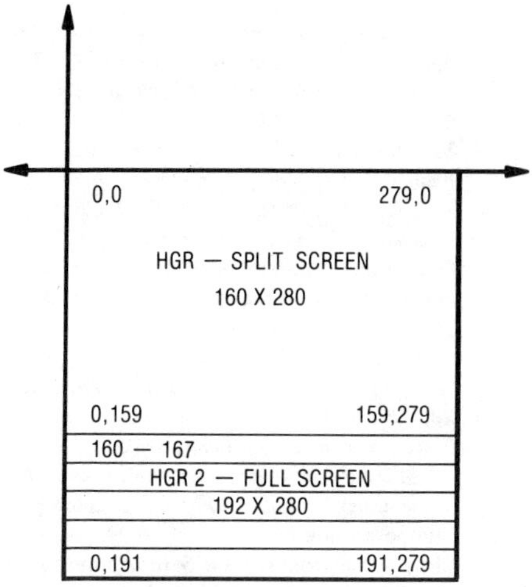

(THE SCREENS ARE NOT TO SCALE)

Fig. 28-2. High resolution graphics screen.

0	Black 1	1	Green (depends on TV)
2	Blue (depends on TV)	3	White 1
4	Black 2	5	(depends on TV)
6	(depends on TV)	7	White 2

Fig. 28-3. High resolution graphics color names and related numbers.

columns (0,279), and 160 rows (0,159). The bottom four lines are reserved for text. Each seven high resolution graphics columns represent one text column. There are 40 text columns and 280 graphics columns. Every eight high resolution graphics rows represent one text row. There are 20 text rows and 160 graphics rows.

The full screen high resolution screen (Fig. 28-2) contains 280 columns (0,279) and 192 rows (0,191).

The high resolution graphics screen is divided into two distinct sets of lines. There are columns with odd numbered lines and columns with even numbered lines. The color statement (HCOLOR =) is related to the odd-even line system. The odd number lines are colored by the odd numbered colors (Fig. 28-3) and the even numbered lines are colored by the even numbered colors.

Two programs are presented in Lesson 28, (1) HI – RES EXPLAINER (Fig. 28-7) and (2) ORBITAL WAR GAME (Fig. 28-9).

The HI – RES EXPLAINER details the use of the high resolution graphics commands and statements (Fig. 28-4).

Line 10 of the HI – RES EXPLAINER sets the TEXT mode, clears

DRAW 1 AT 30,40	Draws shape as defined in the shape table. Shape #1 is drawn at X location 30, Y location 40. The color, scale, and rotation must be specified before DRAW is executed. See line 10 of Fig. 28-8.
HCOLOR=3	Sets the color of the screen to white. Color values range from 0-7 (Fig. 28-4). Even color values print on even numbered lines on the screen. Odd color values print on odd numbered lines on the screen.
HGR	Sets high resolution, split screen, graphics mode to 160 X 280 for the screen. Leaves four lines for TEXT at the bottom of the screen. Sets COLOR = 0 (black). HGR IS AVAILABLE ONLY ON APPLESOFT IN ROM.
HGR 2	Sets high resolution, full screen, graphics mode to 192 X 280 on the screen.
HPLOT 10,20	Places a dot at X location 10, Y location 20, using last HCOLOR designation. X is even numbered line, so HCOLOR value must be even. Odd value color prints black on even numbered line.
HPLOT 9,0 TO 271,0	Plots a line from column 9 to column 271 at row 0.
HPLOT TO 159,271	Plots a line from the last designated point (271,0) to the next designated point (159,271).
ROT=	Value ranges from 0 to 64. Causes a shape to be rotated clockwise after a DRAW or XDRAW.
SCALE	Value ranges from 0-255. Scale 1 is the smallest size, and scale 0 is the largest size. See line 1000, Fig. 28-8.
SHLOAD	Loads a shape table from cassette tape.
TEXT	Sets the screen to the TEXT mode of 24 rows and 40 columns.
XDRAW 1 AT 30,40	Draws shape 1, from previously loaded shape table, at X location 30, Y location 40.

Fig. 28-4. High resolution graphics commands and statements.

the screen, and places the HI – RES EXPLAINER PROGRAM in the center of the screen.

```
10 TEXT : HOME : VTAB 8 : PRINT " HI — RES EXPLAINER PROGRAM"
20 GOSUB 1000 : HOME : HGR : VTAB 21 : PRINT "—————————THIS IS
   THE BOTTOM LINE—————————"
```

In line 20, GOSUB 1000 is a delay loop to allow the user time to view the results as the program progresses. HOME clears the screen. HGR is the statement that places the screen in high resolution split screen graphics (most high resolution graphics statements are prefaced with the letter "H" to distinguish them from low resolution graphics statements). THIS IS THE BOTTOM LINE is printed at line 21 in the text section of the graphics screen. Line 20 is not usable because of computer design.

Lines 30 through 34 set up the basic data to plot rectangles, one in each corner of the screen (Fig. 28-5).

```
30 FOR J = 1 TO 4 : ON J GOTO 31, 32, 33, 34
31 XP = 1 : YP = 0 : GOTO 40
32 XP = 277 : YP = 0 : GOTO 40
```

```
33  XP = 277 : YP = 157 : GOTO 40
34  XP = 1 : YP = 157
40  HCOLOR = 1 : HPLOT XP,XY TO XP + 2,YP TO XP + 2,YP + 2 TO
    XP,YP + 2 TO XP,YP : NEXT J : GOSUB 1000
```

In line 40, HCOLOR = 1 sets the color to green (Fig. 28-4). The color green has a value of 1. All colors with an odd value print only on the odd numbered lines. All colors with an even value print on the even numbered lines.

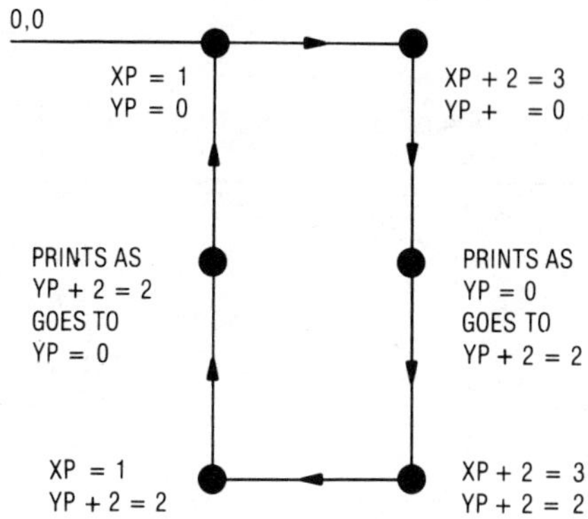


```
31  XP = 1 : YP = 0 : GOTO 40
40  HCOLOR = 1 : HPLOT XP,YP TO XP + 2,YP TO XP + 2,YP + 2 TO
    XP,YP + 2, TO XP,YP : NEXT J : GOSUB 1000
```

Fig. 28-5. HPLOT diagram. HCOLOR = 1 (Prints on odd numbered lines).

HPLOT XP,YP TO XP + 2,YP prints on the dot whose value is XP = 1, YP = 0. The XP value is odd, so the odd value of the color is printed at 1,0. The next dot printed is 3,0. The color on column #2 prints on an even color value, so column #2 is black (Fig. 28-5).

If no dot is specified, HPLOT plots from the last printed dot. The last printed dot is 3,0 (XP + 2,YP). The HPLOT continues from 3,0 to plot XP + 2, YP + 2. An increment of 2 is added to the Y value, so a dot is placed at 3,2. In placing the dot at 3,2 a dot is also placed at 3.1 (Fig. 28-5).

The plot continues from 3,2 to XP,YP + 2, or from 3,2 to 1,2. The color value is odd, so the even valued line does not show a print. The square would be three dots wide by three dots long, but the color value is odd. This causes the square to look like a 2 × 3 rectangle (Fig. 28-5).

The NEXT J in line 40 causes a rectangle to be placed in each corner of the screen.

GOSUB 1000 branches to a delay loop at line 1000 that delays for a count of 1500 to enable the viewer time to view the dots.

```
50   FOR J = 0 TO 150 STEP 157 : FOR K = 0 TO 2 : HPLOT 9,J + K
     TO 271,J + K : NEXT K,J : GOSUB 1000
```

FOR J = 0 TO 157 STEP 157 sets up to print a line at row 0, and a line at row 157. FOR K = 0 to 2 sets up to print three lines. The three lines in columns 0, 1, 2 produce a line 3 rows wide (Fig. 28-6).

HPLOT 9,J + K TO 271,J + K plots three lines,

9, J + K .... 271, J + K
9,0 271,0
9,1 271,1
9,2 271,2

and also plots three lines at 9, J + K TO 271, J + K.

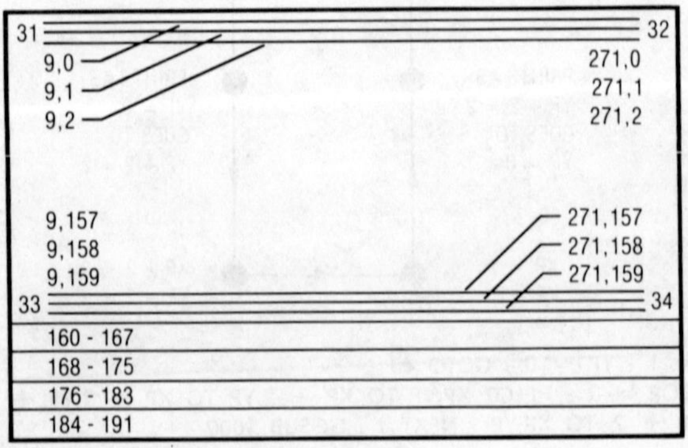


```
30   FOR J = 1 TO 4 : ON J GOTO 31, 32, 33, 34
31   XP = 1 : YP = 0 : GOTO 40
32   XP = 277 : YP = 0 : GOTO 40
33   XP = 277 : YP = 157 : GOTO 40
34   XP = 1 : YP = 157
40   HCOLOR = 1 : HPLOT XP,YP TO XP + 2,YP TO XP + 2,YP + 2 TO XP,
     YP + 2, TO XP,YP : NEXT J : GOSUB 1000
50   FOR J = 0 TO 157 STEP 157 : FOR K = 0 TO 2 : HPLOT 9,J + K TO
     271, J + K : NEXT K, J : GOSUB 1000
```

Fig. 28-6. High resolution explainer.

9,J + K .... 271,J + K
9,157 271,157
9,158 271,158
9,159 271,159

Line 60 causes two vertical lines (of three lines each) to be printed on the right and left sides of the screen. The statement FOR K = 1 TO 3 STEP 2 prints on the odd lines one and three, and steps over the even line because the color value of green (1) does not print on even numbered lines.

```
5     REM : HI-RES EXPLAINER
10    TEXT : HOME : VTAB 8: HTAB 8: PRINT "HI-RES EXPLAINER PROGRAM"
20    GOSUB 1000: HOME : HGR : VTAB 21; PRINT "———————————THIS IS
      THE BOTTOM LINE——————————"
30    FOR J = 1 TO 4: ON J GOTO 31,32,33,34
31    XP = 1:YP = 0: GOTO 40
32    XP = 277:YP = 0: GOTO 40
33    XP = 277:YP = 157: GOTO 40
34    XP = 1:YP = 157
40    HCOLOR= 1: HPLOT XP,YP TO XP + 2,YP TO XP + 2,YP + 2 TO XP,
      YP + 2 TO XP,YP: NEXT J: GOSUB 1000
50    FOR J = 0 TO 157 STEP 157: FOR K = 0 TO 2: HPLOT 9,J + K TO
      271,J + K: NEXT K,J: GOSUB 1000
60    FOR J = 0 TO 276 STEP 276: FOR K = 1 TO 3 STEP 2: HPLOT J + K,5
      TO J + K,154: NEXT K,J: GOSUB 1000
70    HPLOT 9,79: FOR J = 0 TO 130: X = J * 2 + 11: HPLOT TO X,
      INT (((X - 139) ↑ 2) * .00435 + 4.5): NEXT J
80    VTAB 22: PRINT "PLOT: Y=.00435*(X-139)↑2+4.5": GOSUB 1000

90    FOR J = 129 TO 0 STEP - 1:X = J * 2 + 9: HPLOT TO X,( INT
      (151 - ((X - 139) ↑ 2) * .00435 + 4.5)): NEXT J
100   VTAB 23: PRINT "PLOT: Y=151-.00435*(X-139)↑2+4.5";: GOSUB 1000
110   FOR J = 1 TO 129 STEP 2:X = J * 2 + 9:Y = INT (((X - 139) ↑ 2)
      * .00435 + 4.5):X2 = 271 - J * 2:Y2 = INT (151 - ((X - 139)
      ↑ 2) * .00435 + 4.5): HPLOT X,Y TO X2,Y2: NEXT J
999   END
1000  FOR J = 0 TO 1500: NEXT J: RETURN
```

Fig. 28-7. HI-RES EXPLAINER program.

Line 70 causes the graph of a parabola to be sized and printed, with its apex toward the top of the screen. The parabola at line 70 is printed in the upper half of the screen. Steps similar to those in Lesson 25 are used to size and print the graph of the parabola.

```
70 HPLOT 9,79 : FOR J = 0 TO 130 : X = J*2 + 11: HPLOT TO X,
   INT(((X - 139) ∧ 2)* .00435 + 4.5) : NEXT J
```

HPLOT 9,79 designates the location of the first dot to be printed in the graph. FOR J = 0 TO 130 prints 131 dots in the graph (Fig. 28-7).

X = J*2 + 11 is the formula used to compute the value along the X axis. When J = 0, the second dot is placed at 11, along the X axis. The first dot is plotted at HPLOT 9,79. The last value of X is equal to 130*2 + 11 = 271.

The value along the Y axis is plotted by the formula INT((((X − 139)∧2)* .00435)+ 4.5). The graph is plotted in the center of the screen by dividing the range (0,279) by 2 = 139. The center of the X axis is X − 139.

The graph is sized to the usable space between columns 9 and 271, and rows 4 to 79. The Y range = 75.

$X = 9 : (9-139)^2 * CONSTANT = 75$

$CONSTANT = 75/(130)^2 = .00437$

The constant, .004437 is reduced by guesstimate to .00435 to make sure the graph does not extend past the screen limits. The formula is now.

$Y = (X - 139)^2 * .00453.$

Vertical lines are printed along the left side of the screen to form a border. Three vertical lines are printed from row 5 to 154, at columns 0, 1, and 2. The left edge of the parabola starts at column 4. The 4 is added to the formula.

$Y = (X - 139)^2 * .00435 + 4$

To make sure the integer function is always rounded properly, .5 is added to the formula. The final formula is

$Y = (X - 139)^2 * .00435 + 4.5.$

The formula is converted to a program statement, and the data is in Fig. 28-8.

```
HPLOT TO X,INT(((X - 139)^2)*.00435 + 4.5)

80  VTAB 22 : PRINT "PLOT: Y = .00453 * (X-139) ^ 2 + 4.5" :
    GOSUB 1000
```

Line 80 VTAB's to row 22 and prints out the formula used to graph the parabola.

J	J*2+11	INT(((X−139)↑2)*.00435)+4.5)
0	11	75
1	13	73
2	15	71
3	17	69
4	19	67
5	21	65
6	23	63
7	25	61
8	27	59
9	29	57
10	31	55
11	33	53
12	35	51
13	37	49
14	39	48
15	41	46
16	43	44
17	45	42
18	47	41

Fig. 28-8. Data to plot graph.

19	49	39
20	51	38
21	53	36
22	55	35
23	57	33
24	59	32
25	61	30
26	63	29
27	65	28
28	67	27
29	69	25
30	71	24
31	73	23
32	75	22
33	77	21
34	79	20
35	81	19
36	83	18
37	85	17
38	87	16
39	89	15
40	91	14
41	93	13
42	95	12
43	97	12
44	99	11
45	101	10
46	103	10
47	105	9
48	107	8
49	109	8
50	111	7
51	113	7
52	115	7
53	117	6
54	119	6
55	121	5
56	123	5
57	125	5
58	127	5

J	J*2+11	INT(((X−139)↑2)*.00435)+4.5)
59	129	4
60	131	4
61	133	4
62	135	4
63	137	4
64	139	4
65	141	4
66	143	4
67	145	4
68	147	4
69	149	4
70	151	5

Fig. 28-8. (Cont) Data to plot graph.

J	J*2+11	INT(((X−139)↑2)*.00435)+4.5)
71	153	5
72	155	5
73	157	5
74	159	6
75	161	6
76	163	7
77	165	7
78	167	7
79	169	8
80	171	8
81	173	9
82	175	10
83	177	10
84	179	11
85	181	12
86	183	12
87	185	13
88	187	14
89	189	15
90	191	16
91	193	17
92	195	18
93	197	19
94	199	20
95	201	21
96	203	22
97	205	23
98	207	24
99	209	25
100	211	27
101	213	28
102	215	29
103	217	30
104	219	32
105	221	33
106	223	35
107	225	36
108	227	38
109	229	39
110	231	41
111	233	42
112	235	44
113	237	46
114	239	48
115	241	49
116	243	51
117	245	53
118	247	55
119	249	57
120	251	59
121	253	61

Fig. 28-8. (Cont) Data to plot graph.

122	255	63
123	257	65
124	259	67
125	261	69
126	263	71
127	265	73
128	267	75
129	269	78
130	271	80
J	J*2+11	INT(((X−139)↑2)*.00435)+4.5)
J	J*2+11	INT(((X−139)↑2)*.00435)+4.5)

Fig. 28-8. (Cont) Data to plot graph.

```
90  FOR J = 129 TO 0 STEP −1 : X = J*2 + 9 : HPLOT TO X,
    (INT(151 − ((X − 139 ) ∧ 2) * .00435 + 4.5)) : NEXT J
```

Line 90 prints the graph of a parabola starting from the right hand side of the screen. The parabola is in the lower half of the screen, with its apex pointing down. FOR J = 129 TO 0 STEP −1, joins point 130,261 and plots the graph clockwise to point 4,6.

```
100 VTAB 23 : PRINT "PLOT: Y = 151 − .00435*(X−139) ∧ 2 + 4.5"
    ; : GOSUB 1000
```

Line 100 VTAB's to row 23 and prints out the formula to graph the parabola in the lower half of the screen.

```
110 FOR J = 1 TO 129 STEP 2 : X = J * 2 + 9 : Y = INT (((X − 139)
    ∧ 2) * .00435 + 4.5) : X2 = 271 − J * 2 : Y2 = INT (151−
    ((X − 139) ∧ 2) * .00435 + 4.5) : HPLOT X,Y TO X2,Y2 : NEXT J
```

Line 110 causes lines to be printed from the upper graph boundary, through the center of the screen, to the lower graph boundary. The loop causes 129 points to be plotted beginning at the junction of the graphs on the left to the junction of the graphs on the right. Two sets of X points are computed and plotted, X and X2. X is the point on the boundary of the upper graph. X2 is the point on the boundary of the lower graph.

Two sets of Y points are computed, Y and Y2. Y is the point on the boundary of the upper graph. Y2 is the point on the boundary of the lower graph.

The two points, X,Y and X2,Y2, are the opposite ends of a series of clockwise lines filling the interior of the two graphs.

```
X = J * 2 + 9
Y = (((X − 139) ∧ 2) * .00435 + 4.5)

X2 = 271 − J * 2
Y2 = INT (151 − ((X − 139) ∧ 2) * .00435 + 4.5)
```

HPLOT X,Y TO X2,Y2 plots the lines related to the FOR J = 1 TO 129 STEP 2 loop.

The second program written for Lesson 28 is called ORBITAL WAR GAME (Fig. 28-9). *The game runs only on Apple Computers.*

```
1     REM : ORBITAL WAR GAME
2     GOSUB 1600
5     GOTO 1000
10    FOR J = 0 TO 1: HCOLOR= 0: DRAW J + 1 AT VS(J,4),VS(J,5):
      HCOLOR= ABS (VS(J,0)): DRAW J + 1 AT VS(J,6),VS(J,7):VS(J,2) = VS
      (J,2) + VS(J,3)
20    VS(J,4) = VS(J,6):VS(J,5) = VS(J,7):VS(J,6) = COS (VS(J,2)) * VS(J,9) +
      VS(J,11):VS(J,7) = SIN (VS(J,2)) * VS(J,10) + VS(J,12): IF VS(J,0) > - 1
      THEN 40
30    HCOLOR= 0: FOR K = 0 TO VS(J,16): DRAW 4 - J AT VS(J,4) -
      SD(3 - J,1,0) + RND (1) * 7,VS(J,5) - SD(3 - J,1,1) + RND (1)
      * 9: NEXT :VS(J,16) = VS(J,16) + .47
35    FOR D = 1 TO 180: NEXT D
40    NEXT :VS(1,15) = SQR (((VS(0,4) + SD(0,1,0)) - (VS(1,4) + SD(1,1,0))) ↑
      2 + ((VS(0,5) + SD(0,1,1)) - (VS(1,5) + SD(1,1,1))) ↑ 2): RETURN
50    FOR K = 0 TO 3: IF NOT W(K,O) THEN 70
60    NEXT : GOTO 100
70    W(K,3) = COS (VS(0,15) - C(0,6)) * SD(0,0,0) + VS(0,6) + SD(0,1,0):
      IF W(K,3) < C(0,3) OR W(K,3) > C(0,4) THEN W(K,3) = C(0,4): GOTO 100
80    W(K,4) = SIN (VS(0,15) - C(0,6)) * SD(0,0,1) + VS(0,7) + SD(0,1,0):
      IF W(K,4) < C(1,3) OR W(K,4) > C(1,4) THEN W(K,3) = C(0,4):W(K,4) =
      C(1,4): GOTO 100
90    W(K,0) = 1:W(K,5) = COS (VS(0,15) - C(0,6)) * 18:W(K,6) = SIN
      (VS(0,15) - C(0,6)) * 8:VS(0,14) = VS(0,14) - VS(0,13)
100   FOR J = 0 TO 3: HCOLOR= 0: DRAW 3 AT W(J,1),W(J,2): HCOLOR=
      W(J,0): DRAW 3 AT W(J,3),W(J,4):W(J,1) = W(J,3):W(J,2) = W(J,4):W(J,3)
      = W(J,3) + W(J,5):W(J,4) = W(J,4) + W(J,6)

110   IF W(J,3) < C(0,3) OR W(J,3) > C(0,4) OR W(J,4) < C(1,3) OR W(J,4) >
      C(1,4) THEN W(J,0) = 0:W(J,3) = C(0,4):W(J,4) = C(1,5):W(J,5) = 0:W(J,6)
      = 0
120   NEXT : RETURN
140   FOR J = 0 TO 3: IF W(J,0) = 0 OR VS(1,0) < > 1 THEN 170

150   IF ABS (VS(1,4) + SD(1,1,0) - W(J,1) - SD(2,1,0)) < 9 AND ABS (VS(1,5)
      + SD(1,1,1) - W(J,2) - SD(2,1,1)) < 5 THEN VS(1,0) = - 1: VTAB 24:
      HTAB 1: PRINT "INTRUDER DESTROYED";:VS(1,16) = 0:DC = DC + 1:
      GOTO 475
170   NEXT :VS(0,15) = PDL (0) * C(0,5):VS(0,14) = VS(0,14) + VS(0,8):
      VTAB 23: HTAB 17: PRINT INT (VS(0,15) * C(1,5) + .5); SPC( 3);: RETURN
390   HCOLOR= 0: DRAW 4 AT W(4,1), W(4,2): IF VS(1,15) > VS(1,14) OR
      VS(1,0) < 1 THEN W(4,3) = C(0,4):W(4,4) = C(1,4): FOR J = 0 TO 300:
      NEXT : RETURN

400   VS(1,8) = (1 - VS(1,15) < VS(1,13)) * ((VS(1,15) - VS(1,13)) /
      (VS(1,14) - VS(1,13))):W(4,5) = VS(1,6) - VS(0,6): IF ABS (W(4,5)) < .001
      THEN W(4,5) = C(0,6) + (VS(1,7) > VS(0,7)) * PI: GOTO 420
410   W(4,5) = ATN ((VS(1,7) - VS(0,7)) / W(4,5)) + (VS(1,6) > VS(0,6)) * PI
420   W(4,5) = W(4,5) + ( - 1) ↑ INT ( RND (1) + .5) * RND (1) * VS(1,8)
```

Fig. 28-9. ORBITAL WAR GAME program.

```
     * PI / 5:W(4,6) = VS(1,15) + ( - 1) ↑ INT ( RND (1) + .5) * RND
     (1) * VS(1,8) * (VS(1,14) - VS(1,15))
430  W(4,3) = VS(1,6) + COS (W(4,5)) * W(4,6):W(4,4) = VS(1,7) + SIN
     (W(4,5)) * W(4,6): IF W(4,3) < C(0,3) OR W(4,3) > C(0,4) OR W(4,4) <
     C(1,3) OR W(4,4) > C(1,4) THEN FOR J = 0 TO 55: NEXT J: RETURN
440  FOR J = 1 TO 6: HCOLOR= J - INT (J / 2) * 2: HPLOT VS(1,6) +
     SD(2,0,0),VS(1,7) + SD(2,0,1) TO W(4,3),W(4,4): NEXT : HCOLOR= 1:
     DRAW 4 AT W(4,3),W(4,4):W(4,1) = W(4,3):W(4,2) = W(4,4)
450  VS(1,8) = SQR ((W(4,3) - (VS(0,6) + SD(0,1,0))) ↑ 2 + (W(4,4) -
     (VS(0,7) + SD(0,1,1))) ↑ 2)
460  VS(0,14) = VS(0,14) - (VS(1,14) - INT (VS(1,8))) * 6: IF VS(0,14) > 0
     THEN 480
470  VTAB 24: HTAB 1: PRINT "DEFENDER DESTROYED ";:VS(0,0) = - 1:VS(0,16)
     = 0:VS(0,14) = 0:VS(0,8) = 0:IC = IC + 1
475  HCOLOR= 0: DRAW 4 AT W(4,1),W(4,2): RETURN
480  W(4,3) = C(0,4):W(4,4) = C(1,4): RETURN
610  GOSUB 140
620  GOSUB 10: VTAB 22: HTAB 15: PRINT VS(0,14); SPC( 2);: HTAB 34: PRINT
     INT (VS(1,15) + .5); SPC( 3);
640  IF VS(0,0) + VS(1,0) = 2 AND PEEK ( - 16287) > 127 AND VS(0,14) >
     VS(0,13) THEN GOSUB 50: GOTO 740
660  GOSUB 100
740  GOSUB 140: IF VS(0,0) + VS(1,0) = 2 THEN GOSUB 390
800  IF VS(0,16) < 5 AND VS(1,16) < 5 THEN 610
840  IF VS(0,0) < 0 THEN VS(0,0) = 0
850  IF VS(1,0) < 0 THEN VS(1,0) = 0
860  FOR K = 0 TO 7: GOSUB 10: FOR D = 1 TO 500: NEXT D,K
998  RETURN
1000 DIM VS(1,16),W(4,7): POKE 232,0: POKE 233,3:J = 0: SCALE= 1: ROT=
     0:K = 0
1010 DIM C(1,6),SD(3,1,1),OV(1): PI = 3.14159
1020 FOR J = 0 TO 3: FOR K = 0 TO 1: FOR L = 0 TO 1: READ SD(J,K,L):
     NEXT L,K,J
1030 FOR K = 0 TO 1: FOR J = 0 TO 4: READ C(K,J): NEXT J,K: READ
     C(0,5),C(1,5)
1040 OV(1) = 5 / 57.2958:OV(0) = OV(1) / 1.5435
1050 GOSUB 3000
1070 IC = 0:DC = 0:VS(0,16) = 0:VS(1,16) = 0:C(0,6) = 1.5707
1080 VS(0,0) = 1:VS(1,0) = 0:VS(0,1) = INT ( RND (1) + .5):VS(1,1) = INT
     ( RND (1) + .5):VS(0,2) = RND (2 * PI):VS(1,2) = VS(0,2) + PI +
     ( - 1) ↑ ( INT ( RND (1) + .5)) * RND (PI)
1090 VS(0,3) = OV(VS(0,1)) * (1 - 2 * INT ( RND (1) + .5)):VS(1,3) =
     OV(VS(1,1)) * (1 - 2 * INT ( RND (1) + .5))
1100 FOR J = 0 TO 4:W(J,0) = 0:W(J,3) = C(0,4):W(J,4) = C(1,4):W(J,5) =
     0:W(J,6) = 0:W(J,1) = W(J,3):W(J,2) = W(J,4): NEXT
1110 FOR K = 0 TO 1:VS(K,9) = C(VS(K,1),0) - SD(K,0,0) / 2:VS(K,10) =
     C(VS(K,1),1) - SD(K,0,1) / 2:VS(K,11) = C(0,2) - SD(K,1,0):VS(K,12) =
     C(1,2) - SD(K,1,1): NEXT K
1120 FOR K = 0 TO 1:VS(K,4) = COS (VS(K,2)) * VS(K,9) + VS(K,11):VS(K,6)
     = VS(K,4):VS(K,5) = SIN (VS(K,2)) * VS(K,10) + VS(K,12):VS(K,7) =
     VS(K,5): NEXT K
1130 VS(0,8) = 85:VS(0,13) = 134:VS(1,13) = 40:VS(1,14) = 120
```

Fig. 28-9. (Cont) ORBITAL WAR GAME program.

```
1140 HGR : VTAB 21: HOME : VTAB 21: PRINT "DEFENDER = ";DC;: HTAB 23:
     PRINT "INTRUDER =";IC
1150 PRINT "ENERGY LEVEL ="; SPC(8);"DISTANCE ="
1160 PRINT "FIRE DIRECTION ="
1170 HCOLOR= 1: HPLOT 1,0 TO 279,0 TO 279,159 TO 1,159 TO 1,0: DRAW 1
     AT VS(0,4),VS(0,5):VS(0,16) = 0:VS(1,16) = 0
1180 FOR K = 0 TO 8: GOSUB 10: FOR D = 1 TO 550: NEXT D,K: VTAB 24:
     FLASH : PRINT "WARNING! ! INTRUDER APPROACHING";
1190 NORMAL : FOR K = 0 TO 4: GOSUB 10: FOR D = 1 TO 550: NEXT D,K:
     VTAB 23: CALL - 958:VS(1,0) = 1:VS(0,14) = 3000
1200 GOSUB 610: IF IC < 5 AND DC < 5 THEN 1080
1210 VTAB 23: HTAB 24: INPUT "TRY AGAIN ?";Q$: IF Q$ <> "N"
     THEN 1070
1220 TEXT : HOME : END
1600 FOR K = 768 TO 1000: READ J: IF J = - 1 THEN 1840
1610 POKE K,J: NEXT K: GOTO 1840

1620 DATA 4,0,10,0,105,0,189,0,202,0
1630 DATA 45,5,45,5,45,5,45,5,73,58,7
1640 DATA 63,7,63,7,63,7,63,7,63,5,63,7
1650 DATA 191,73,73,105,5,45,5,141,251,63,7,255
1660 DATA 74,45,5,109,21,7,59,7,7,255,31,7
1670 DATA 74,45,5,7,45,5,45,5,13,5,250,63
1680 DATA 7,63,7,7,255,31,7,155,41,5,45,5
1690 DATA 45,5,45,5,45,5,45,5,45,5,218,59
1700 DATA 7,63,7,63,7,63,7,7,63,7,7,0
1710 DATA 77,9,5,73,77,77,58,7,63,7,63
1720 DATA 7,31,7,63,7,63,7,159,45,5,45,5
1730 DATA 45,5,45,5,45,5,45,7,7,5,45,5
1740 DATA 45,5,218,59,7,63,5,63,7,63,7,15
1750 DATA 63,7,63,7,5,63,25,191,73,13,5,45
1760 DATA 5,45,5,5,45,5,209,31,7,63,7,63
1770 DATA 7,63,7,159,41,5,105,41,5,73,5,45,0
1780 DATA 77,250,31,7,155,9,5,105,77,218,27
1790 DATA 7,0
1800 DATA 77,109,58,7,63,7,255,87,41,5,5
1810 DATA 9,5,13,5,218,63,7,5,63,7,255,87
1820 DATA 9,5,9,5,5,0
1830 DATA -1
1840 RETURN
2100 DATA 10,10,4,2
2110 DATA 11,7,3,3
2120 DATA 3,4,0,1
2130 DATA 5,5,1,2
2140 DATA 128,75,138,5,270
2150 DATA 92,60,80,5,150
2160 DATA .02464,57.2958
3000 HOME : VTAB 8: HTAB 8: PRINT "=== ORBITAL WAR GAME ===" :
     PRINT : PRINT : HTAB 12: PRINT 'BRIAN BLACKWOOD"
3010 PRINT : PRINT : HTAB 12: PRINT "7020 BURLINGTON": PRINT : PRINT :
     HTAB 12: PRINT "BEAUMONT TX, 77706"
3020 PRINT : PRINT : HTAB 12: PRINT "COPYRIGHT JULY 20,1980"
3030 FOR J = 1 TO 1500: NEXT J: RETURN
```

Fig. 28-9. (Cont) ORBITAL WAR GAME program.

with Applesoft in ROM. It can be loaded from tape and saved to tape. The shape tables are written into the program in data statements. The information necessary to create and save shape tables is found in *Applesoft Basic Programming Manual,* pages 91 to 100, published by Apple Computer Inc.®

The program will not be explained in detail because this is the final examination. The lessons in the book give sufficient information and detail for all the sharp students to replicate the program. This program draws on logic, graphics, mathematics, science, and programming ability to create an interesting game.

The program creates four shapes: defender, intruder, defender's missiles, and intruder's space rays. The defender and intruder move in either of two randomly selected orbits, an inner orbit, and an outer orbit.

The defender has four missiles to fire at the intruder that are controlled and fired by the player through game paddle zero (0). Each missile is replenished when it leaves the screen, so the defender has an unlimited number of missiles, within a controlled time frame.

The intruder automatically fires its space rays when the defender is in range. The invader has an unlimited number of space rays to fire, but they are only effective within a specified range.

The game ends when either adversary has five kills.

The game is written entirely in Applesoft BASIC for teaching purposes. In Applesoft the game is a bit slow. If the orbital and firing routines were written in assembly language, the game would be faster.

```
CONSTANTS
  Orbit values — 2 orbits
  DIM C(1,6)
  C(A,B)
    A = orbit 0 or 1
    B = range of orbit
      0 = X range
      1 = Y range
  C(0,0), C(0,1), C(1,0), and C(1,1) = orbit values
  (SCREEN LIMITS)
  C(A,B)
    A = 0 = X axis value
    A = 1 = Y axis value
    B = 2 = offset
    B = 3 = minimum
    B = 4 = minimum on selected axis
    B = 5 = maximum on selected axis
  C(1,3) = minimum on Y axis
  C(1,4) = maximum on Y axis
  C(0,5) = conversion factor of paddle zero (0-255) to radians (0, pi)
```

Fig. 28-10. Orbital war game variables.

C(1,5) = conversion factor of radians to degrees (57.2958)
C(0,6) = conversion of paddle value to degrees on the screen
360 — North, 90 — East, 180 — South, and 270 — West
C(1,6) = # of times to draw space ship destruction
DC = defender count — the number of kills
IC = intruder count — the number of kills
J, K = loop and temporary variables

ORBITAL
OV(0) = angular velocity of outer orbit #0
OV(1) = angular velocity of inner orbit #1
PI = 3.1417
ROT = 0 = HGR rotation value (value range from 0-64)
SCALE = 1 = HGR scaling factor — value range 0-255-1 smallest 0 largest

SHAPE DATA—four different shapes
0 = defender
1 = intruder
2 = missile (defender)
3 = space ray (intruder)
SD(3,1,1) = shape data
SD(A,B,C)
A = 0 to 3 shape number
B = 0 = range
B = 1 = offset—center of space ship to center position of the screen from position 0,0
C = 0 = X axis value
C = 1 = Y axis value
SD(0,1,1) = Y axis, offset of the shape 0
SD(3,0,0) = X axis, range of shape 3

VEHICLE STATUS
VS(1,15)
VS(0,?) = defender
VS(1,?) = intruder
VS(A,B)
A = 0 = defender
A = 1 = intruder
B = 0 = status
VS(1,0) = 0—intruder does not exist
VS(1,0) = 1—intruder functional
VS(1,0) = −1—intruder damaged
B = 1 = orbit
VS(0,1) = 0—defender is in the outer orbit
VS(0,1) = 1—defender is in the inner orbit
B = 2 = angle value
B = 3 = orbital velocity
B = 4 = X axis value
B = 5 = Y axis value
B = 6 = next X axis value
B = 7 = next Y axis value
VS(0,8) = energy increment
VS(1,8) = accuracy factor or distance to defender by intruder's space rays
B = 9 = X range
B = 10 = Y range
B = 11 = X offset
B = 12 = Y offset

Fig. 28-10. (Cont) Orbital war game variables.

```
VS(0,13) = defender's energy base
VS(1,13) = intruder's base firing distance
VS(0,14) = defender's energy level
VS(1,14) = intruder's maximum firing distance
VS(0,15) = defender's fire direction
VS(1,15) = intruder's distance to the defender
VS(0,16) = defender's damage count
VS(1,16) = intruder's damage count
WEAPON STATUS
W(4,6) = weapon data
W(A,B) = weapon data
A = 0, 1, 2, 3—defender has 4 missiles
A = 4—intruder has unlimited space rays at specified range
(DEFENDER'S WEAPONS)
B = 0 = HCOLOR = 0 (black) or HCOLOR = 1 (green)
W(1,0) = 0—HCOLOR = 0 (black)
W(1,0) = 1—HCOLOR = 1 (green)
B = 1 = X position value
B = 2 = X positive value
B = 3 = next X positive value
B = 4 = next Y positive value
(INTRUDER'S WEAPON)—same B1 through B4
B = 5 = change in X value random value
B = 6 = change in Y value random value
```

Fig. 28-10. (Cont) Orbital war game variables.

The variables in the program are shown in Fig. 28-10.

Line 1 GOSUB 1600 causes the shape tables to be loaded into memory.

```
1600  FOR K = 768 TO 1000 : READ J : IF J = −1 THEN 1840
1610  POKE K, J : NEXT K : GOTO 1840
```

Line 1600 sets up the number of memory addresses (decimal) into which the shape table data is placed. READ J reads the data.

IF J = −1 THEN 1840 is a clean way to end a READ-DATA statement without getting a processing error.

POKE K, J fills a specific memory address with specific data. NEXT K continues processing the data until it has all been placed in memory.

The program RETURNS to line 2, which is GOTO 1000.

Lines 1000 to 1040 contain the initialization of constants. These constants are set up one time and do not change throughout the program. The constants initialized are vehicle status (VS), weapon status (W), SCALE = 1, ROT = 0, constants (C), shape data (SD), orbital value (OV), and pi = 3.14159. OV(1) produces the angular velocity of orbit 1, the inner orbit. OV(0) is the angular velocity of the outer orbit (Fig. 28-10).

```
1020  FOR J = 0 TO 3 : FOR K = 0 TO 1 : FOR L = 0 TO 1 :
      READ SD(J, K, L) : NEXT L, K, J
```

Line 1020 reads the shape data at lines 2100 through 2130. This data tells the height and width of the shape, and the distance from the shape's center to the first plot of the shape. This is the offset of the vehicle from the center of the screen.

```
1030  FOR K = 0 TO 1 : FOR J = 0 TO 4 : READ C(K,J) : NEXT J,K :
      READ C(0,5), C(1,5)
```

Line 1030 reads the data in lines 2140 through 2160 to set up the constant array values. C(0,5) is the conversion factor of the paddle range (0-255) to radians. C(1,5) is the conversion factor of radians to degrees (Fig. 28-10).

1050 GOSUB 3000 branches to line 3000 to display the name of the game, the author's name and address, and the copyright date.

Lines 1070 through 1130 initialize all flight and gunnery information before the start of the program. Such information includes the orbit number, direction of motion, initial angle between space ships, shape data, vehicle status, weapon status, and constants.

Lines 1130 through 1170 set up the screen display headers in the text portion of the screen. The headers include the defender count of the number of kills, the intruder count of the number of kills, the energy level of the defender, the distance of the defender to the intruder, and the fire direction of the defender to the intruder.

Line 1180 sets up the preconflict movement by flashing WARNING !! INVADER APPROACHING.

```
1200  GOSUB 610 : IF IC < 5 AND DC < 5 THEN 1080
```

The lines from 610 through 850 tie all actions together and create the battle.

```
610  GOSUB 140
```

Lines 140 through 170 determine if the defender's missile has destroyed the intruder. This routine returns to 620, which begins with the statements GOSUB 10.

Line 10 DRAWS and redraws both space ships at the old position. It also draws the space ships at the new position.

Line 20 calculates the next position of the space ships.

Line 30 blacks out part of the damaged space ship and increments the damage count which is held in VS(0,16) for the defender, and VS(1,16) for the intruder.

Line 35 FOR D = 1 TO 180 : NEXT D is a timing loop so projectiles and space ships run at the same speed. This timing loop causes a delay before the program can continue. If a space ship is damaged, its weapons will not fire during this delay.

Line 40 calculates the distance between defender and intruder and RETURNS to the second statement in line 620, to print out the defender's energy level, and the intruder's distance to the defender.

In line 640, if both space ships are functional, if the paddle key is pressed, and if the defender's energy level is greater than the defender's base energy level, the program jumps to line 50.

Lines 50 and 60 determine if a missile is available to fire. If it is, and if the paddle firing button was pressed, a missile is fired (if a missile is available, go to line 70. If no missile is available, go to line 100).

Lines 70, 80, and 90 set the missile firing direction, give missile speed, and fire the missile.

Lines 100, 110, and 120 move the defender's missile toward the intruder. The program returns to line 740, which is GOSUB 140.

Lines 140, 150, and 170 determine if the defender's missile has destroyed the intruder. If the defender's missile has not, the program branches to line 390.

Lines 390 through 480 calculate the action, angle, range, and distance to the defender. This information prepares the intruder's space ray to fire on the defender.

Line 440 creates a series of flashes and explosions when the intruder's space ray is fired and when it hits the defender. Line 440 plots an HCOLOR = 1 three times, and wipes out the lines. This routine causes a flashing line from the intruder at the point where the space ray is going to appear. The area flashes three times, and then the space ray appears on the screen. This is to simulate an explosion. This brings the program back to lines 610 through 998 to continue the action of the program.

This is a general outline of the program:

I. Line 1 – GOSUB 1600
   A. Loads the shape tables at lines 1600 through 1840
II. Line 2 – GOTO 1000
   A. Lines 1000 — 1050 initialize constants and display copyright information at lines 3000 – 3020
III. Lines 10 – 40
   A. Draws space vehicles
   B. Line 30 – if either vehicle is damaged, part of the interior is blacked out
IV. Lines 50 – 90
   A. Fires defender's missile
V. Lines 100 – 120
   A. Moves defender's missile
VI. Lines 140 – 170
   A. Determine if defender's missile destroyed the intruder
VII. Lines 390 – 480
   A. Calculate action, range, angle, fire, and damage to defender by intruder's space ray

=== ORBITAL WAR GAME ===

WELCOME TO THE WORLD OF ORBITAL DEFENSE. YOU HAVE BEEN ASSIGNED DUTY ON AN ORBITING SPACE STATION. YOUR ORDERS ARE TO SCAN DEEP SPACE AND STOP ANY INTRUDING ALIEN VEHICLE FROM REACHING THE EARTH. WHEN YOU HAVE DESTROYED FIVE ENEMY CRAFT YOU WILL BE TRANSFERRED TO A NEW UNIT. (YOUR VEHICLE IS THE CYLINDRICAL CRAFT)

THERE ARE TWO ORBITS FOR THIS PROGRAM. BOTH YOUR VEHICLE AND THE INTRUDER CAN BE IN EITHER ORBIT. IN ADDITION THE VEHICLES CAN MOVE IN A CLOCKWISE OR COUNTER-CLOCKWISE DIRECTION. THIS IS DETERMINED RANDOMLY BEFORE EACH ENCOUNTER. THE TWO CRAFT FOLLOW GRAVITATIONAL FORCES AND CANNOT BE MANEUVERED.

YOU WILL HAVE TIME TO PREPARE FOR COMBAT BEFORE THE INTRUDER APPEARS. ALSO, YOU WILL RECEIVE A MESSAGE JUST BEFORE THE INTRUDER RETURNS FROM HYPERSPACE TRAVEL. THEN THE BATTLE WILL COMMENCE.

SCREEN DISPLAY WILL AUTOMATICALLY INDICATE DISTANCE TO INTRUDER, YOUR ENERGY LEVEL, AND THE DIRECTION YOUR MISSILES ARE AIMED. THIS DIRECTION IS STANDARD COMPASS ANGLES (0 AND 360-STRAIGHT UP, 90-RIGHT, 180-DOWN, 270-LEFT). TO CHANGE DIRECTION ROTATE PADDLE ZERO. TO FIRE MISSILES PUSH PADDLE ZERO BUTTON. YOU CAN HAVE ONLY FOUR MISSILES ON THE SCREEN AT ANY ONE TIME. THESE ARE AUTOMATICALLY RESTOCKED AS THEY LEAVE THE SCREEN. THESE MISSILES TRAVEL SLOWLY SO YOU WILL HAVE TO FIRE AT AN ANGLE THAT WILL LEAD THE PATH OF THE INTRUDER.

THE INTRUDER'S WEAPON IS SLIGHTLY DIFFERENT THAN THE DEFENDER'S. WHEN IT IS WITHIN A DISTANCE OF 120 THEN HE WILL FIRE HIS RAY BEAM AT YOU. LUCKILY, HIS WEAPON IS INEXACT AND HE WON'T HIT YOU DEAD CENTER WITH EVERY SHOT. HIS BLASTS DRAIN YOUR ENERGY UNTIL YOU HAVE ZERO LEFT. THEN YOU ARE GONE.

Fig 28-11. Orbital war game instructions.

VIII. Lines 610 – 998
- A. Loop that ties all program actions together
- B. Post destruction let down at lines 860 – 998

IX. Lines 1000 – 1070
- A. Initializes all battle variables
- B. Screen display headers at lines 1140 – 1170

X. Lines 1180 – 1220
- A. Pre-conflict movement
- B. Intruder warning period at line 1190
- C. Call subroutine for battle at line 1200
- D. Another game and END at lines 1210 – 1220

XI. Lines 1600 – 1840
- A. Shape table data

XII. Lines 2100 – 2160
- A. Shape data at lines 2100 – 2130
- B. Constant array values at lines 2140 – 2160

XIII. Lines 3000 – 3030
- A. Copyright information

TO THE READER

Sams Computer books cover Fundamentals — Programming — Interfacing — Technology written to meet the needs of computer engineers, professionals, scientists, technicians, students, educators, business owners, personal computerists and home hobbyists.

Our Tradition is to meet your needs and in so doing we invite you to tell us what your needs and interests are by completing the following:

1. I need books on the following topics:

____

____

____

____

____

____

2. I have the following Sams titles:

____

____

____

____

____

____

3. My occupation is:

_____ Scientist, Engineer
_____ Personal computerist
_____ Technician, Serviceman
_____ Educator
_____ Student
_____ D P Professional
_____ Business owner
_____ Computer store owner
_____ Home hobbyist
Other ______________________

____

Name (print) ______________________________________

Address ______________________________________

City ____________________ State ______________ Zip ______________

Mail to: **Howard W. Sams & Co., Inc.**
Marketing Dept. #CBS1/80
4300 W. 62nd St., P.O. Box 7092
Indianapolis, Indiana 46206